THE GOSPEL OF THOMAS

Also by Jean-Yves Leloup

The Gospel of Mary Magdalene

The Gospel of Philip:
Jesus, Mary Magdalene, and the Gnosis of Sacred Union

THE GOSPEL OF THOMAS

THE GNOSTIC WISDOM OF JESUS

Translation from the Coptic, introduction,
and commentary by
JEAN-YVES LELOUP

English translation and notes by
JOSEPH ROWE

Inner Traditions
Rochester, Vermont

Inner Traditions
One Park Street
Rochester, Vermont 05767
www.InnerTraditions.com

Originally published in French under the title *L'Évangile de Thomas* by Albin Michel, 22, rue Huyghens, 75014 Paris
First U.S. edition published in 2005 by Inner Traditions

LIBRARY OF CONGRESS CATALOGING-IN-PUBLICATION DATA

Gospel of Thomas (Coptic Gospel). English.
  The Gospel of Thomas : the gnostic wisdom of Jesus / translation from the Coptic, introduction, and commentary by Jean-Yves Leloup ; English translation and notes by Joseph Rowe.
    p. cm.
  Includes bibliographical references.
  ISBN 1-59477-046-8 (pbk.)
  1. Gospel of Thomas (Coptic Gospel)—Criticism, interpretation, etc. I. Gospel of Thomas (Coptic Gospel). English. II. Leloup, Jean-Yves. III. Rowe, Joseph, 1942- IV. Title.
  BS2860.T52G6713 2005
  229'.8—dc22

                                                                2004027022

Printed and bound in the United States at Lake Book Manufacturing, Inc.
10 9 8 7 6 5 4 3 2 1

Text design and layout by Priscilla Baker
This book was typeset in Caslon, with Copperplate used as a display typeface

CONTENTS

FOREWORD

Among all the astonishing documents accidentally—or fatefully—unearthed in 1945 near the desert village of Nag Hammadi in Upper Egypt, the Gospel of Thomas has made the greatest impact on our understanding of Christianity. The first English rendering of this text was published in 1959 and was greeted with intense interest by scholars and theologians alike. But the impact of this document was soon felt far beyond the circles of specialists, almost as though an audible recording of the voice of Jesus had been discovered. That is to say that even across the reaches of millennial time and even through the curtain of translation from languages known to but a few, for many of us the words in this text have the power to touch an unknown part of ourselves that brings with it an undeniable recognition of truth and hope. When it was said of Jesus, by those who were at first bewildered by him, that he spoke "as one having authority," what is surely meant is that he and his teaching authenticated itself by their power to awaken that same hidden, self-authenticating part of the human heart and mind.

Here we have the key to approaching the fundamental category that scholars and theologians have applied to this document and those like it—the technical term *gnosticism*. It is a word that in fact points to something of great importance to our understanding of all the spiritual traditions of the world and, as such, of great importance to our understanding of human life itself.

When scholars apply the label *gnostic* to the documents found at Nag Hammadi, they are generally assigning them to the current of religious doctrines and practices that flourished in the early centuries of the Christian era and were condemned as heresy in a movement spearheaded in the second century by the redoubtable bishop of Lyons, Irenaeus. The eventual result of this condemnation was the widespread suppression of these heresies and the relentless destruction of their constitutive texts. Until now, most of what was known of these teachings was based on the adversarial accounts of them provided in Irenaeus's vastly influential work, *Against the Heresies.* The immense historical significance of the Nag Hammadi documents consists in the likelihood that they were buried by members of more of these communities in order to preserve them from the storm of the ecclesiastical book burning of the time. Thus, nearly two thousand years after the suppression of these so-called heresies, we now suddenly have the opportunity to look directly at aspects of their teachings instead of seeing them largely through the eyes of their enemies.

But although the texts themselves can now be directly seen for the first time in nearly two thousand years, really to see them is a task that invites us to something much more demanding and joyous than simply reading them off the pages of ancient scrolls or modern translations and interpreting them according to familiar habits of intellectual analysis.

It is not for nothing that in this document the very first words of Jesus, here called by the Aramaic name Yeshua, are these: "Whoever lives the interpretation of these words will no longer taste death." Is this merely a figure of speech? Or do these words speak to some kind of knowledge and knowing that have an action upon the very flesh and blood of a human being, an action that is incomparably more penetrating than anything we call "knowledge" or "knowing"—including even our inspired moments of intellectual insight or passionate realization? Is there some kind of knowing that can transform our being to the point—dare we imagine—of bringing forth a life that does not die when the body dies? Such knowing as this is inseparable from the action of faith—considered not simply as a set of emotionally charged beliefs, but as a movement within the human psyche that generates a magnetic current flowing between our individual human life and the source of human life itself; and that deposits into our human life the spiritualized matter of what is called the "new Adam"; and that enables a man or woman actually to answer in an entirely new way the great cry of St. Paul: "For the good that I would, that I do not; and that which I hate, that do I," or, in other words, to answer with the actions of love rather than with brittle promises of future virtue. Such transformational knowing actually has little or nothing to do with what we ordinarily call thought. It has to do with energy, the energy of consciousness. This energy is at the heart of what is signified by the ancient word *gnosis,* from which *gnosticism* is derived.

In applying the term *gnosticism* to these teachings, scholars and theologians understandably call our attention to the emphasis that most of the Nag Hammadi documents place on the role of knowledge in the religious life—in apparent contrast to the demand for faith that became the central tenet of the Church over the centuries, especially in the West. There are numerous other doctrines that are sometimes identified with gnosticism—such as its apparent metaphysical dualism and condemnation of the world. But it is the notion of gnosis as transformational knowing that is of utmost importance and that cries out for deeper inquiry in the world we now live in, a world—a civilization—which is deeply, perhaps fatally, afflicted with an ever-widening disconnect between what we know with the mind and what we know in our heart and in our instincts.

Both in our civilization and in our personal lives, the growth of knowledge far outstrips the growth of being, endlessly complicating our existence and taking away from us far more than it gives us. In relation to the advances and applications of scientific knowledge, we are like children restlessly sitting at the controls of a locomotive. Without a corresponding growth of inner, moral power, our intellectual power seems now to be carrying us toward disaster—in the form of the catastrophic destruction of the natural world, in the decay of ethical values, in the secrets of biological life falling under the sway of blind commerce or blind superstition, and above all, in the impending worldwide nuclear terror. May we not therefore say, as Plato said 2,500 years ago, that such "knowledge" as we have does not really deserve the label *knowledge?* Can we listen to him as he tells us that knowledge without virtue can neither bring us good nor show us truth? This is to say that such knowing as we have is not transformational; it does not elevate our level of being and it does not nourish the development of moral power.

It is only the fully developed human being, which means only the fully developed human mind in which the intuition of objective value is an essential component, that can see the world as it really is, and that, through its action upon our instincts and impulses, can lead us toward the capability to act in the service of the Good.

The present text is offered to us by Jean-Yves Leloup not so much as a commentary on these words of Jesus, but "as a meditation that arises from the tilled earth of our silence." I take this to mean that it is through the author's own inner opening toward the Self that his scholarly and theological skills take their ultimate direction in translating and interpreting what he rightly calls "this sublime jewel of a gospel." In other words, there may be, and I believe there are, two kinds or levels of knowing operating in this book. On one level, the visible level of words and concepts, there are the insights and explanations that will help every serious reader think in a new way about the meaning of the teaching of Jesus, a way that does not in any way deny the greatness of Christian doctrine that has brought comfort to countless millions of men and women throughout the ages. But for Leloup, this kind of knowing about the Christian religion, precious as it is, is secondary to a deeper kind given through the grace that is the fruit of the inner work of meditation.

And what words can characterize passage to this deeper level of knowing? Leloup puts it this way: "There exists a relative consciousness formed and acquired through readings, encounters, and the thoughts of others." And he goes on to say: "But there is also a consciousness that arises directly from knowledge of ourselves, of the 'Living One' within us. It is toward this consciousness, this gnosis, that Yeshua invites us in the Gospel of Thomas—not in order to become 'good Christians,' but to become christs—in other words, gnostics, or awakened human beings." This deeper knowing may properly be called pure consciousness—or, perhaps more precisely, the pure energy of consciousness. It is an energy, no doubt itself existing at many levels, that can be allowed to descend into the body, heart, and mind and, through its own active force, make of us the being called *anthropos,* the awakened, fully human being.

This energy is not what we ordinarily call *thought.* But it is this energy that has the power to do what we have wrongly imagined our ordinary thought can do: It can direct all our functions, including our mental thought. This book, therefore—as is true of Jean-Yves Leloup's presentations of the Gospel of Mary and the Gospel of Philip (which are also gnostic texts)—is in itself a step toward the work of the mind that desperately needs to be rediscovered in our era. The proper work of the mind is to function at two levels, the level of silence and the level of expression. And it is expression that is secondary—that is, truth in the form of words and formulations can come only out of silence, the state of the pure energy of consciousness anterior to its assumption of forms; words; ideas; associations; the organization of impressions, images, programs . . .

The mind alone—the mind that is not nourished by the silence of the fertile void of pure Being—as such is incapable of guiding human life. The ordinary, isolated intellect, no matter how brilliant or inspired, has not the energy to command our thoughts, words, impulses, memories and experiences in a way that conforms to truth and the Good. This, in sum, is the tragedy of our era, of our knowledge in the modern world. All that science has brought us—the phenomenal, wondrous discoveries it has brought us about life, matter and the universe—will eventually bring us nothing but destruction because we have forgotten that the mind alone cannot direct itself or the whole of ourselves. It does not have the energy for this. It is an energy that must come from another, higher level within the human psyche, a level that is experienced as silence.

Whatever we wish to call it, then—gnosticism, esotericism, mysticism, each in its authentic rather than imitative form—spiritual work has to do with energy rather than solely with what we call thought. Gnosis is a force, not just a set of ideas, symbols, or concepts. To the extent that we render our religious or moral teachings only in words, no matter how beautiful or systematic, we are bound to become the prey of academicism, dogmatism, or fanaticism. What our modern world has suffered from most of all is runaway ideology, the agitated attachment to ideas that thereby become the playthings of infrahuman energies. This is the great danger of all ideologies, whether political, religious, or academic.

"Is it possible," Leloup asks, "to read these logia [these sayings of Yeshua] in a way that allows them to make their way into the mind and the heart of our humanity, leading us into a voyage of transformation, toward a full realization of our being?" Within this question lie both the effort and the reward, the demand and the gift, offered by this and all truly sacred writings. What would it mean to attend to our inner state of being even as we try with all our might to grasp the meaning of these sayings— alone in our room or in our exchanges with companions and colleagues or, for that matter, in our inner confrontations with all the views that we may have previously taken as the sole truth? What would it bring to us now to keep a quiet mind alongside the passionate commitment to independent thought that once brought such hope to our modern world? "It is my belief," Leloup concludes, "that it is from this ground [of inner silence], rather than from mental agitation, that these words [of Yeshua] can bear their fruit of light."

JACOB NEEDLEMAN,
DEPARTMENT OF PHILOSOPHY,
SAN FRANCISCO STATE UNIVERSITY,
AND AUTHOR OF *LOST CHRISTIANITY AND THE AMERICAN SOUL*

ABBREVIATIONS

I Cor, II Cor	First Corinthians, Second Corinthians
I John	First Letter of John
I Peter	First Letter of Peter
I Thess, II Thess	First Thessalonians, Second Thessalonians
I Tim	First Timothy
Col	Colossians
Dan	Daniel
Deut	Deuteronomy
Eccus	Ecclesiasticus/Sirach
Eph	Ephesians
Ex	Exodus
Ezek	Ezekiel
Gal	Galatians
Gen	Genesis
Heb	Hebrews
James	Epistle of James
Jer	Jeremiah
John	The Gospel of John
Lev	Leviticus
Luke	The Gospel of Luke
Mark	The Gospel of Mark
Matt	The Gospel of Matthew
Num	Numbers
Phil	Philippians
Prov	Proverbs
Rev	Revelation
Rom	Romans
Zach	Zachariah

Introduction

The Discovery

It happened in 1945, in upper Egypt, in the area where Khenoboskion, the ancient monastic community founded by St. Pachomius, had once stood. There was nothing unusual about that particular stretch of land, near the Arab village of Nag Hammadi, and nothing unusual about the peasant digging there in search of fertilizer. It was by accident that his blade struck the treasure in the buried jar.

It was a treasure not of gold, but of words, emerging from the shroud of many centuries, written on parchment that had been slowly decaying under the sands: a gnostic library hidden in amphoras normally used to age wine. The library consisted of fifty-three parchments written in Sahidic Coptic, the last remaining language still close to the extinct ancient Egyptian pharaonic language. (The word Copt is derived from the Arabic *qibt*, which in turn derives from the Greek Aiguptios, Egypt.)

Among these fifty-three manuscripts, in Codex II, there is a gospel, or "good news," attributed to Jesus' disciple Thomas. This gospel contains no apocalyptic proclamations and no prophecies. Instead, it reveals what we have always carried within ourselves: an infinite Space, which is the same within us and without us. All that is needed is to break open the man-made jar that hides it from us.

This Gospel of Thomas contains no biography of Jesus (Yesu in Greek and Coptic, Yeshua in Aramaic), nor any account of his miracles. It is a collection of 114 sayings, called *logia* in Greek (singular: *logion*). These are said to be the naked words attributed to the Master, "the Living Jesus," written down by Didymus Judas Thomas, the Twin. Who was the

1

latter? Was he the "twin" (*didymos* in Greek, and *thomas* or *te'oma* in Aramaic) of Jesus in some sense of an alter ego or closest disciple? The sayings themselves do not elaborate on this, for they are anything but loquacious narratives. Many of them seem as terse and enigmatic as Zen koans. But if we allow them to penetrate into the ever-grinding cogs of our ordinary mental apparatus, they will sprout like living seeds and grow there—given time, they may bring the turning wheels to a full halt and a silence . . . a transformation of consciousness.

CRITICAL REACTION

This gospel has elicited a wide range of reactions from critics. For some scholars it represents one of many apocryphal writings, an item of academic interest in the study of gnostic texts. For others, it is a mere collage of the words of Jesus derived from the canonical gospels and mixed with heterodox traditions that claim to originate with Jesus. For still others, it is the closest document we have to the very source that the canonical gospels themselves drew upon, a tradition that predates them. In this view, the Gospel of Thomas is the "protogospel" that we have so long been seeking, the only one that transmits the authentic words of Jesus.

But whether we like it or not, Yeshua of Nazareth was not a writer. It is therefore impossible to speak of "the authentic words of Jesus." Every saying of his that we possess consists of words that have been *heard*— words that bear the imprint of a listener whose listening may be crude or subtle. The gospels of Mark, Matthew, Luke, John, Thomas, and a number of others represent at least five different ways of listening to the Word. Each also represents different ways of understanding, interpreting, and translating cultural and linguistic differences according to the quality of his own intimacy with the Master, and according to his own levels of evolution, openness, and awareness. None of these ways of listening can pretend to circumscribe the Word. Each has truth, but none contains the whole truth.

Thomas seems to have a less "Jewish" ear than does Matthew; he is less interested in stories of miracles than is Mark; and he does not share Luke's interest in the annunciation of God's Mercy, "even to the pagans." What interests Thomas is the transmission of Yeshua's teaching. Every saying received from the Master is treated as a seed, with the potential of growing a new kind of fully conscious human being. In this way, Thomas and other authors of the lineage of that "infinitely skeptical and infinitely believing" disciple see Yeshua as a gnostic, like themselves.

WAS YESHUA A GNOSTIC?

When Yeshua asks his disciples "Who am I to you?" only Thomas refuses to answer: "Master, my mouth could never utter what you are like." It is a good answer, recalling Yeshua's own answer of silence to Pilate's question "What is Truth?" Perhaps we, too, would do well to keep silent, instead of answering "Jesus is this" or "Jesus is that." This is in harmony with the practice of gnostics, who are not theologians concerned with finding names for the unnamable, but rather practitioners of "knowing silence."

Yeshua "Is What He Is." No one possesses a total and complete vision of Him. Yeshua only affirms, with love and power, a pure and simple "I Am." And this affirmation awakens a mysterious echo in each of us.

But what is his teaching? It is in relation to this question that the Gospel of Thomas can be considered a "gnostic" gospel— but only if *gnosis*[1] is understood to be nondualistic and is not confused with certain forms of dualistic or Manichean Gnosticism. Indeed, Yeshua appears in this gospel as a Being who seeks to awaken us to our own state of consciousness. This is also consonant with a passage in the Gospel of John, in which he says: "Where I am, I also wish you to be . . . the Spirit given me by my Father, I also have given to you . . . I am in you, and you are in me . . ." and so on.

Like the Eastern sages, Yeshua speaks in paradoxical aphorisms that invite us to become conscious of our uncreated origin, of our boundless freedom, even in the midst of the most severe contingencies. Thus we awaken to absolute Reality, right in the heart of the bleakest and most relative of realities.

---

1. [The Greek word *gnosis* is related, through its Indo-European root *gnô-*, to the English word *knowledge*, the French word *connaître*, the Latin *cognoscere*, the Sanskrit *jñana*, and many others. —*Trans.*]

Gnosis is a twofold lucidity regarding the human condition, at once a unitary witnessing and a dual awareness of both absurdity and grace. Relative reality shows us that we are dust and return to dust. "All that is composed, shall be decomposed," as Yeshua says in the Gospel of Mary Magdalene. But there is another reality, one that shows: "We are light, and return to light." Within us is a sun that never sets, a peace and wakefulness toward which our infinite desire yearns unceasingly. Relative reality shows us that we are either male or female; but full reality shows us that we are both.

Gnostics claim that an integration of our masculine and feminine polarities is possible, reaching toward a realized human beingness that does not love from lack, but rather from fullness. Then our love becomes not merely a thirst, but instead an overflowing fountain.

We must cross unceasingly from limited to unlimited consciousness. "Be passersby!" the Gospel of Thomas commands. There exists a relative consciousness formed and acquired through readings, encounters, and the thoughts of others. But there is also a consciousness that arises directly from knowledge of ourselves, of the "Living One" within us. It is toward this consciousness, this *gnosis,* that Yeshua invites us in the Gospel of Thomas, not in order to become "good Christians," but to become christs—in other words, gnostics, or awakened human beings. Gnosis is not some state of mental expansion or ego-inflation. On the contrary, it means putting an end to the ego. It is a transparency with regard to "the One who Is" in total innocence and simplicity. This is why the qualities of the gnostic are said to be unconditioned, to resemble those of "an infant seven days old."

Is the Yeshua of Thomas different from the Yeshua of the other gospels? Undoubtedly! But this difference resides not so much in the ultimate nature of the Christ as in the presentation of his teaching. It is a difference of hearing, rather than of words. Thus it is possible to read this gospel in a Catholic, Orthodox, or other manner, just as we read Luke, Mark, Matthew, and John in different ways. There is no need to enter into a dualistic polemic, setting the Gospel of Thomas against the canonical gospels, considering it superior to them and the only authentic gospel. To do so would, after all, be merely to give in to a reaction against the other dualistic polemic that has branded the Thomas Gospel as a fabrication of lies and heresies. (This is not unlike the former neglect of the Gospel of John, which many exegetes branded as either too Greek or too Gnostic . . . and today, there are those who say exactly the opposite.)

Might it not be that our task is to read all the gospels *together*, seeing them as different points of view of the Christ, different points of view that exist both within us and outside of us, in historical and meta-historical dimensions? Does not the Nag Hammadi discovery, with this sublime jewel of a gospel, reveal to us new facets of the unchanging Eternal Jewel? Is it not our task to go beyond both naive enthusiasm and doctrinaire suspicion to cultivate the ear of the golden mean and to learn to listen to the Spirit, which speaks to all human beings, beyond all Churches, religions, and elites?

THE TRANSLATION

In this translation of this gospel I have used the Coptic text as established by Yves Haas, as well as the Oxyrhynchus papyri and the Greek retroversion of Rudolf Kasser. I have also made use of the work of Professor Puech and of Professor Ménard, with whom I worked for some years at the University of Strasbourg on another great gnostic text, the Gospel of Truth. I make no claim here of presenting a "definitive" version of the Gospel of Thomas. This translation is one interpretation among a number of others, informed by my desire to be faithful to the breath, or spirit, as well as to the letters, of these words.

Pope Gregory I said that only a prophet could understand the prophets. And it is said that only a poet can understand a poet. Who, then, must we be in order to understand Yeshua?

THE COMMENTARY

Without underestimating the importance of scholarly expertise, yet determined to distance ourselves from the quarrels of scholars and esotericists, we must ask the question: Is it possible to truly *read* the Gospel of Thomas today? Is it possible to read it as a scripture unencumbered by the glosses of textual criticism or of subjective excess, allowing it to speak for itself and to inspire us? Is it possible to read these logia in a way that allows them to make their way into the mind and the heart of our humanity, leading us into a voyage of transformation, toward a full realization of our being?

If so, then what I propose is not so much a "commentary" on these words of Yeshua of Nazareth as it is a meditation that arises from the tilled earth of our silence. It is my belief that it is from this ground, rather than from mental agitation, that these words can bear their fruit of light.

THE TEXT OF THE
GOSPEL OF THOMAS

ⲚⲀⲈⲒ ⲚⲈ Ⲛ̄·ϢⲀϪⲈ ⲈⲐⲎⲠ` ⲈⲚⲦⲀ·Ⲓ̄Ⲥ̄ ⲈⲦ·ⲞⲚⲌ
·ϪⲞ·ⲞⲨ ⲀⲨⲰ Ⲁϥ·ⲤⲌⲀⲒⲤⲞⲨ Ⲛ̄ϬⲒ·ⲆⲒⲆⲨⲘⲞⲤ ϮⲞⲨⲆⲀⲤ ⲐⲰⲘⲀⲤ

1 ⲀⲨⲰ ⲠⲈⲬⲀ·ϥ` ϪⲈ ⲠⲈⲦⲀ·ⲌⲈ
Ⲉ̄·ⲐⲈⲢⲘⲎⲚⲈⲒⲀ Ⲛ̄·ⲚⲈⲈⲒ·ϢⲀϪⲈ ϥ·ⲚⲀ·
·ϪⲒ·ϮⲠⲈ ⲀⲚ Ⲙ̄·Ⲡ·ⲘⲞⲨ`

2 ⲠⲈⲬⲈ·Ⲓ̄Ⲥ̄ <> Ⲙ̄Ⲛ̄ⲦⲢⲉϥ`
·ⲖⲞ Ⲛ̄ϬⲒ·ⲠⲈⲦ·`·ϢⲒⲚⲈ Ⲉϥ·`·ϢⲒⲚⲈ ϢⲀⲚⲦⲉϥ`
·ϬⲒⲚⲈ ⲀⲨⲰ ⲌⲞⲦⲀⲚ` Ⲉϥ·ϢⲀⲚ·ϬⲒⲚⲈ ϥ·ⲚⲀ·
·ϢⲦⲢ̄Ⲧ̄Ⲣ̄ ⲀⲨⲰ Ⲉϥ·ϢⲀⲚ·`·ϢⲦⲞⲢⲦⲢ̄ ϥ·ⲚⲀ·Ⲣ̄·
[   ] ·ϢⲠⲎⲢⲈ ⲀⲨⲰ ϥ·ⲚⲀ·Ⲣ̄·
·Ⲣ̄ⲢⲞ ⲈϪⲘ̄·Ⲡ·ⲦⲎⲢ·ϥ

3 ⲠⲈⲬⲈ·Ⲓ̄Ⲥ̄ ϪⲈ ⲈⲨ·ϢⲀ·
·ϪⲞ·ⲞⲤ ⲚⲎ·ⲦⲚ̄ Ⲛ̄ϬⲒ·ⲚⲈⲦ·`·ⲤⲰⲔ ⲌⲎⲦ·`·ⲦⲎⲨⲦⲚ̄
ϪⲈ ⲈⲒⲤ·ⲌⲎⲎⲦⲈ Ⲉ·Ⲧ·`·Ⲙ̄Ⲛ̄ⲦⲈⲢⲞ ⲌⲚ̄·Ⲧ·ⲠⲈ ⲈⲒⲈ
Ⲛ̄·ⲌⲀⲖⲎⲦ` ·ⲚⲀ·Ⲣ̄·ϢⲞⲢⲠ` ⲈⲢⲰ·ⲦⲚ̄ Ⲛ̄ⲦⲈ·
·Ⲧ·ⲠⲈ ⲈⲨ·ϢⲀⲚ·ϪⲞ·ⲞⲤ ⲚⲎ·ⲦⲚ̄ ϪⲈ Ⲥ·ⲌⲚ̄·ⲐⲀⲖⲀⲤⲤⲀ
ⲈⲒⲈ Ⲛ̄·ⲦⲂⲦ` ·ⲚⲀ·Ⲣ̄·ϢⲞⲢⲠ` ⲈⲢⲰ·ⲦⲚ̄
ⲀⲖⲖⲀ Ⲧ·Ⲙ̄Ⲛ̄ⲦⲈⲢⲞ Ⲥ·Ⲙ̄·ⲠⲈⲦⲚ̄·ⲌⲞⲨⲚ` ⲀⲨⲰ
Ⲥ·Ⲙ̄·ⲠⲈⲦⲚ̄·ⲂⲀⲖ` ⲌⲞⲦⲀⲚ ⲈⲦⲈⲦⲚ̄·ϢⲀⲚ·
·ⲤⲞⲨⲰⲚ·ⲦⲎⲨⲦⲚ̄ ⲦⲞⲦⲈ ⲤⲈ·ⲚⲀ·ⲤⲞⲨⲰ ̄
·ⲦⲎⲚⲈ ⲀⲨⲰ ⲦⲈⲦⲚⲀ·ⲈⲒⲘⲈ ϪⲈ Ⲛ̄·ⲦⲰ·ⲦⲚ̄ ⲠⲈ
Ⲛ̄·ϢⲎⲢⲈ Ⲙ̄·Ⲡ·ⲈⲒⲰⲦ` ⲈⲦ·ⲞⲚⲌ ⲈϢⲰⲠⲈ ⲆⲈ
ⲦⲈⲦⲚⲀ·ⲤⲞⲨⲰⲚ·ⲦⲎⲨⲦⲚ̄ ⲀⲚ ⲈⲒⲈ ⲦⲈⲦⲚ̄·
·ϢⲞⲞⲠ` ⲌⲚ̄·ⲞⲨ·Ⲙ̄Ⲛ̄Ⲧ·ⲌⲎⲔⲈ ⲀⲨⲰ Ⲛ̄·ⲦⲰ·ⲦⲚ̄
ⲠⲈ Ⲧ·Ⲙ̄Ⲛ̄Ⲧ·ⲌⲎⲔⲈ

4 ⲠⲈⲬⲈ·Ⲓ̄Ⲥ̄ <> ϥ·ⲚⲀ·ϪⲚⲀⲨ ⲀⲚ
Ⲛ̄ϬⲒ·Ⲡ·ⲢⲰⲘⲈ Ⲛ̄·ⲌⲀⲖⲞ ⲌⲚ̄·ⲚⲈϥ·ⲌⲞⲞⲨ Ⲉ·ϪⲚⲈ·
·ⲞⲨ·ⲔⲞⲨⲈⲒ Ⲛ̄·ϢⲎⲢⲈ·ϢⲎⲘ Ⲉϥ·ⲌⲚ̄·ⲤⲀϢϥ̄
Ⲛ̄·ⲌⲞⲞⲨ ⲈⲦⲂⲈ·Ⲡ·ⲦⲞⲠⲞⲤ Ⲙ̄·Ⲡ·ⲰⲚⲌ ⲀⲨⲰ
ϥ·ⲚⲀ·ⲰⲚⲌ ϪⲈ ⲞⲨⲚ̄·ⲌⲀⲌ Ⲛ̄·ϢⲞⲢⲠ` ·ⲚⲀ·Ⲣ̄·ⲌⲀⲈ
ⲀⲨⲰ Ⲛ̄ⲤⲈ·ϢⲰⲠⲈ ⲞⲨⲀ ⲞⲨⲰⲦ

These are the words of the Secret.
They were revealed by the Living Yeshua.
Didymus Judas Thomas wrote them down.

1   Yeshua said:
Whoever lives the interpretation of these words
will no longer taste death.

2   Yeshua said:
Whoever searches
must continue to search
until they find.
When they find,
they will be disturbed;
and being disturbed, they will marvel
and will reign over All.

3   Yeshua said:
If those who guide you say: Look,
the Kingdom is in the sky,
then the birds are closer than you.
If they say: Look,
it is in the sea,
then the fish already know it.
The Kingdom is inside you,
and it is outside you.
When you know yourself, then you will be known,
and you will know that you are the child of the Living Father;
but if you do not know yourself,
you will live in vain
and you will be vanity.

4   Yeshua said:
An aged person will not hesitate to ask a seven-day-old infant
about the Place of Life, and that person will live.
Many of the first will make themselves last, and they will
become One.

5   ⲡⲉⲭⲉ·ⲓ̅ⲥ̅ ⲥⲟⲩⲱⲛ·ⲡⲉⲧ·ⲙ̄·ⲡ·ⲙ̄ⲧⲟ ⲙ̄·ⲡⲉⲕ·ⲋⲟ ⲉⲃⲟⲗ`
    ⲁⲩⲱ ⲡⲉⲑⲏⲡ` ⲉⲣⲟ·ⲕ` ⳝ·ⲛⲁ·ϭⲱⲗⲡ` ⲉⲃⲟⲗ
    ⲛⲁ·ⲕ` ⲙ̄·ⲗⲁⲁⲩ ⲅⲁⲣ ⲉⳝ·ⲋⲏⲡ` ⲉⳝ·ⲛⲁ·ⲟⲩⲱⲛⲋ
    ⲉⲃⲟⲗ ⲁⲛ

6   ⲁⲩ·ⲭⲛⲟⲩ·ⳝ ⲛ̄ϭⲓ·ⲛⲉ·ⳝ·`·ⲙⲁⲑⲏⲧⲏⲥ
    ⲡⲉⲭⲁ·ⲩ ⲛⲁ·ⳝ` ⲭⲉ ⲕ·`·ⲟⲩⲱ·ϣ ⲉⲧⲣⲛ̄·ⲣ̄·ⲛⲏⲥⲧⲉⲩⲉ
    ⲁⲩⲱ ⲉ·ϣ ⲧⲉ ⲑⲉ ⲉⲛⲁ·ϣⲗⲏⲗ ⲉⲛⲁ·†·ⲉⲗⲉⲏⲙⲟⲥⲩⲛⲏ
    ⲁⲩⲱ ⲉⲛⲁ·ⲣ̄·ⲡⲁⲣⲁⲧⲏⲣⲉⲓ ⲉ·ⲟⲩ
    ⲛ̄·ϭⲓ·ⲟⲩⲱⲙ` ⲡⲉⲭⲉ·ⲓ̅ⲥ̅ ⲭⲉ ⲙ̄·ⲡⲣ̄·ⲭⲉ·ϭⲟⲗ ⲁⲩⲱ
    ⲡⲉⲧⲉⲧⲙ̄·ⲙⲟⲥⲧⲉ ⲙ̄·ⲙⲟ·ⳝ` ⲙ̄·ⲡⲣ̄·ⲁ·ⲁⳝ ⲭⲉ
    ⲥⲉ·ϭⲟⲗⲡ` ⲧⲏⲣ·ⲟⲩ ⲉⲃⲟⲗ ⲙ̄·ⲡⲉ·ⲙⲧⲟ ⲉⲃⲟⲗ
    ⲛ̄·ⲧ·ⲡⲉ ⲙ̄·ⲗⲁⲁⲩ ⲅⲁⲣ ⲉⳝ·ⲋⲏⲡ` ⲉⳝ·ⲛⲁ·ⲟⲩⲱⲛⲋ
    ⲉⲃⲟⲗ ⲁⲛ ⲁⲩⲱ ⲙ̄·ⲗⲁⲁⲩ ⲉⳝ·ⲋⲟⲃⲥ̅ ⲉⲩ·
    ·ⲛⲁ·ϭⲱ ⲟⲩⲉ·ϣⲛ̄·ϭⲟⲗⲡ·ⳝ`

7   ⲡⲉⲭⲉ·ⲓ̅ⲥ̅ <> ⲟⲩ·
    ·ⲙⲁⲕⲁⲣⲓⲟⲥ ⲡⲉ ⲡ·ⲙⲟⲩⲉⲓ ⲡⲁⲉⲓ ⲉⲧⲉ
    ⲡ·ⲣⲱⲙⲉ ·ⲛⲁ·ⲟⲩⲟⲙ·ⳝ ⲁⲩⲱ ⲛ̄ⲧⲉ·ⲡ·ⲙⲟⲩⲉⲓ
    ·ϣⲱⲡⲉ ⲣ̄·ⲣⲱⲙⲉ ⲁⲩⲱ ⳝ·ⲃⲏⲧ` ⲛ̄ϭⲓ·ⲡ·ⲣⲱⲙⲉ
    ⲡⲁⲉⲓ ⲉⲧⲉ ⲡ·ⲙⲟⲩⲉⲓ ·ⲛⲁ·ⲟⲩⲟⲙ·ⳝ ⲁⲩⲱ
    ⲡ·ⲙⲟⲩⲉⲓ ·ⲛⲁ·ϣⲱⲡⲉ ⲣ̄·ⲣⲱⲙⲉ

8   ⲁⲩⲱ ⲡⲉⲭⲁ·ⳝ
    ⲭⲉ ⲉ·ⲡ·ⲣⲱⲙⲉ ·ⲧⲛ̄ⲧⲱⲛ ⲁ·ⲩ·ⲟⲩⲱϩⲉ
    ⲣ̄·ⲣⲙ·ⲛ̄·ϩⲏⲧ` ⲡⲁⲉⲓ ⲛ̄ⲧⲁϩ·ⲛⲟⲩϫⲉ ⲛ̄·ⲧⲉⳝ·ⲁⲃⲱ
    ⲉ·ⲑⲁⲗⲁⲥⲥⲁ ⲁⳝ·ⲥⲱⲕ ⲙ̄·ⲙⲟ·ⲥ ⲉ·ϩⲣⲁⲓ̈
    ϩⲛ̄·ⲑⲁⲗⲁⲥⲥⲁ ⲉⲥ·ⲙⲉϩ ⲛ̄·ⲧⲃⲧ` ⲛ̄·ⲕⲟⲩⲉⲓ ⲛ̄·
    ·ϩⲣⲁⲓ̈ ⲛ̄·ϩⲏⲧ·ⲟⲩ ⲁⳝ·ϩⲉ ⲁ·ⲩ·ⲛⲟϭ ⲛ̄·ⲧⲃⲧ ⲉ·ⲛⲁⲛⲟⲩ·ⳝ`
    ⲛ̄ϭⲓ·ⲡ·ⲟⲩⲱϩⲉ ⲣ̄·ⲣⲙ·ⲛ̄·ϩⲏⲧ` ⲁⳝ·ⲛⲟⲩϫⲉ
    ⲛ̄·ⲛ̄·ⲕⲟⲩⲉⲓ ⲧⲏⲣ·ⲟⲩ ⲛ̄·ⲧⲃⲧ` ⲉⲃⲟⲗ ⲉ[ⲡ·ⲉ]ⲥⲏⲧ`
    ⲉ·ⲑⲁⲗⲁⲥⲥⲁ ⲁⳝ·ⲥⲱⲧⲡ` ⲙ̄·ⲡ·ⲛⲟϭ ⲛ̄·
    ·ⲧⲃⲧ ⲭⲱⲣⲓⲥ·ϩⲓⲥⲉ ⲡⲉⲧⲉ·ⲟⲩⲛ̄·ⲙⲁⲁϫⲉ ⲙ̄·ⲙⲟ·ⳝ
    ⲉ·ⲥⲱⲧⲙ̄ ⲙⲁⲣⲉⳝ·`·ⲥⲱⲧⲙ̄

9   ⲡⲉⲭⲉ·ⲓ̅ⲥ̅ ⲭⲉ ⲉⲓⲥ·ϩⲏⲏⲧⲉ`
    ⲁⳝ·ⲉⲓ ⲉⲃⲟⲗ ⲛ̄ϭⲓ·ⲡⲉⲧ·`·ⲥⲓⲧⲉ ⳝ·ⲙⲉϩ·ⲧⲟⲟⲧ·ⳝ̄
    ⲁⳝ·ⲛⲟⲩϫⲉ ⲁ·ϩⲟⲉⲓⲛⲉ ⲙⲉⲛ ·ϩⲉ ⲉⲭⲛ̄·ⲧⲉ·ϩⲓⲏ`
    ⲁⲩ·ⲉⲓ ⲛ̄ϭⲓ·ⲛ̄·ϩⲁⲗⲁⲧⲉ ⲁⲩ·ⲕⲁⲧ·ⳝ·ⲟⲩ ϩⲛ̄·ⲕⲟⲟⲩⲉ

5   Yeshua said:
Recognize what is in front of you,
and what is hidden from you will be revealed.
There is nothing hidden that will not be revealed.

6   His disciples questioned him:
"Should we fast? How should we pray? How should we give
    alms? What rules of diet should we follow?"
Yeshua said:
Stop lying.
Do not do that which is against your love.
You are naked before heaven.
What you hide will be revealed,
whatever is veiled will be unveiled.

7   Yeshua said:
Fortunate is the lion eaten by a human,
for lion becomes human.
Unfortunate is the human eaten by a lion,
for human becomes lion.

8   Yeshua said:
A human being is like a good fisherman
who casts his net into the sea.
When he pulls it out, he finds a multitude of little fish.
Among them there is one fine, large fish.
Without hesitation, he keeps it and throws all the small fish
    back into the sea.
Those who have ears, let them hear!

9   Yeshua said:
Once a sower went out
and sowed a handful of seeds.
Some fell on the road,
and were eaten by birds.
Some fell among the thorns,
which smothered their growth,
and the worms devoured them.
Some fell among the rocks,

ⲁⲩ·ϩⲉ ⲉⲭⲛ̄·ⲧ·ⲉⲭⲛ̄·ⲧ·ⲡⲉⲧⲣⲁ ⲁⲩⲱ ⲙ̄ⲡⲟⲩ·ϫⲉ·ⲛⲟⲩⲛⲉ
ⲉ·ⲡ·ⲉⲥⲏⲧ` ⲉ·ⲡ·ⲕⲁϩ ⲁⲩⲱ ⲙ̄ⲡⲟⲩ·ⲧⲉⲩⲉ·ϩⲙ̄ⲥ̄ ⲉ·ϩⲣⲁⲓ
ⲉ·ⲧ·ⲡⲉ ⲁⲩⲱ ϩⲛ̄·ⲕⲟⲟⲩⲉ ⲁⲩ·ϩⲉ ⲉⲭⲛ̄·ⲛ̄·ϣⲟ‾ⲧⲉ
ⲁⲩ·ⲱϭⲧ` ⲙ̄·ⲡⲉ·ϭⲣⲟϭ ⲁⲩⲱ ⲁ·ⲡ·ϥⲛ̄ⲧ ·ⲟⲩⲟⲙ·ⲟⲩ
ⲁⲩⲱ ⲁ·ϩⲛ̄·ⲕⲟⲟⲩⲉ ·ϩⲉ ⲉⲭⲛ̄·ⲡ·ⲕⲁϩ ⲉⲧ·ⲛⲁⲛⲟⲩ·ϥ`
ⲁⲩⲱ ⲁϥ·ϯ·ⲕⲁⲣⲡⲟⲥ ⲉ·ϩⲣⲁⲓ ⲉ·ⲧ·ⲡⲉ ⲉ·ⲛⲁⲛⲟⲩ·ϥ` ⲁϥ·
·ⲉⲓ ⲛ̄·ⲥⲉ ⲉ·ⲥⲟⲧⲉ ⲁⲩⲱ ϣⲉ·ϫⲟⲩⲱⲧ` ⲉ·ⲥⲟⲧⲉ

10 ⲡⲉϫⲉ·ⲓ̄ⲥ̄ ϫⲉ ⲁⲉⲓ·ⲛⲟⲩϫⲉ ⲛ̄·ⲟⲩ·ⲕⲱϩⲧ` ⲉⲭⲛ̄·
·ⲡ·ⲕⲟⲥⲙⲟⲥ ⲁⲩⲱ ⲉⲓⲥ·ϩⲏⲏⲧⲉ ϯ·ⲁⲣⲉϩ ⲉⲣⲟ·ϥ`
ϣⲁⲛⲧⲉϥ·ϫⲉⲣⲟ

11 ⲡⲉϫⲉ·ⲓ̄ⲥ̄ ϫⲉ ⲧⲉⲉⲓ·ⲡⲉ ·ⲛⲁ·ⲣ̄·ⲡⲁⲣⲁⲅⲉ
ⲁⲩⲱ ⲧⲉⲧ·ⲛ̄·ⲧ·ⲡⲉ ⲙ̄·ⲙⲟ·ⲥ ·ⲛⲁ·ⲣ̄·ⲡⲁⲣⲁⲅⲉ
ⲁⲩⲱ ⲛⲉⲧ·ⲙⲟⲟⲩⲧ ⲥⲉ·ⲟⲛϩ ⲁⲛ ⲁⲩⲱ ⲛⲉⲧ·ⲟⲛϩ
ⲥⲉ·ⲛⲁ·ⲙⲟⲩ ⲁⲛ ⲛ̄·ϩⲟⲟⲩ ⲛⲉ·ⲧⲉⲧⲛ̄·ⲟⲩⲱⲙ`
ⲙ̄·ⲡⲉⲧ·ⲙⲟⲟⲩⲧ` ⲛⲉ·ⲧⲉⲧⲛ̄·ⲉⲓⲣⲉ ⲙ̄·ⲙⲟ·ϥ ⲙ̄·ⲡⲉⲧ·ⲟⲛϩ
ϩⲟⲧⲁⲛ ⲉⲧⲉⲧⲛ̄·ϣⲁⲛ·ϣⲱⲡⲉ ϩⲙ̄·ⲡ·ⲟⲩⲟⲉⲓⲛ
ⲟⲩ ⲡⲉ ⲧⲉⲧⲛⲁ·ⲁ·ϥ ϩⲙ̄·ⲫⲟⲟⲩ ⲉⲧⲉⲧⲛ̄·
·ⲟ ⲛ̄·ⲟⲩⲁ ⲁⲧⲉⲧⲛ̄·ⲉⲓⲣⲉ ⲙ̄·ⲡ·ⲥⲛⲁⲩ ϩⲟⲧⲁⲛ ⲇⲉ
ⲉⲧⲉⲧⲛ̄·ϣⲁ·ϣⲱⲡⲉ ⲛ̄·ⲥⲛⲁⲩ` ⲟⲩ ⲡⲉ ⲉⲧⲉⲧⲛ̄·ⲛⲁ·ⲁ·ϥ`

12 ⲡⲉϫⲉ·ⲙ̄·ⲙⲁⲑⲏⲧⲏⲥ ⲛ̄·ⲓ̄ⲥ̄ ϫⲉ ⲧⲛ̄·
·ⲥⲟⲟⲩⲛ ϫⲉ ⲕ·ⲛⲁ·ⲃⲱⲕ` ⲛ̄·ⲧⲟⲟⲧ·ⲛ̄ ⲛⲓⲙ` ⲡⲉ
ⲉⲧ·ⲛⲁ·ⲣ̄·ⲛⲟϭ ⲉ·ϩⲣⲁⲓ ⲉⲭⲱ·ⲛ ⲡⲉϫⲉ·ⲓ̄ⲥ̄ ⲛⲁ·ⲩ
ϫⲉ ⲡ·ⲙⲁ ⲛ̄ⲧⲁⲧⲉⲧⲛ̄·ⲉⲓ ⲙ̄·ⲙⲁⲩ ⲉⲧⲉⲧⲛⲁ·
·ⲃⲱⲕ` ϣⲁ·ⲓ̈ⲁⲕⲱⲃⲟⲥ ⲡ·ⲇⲓⲕⲁⲓⲟⲥ ⲡⲁⲉⲓ ⲛ̄ⲧⲁ·
·ⲧ·ⲡⲉ ⲙ̄ⲛ̄·ⲡ·ⲕⲁϩ ·ϣⲱⲡⲉ ⲉⲧⲃⲏⲧ·ϥ̄

13 ⲡⲉϫⲉ·ⲓ̄ⲥ̄ ⲛ̄·ⲛⲉϥ·ⲙⲁⲑⲏⲧⲏⲥ ϫⲉ ·ⲧⲛ̄ⲧⲱⲛ·ⲧ` ⲛ̄ⲧⲉⲧⲛ̄·
·ϫⲟ·ⲟⲥ ⲛⲁ·ⲉⲓ ϫⲉ ⲉ·ⲉⲓⲛⲉ ⲛ̄·ⲛⲓⲙ ⲡⲉϫⲁ·ϥ ⲛⲁ·ϥ`
ⲛ̄ϭⲓ·ⲥⲓⲙⲱⲛ·ⲡⲉⲧⲣⲟⲥ ϫⲉ ⲉⲕ·ⲉⲓⲛⲉ ⲛ̄·ⲟⲩ·ⲁⲅ`
ⲅⲉⲗⲟⲥ ⲛ̄·ⲇⲓⲕⲁⲓⲟⲥ ⲡⲉϫⲁ·ϥ ⲛⲁ·ϥ ⲛ̄ϭⲓ·ⲙⲁⲑ`
ⲑⲁⲓⲟⲥ ϫⲉ ⲉⲕ·ⲉⲓⲛⲉ ⲛ̄·ⲟⲩ·ⲣⲱⲙⲉ ⲙ̄·ⲫⲓⲗⲟⲥⲟⲫⲟⲥ
ⲛ̄·ⲣⲙ̄·ⲛ̄·ϩⲏⲧ` ⲡⲉϫⲁ·ϥ ⲛⲁ·ϥ ⲛ̄ϭⲓ·ⲑⲱⲙⲁⲥ
ϫⲉ ⲡ·ⲥⲁϩ ϩⲟⲗⲱⲥ ⲧⲁ·ⲧⲁⲡⲣⲟ ·ⲛⲁ·ϣⲁⲡ·ϥ` ⲁⲛ
ⲉⲧⲣⲁ·ϫⲟ·ⲟⲥ ϫⲉ ⲉⲕ·ⲉⲓⲛⲉ ⲛ̄·ⲛⲓⲙ` ⲡⲉϫⲉ·ⲓ̄ⲏ̄ⲥ̄
ϫⲉ ⲁⲛⲟ·ⲕ` ⲡⲉⲕ·`·ⲥⲁϩ ⲁⲛ ⲉⲡⲉⲓ ⲁⲕ·ⲥⲱ ⲁⲕ·ϯϩⲉ
ⲉⲃⲟⲗ ϩⲛ̄·ⲧ·ⲡⲏⲅⲏ ⲉⲧ·ⲃⲣ̄ⲃⲣⲉ ⲧⲁⲉⲓ ⲁⲛⲟ·ⲕ`
ⲛ̄ⲧⲁⲉⲓ·ϣⲓⲧ·ⲥ̄ ⲁⲩⲱ ⲁϥ·ϫⲓⲧ·ϥ̄ ⲁϥ·ⲁⲛⲁⲭⲱⲣⲉⲓ

and could not take root.
Others fell on fertile ground,
and their fruits grew up toward heaven.
They produced sixty and one hundred-twenty units per measure.

10 Yeshua said:
I have sown fire upon the world,
and now I tend it to a blaze.

11 Yeshua said:
This sky will pass away,
and the one above it will also pass away.
The dead have no life,
and the living have no death.
On days when you ate what was dead,
you made it alive.
When you are in the light, what will you do?
When you were One, you created two.
But now that you are two, what will you do?

12 The disciples said to Yeshua:
"We know that you will leave us.
Who will be great among us then?"
Yeshua told them:
When you find yourselves at that point,
go to James[1] the Just:
All that concerns heaven and earth is his domain.

13 Yeshua said to his disciples:
What am I like, for you?
To what would you compare me?
Simon Peter said: "You are like a righteous angel."
Matthew said: "You are like a wise philosopher."
Thomas said: "Master, my mouth could never utter what you
   are like."
Yeshua told him:
I am no longer your Master, because you have drunk, and

---

1. This refers to James (i.e., Jacob), the brother of Yeshua.

ⲁϥ·ⲭⲱ ⲛⲁ·ϥ ⲛ̄·ϣⲟⲙⲧ` ⲛ̄·ϣⲁϫⲉ ⲛ̄ⲧⲁⲣⲉ·ⲑⲱⲙⲁⲥ
ⲇⲉ ·ⲉⲓ ϣⲁ·ⲛⲉϥ·``ϣⲃⲉⲉⲣ` ⲁⲩ·ⲭⲛⲟⲩ·ϥ` ⲭⲉ
ⲛ̄ⲧⲁ·ⲓ̅ⲥ̅·ⲭⲟ·ⲟⲥ ⲭⲉ ⲟⲩ ⲛⲁ·ⲕ` ⲡⲉⲭⲁ·ϥ` ⲛⲁ·ⲩ ⲛ̄ϭⲓ·
·ⲑⲱⲙⲁⲥ ⲭⲉ ⲉⲓ·ϣⲁⲛ·``ⲭⲱ ⲛⲏ·ⲧⲛ̄ ⲟⲩⲁ ⲍ̄ⲛ̄·ⲛ̄·ϣⲁⲭⲉ
ⲛ̄ⲧⲁϥ·ⲭⲟ·ⲟⲩ ⲛⲁ·ⲉⲓ ⲧⲉⲧⲛⲁ·ϥⲓ·ⲱⲛⲉ ⲛ̄ⲧⲉ ⲧⲛ̄·ⲛⲟⲩⲭⲉ
ⲉⲣⲟ·ⲉⲓ ⲁⲩⲱ ⲛ̄ⲧⲉ·ⲟⲩ·ⲕⲱⲍⲧ` ·ⲉⲓ ⲉ ⲃⲟⲗ
ⲍ̄ⲛ̄·ⲛ̄·ⲱⲛⲉ ⲛ̄ⲥ·ⲣⲱⲍⲕ` ⲙ̄·ⲙⲱ·ⲧⲛ̄

14 ⲡⲉⲭⲉ· ⲓ̅ⲥ̅ ⲛⲁ·ⲩ ⲭⲉ ⲉⲧⲉⲧⲛ̄·ϣⲁⲛ·ⲣ̄·ⲛⲏⲥⲧⲉⲩⲉ ⲧⲉⲧⲛⲁ·
·ⲭⲡⲟ ⲛⲏ·ⲧⲛ̄ ⲛ̄·ⲛⲟⲩ·ⲛⲟⲃⲉ ⲁⲩⲱ ⲉⲧⲉⲧⲛ̄·ϣⲁ¯·
·ϣⲗⲏⲗ` ⲥⲉ·ⲛⲁ·ⲣ̄·ⲕⲁⲧⲁⲕⲣⲓⲛⲉ ⲙ̄·ⲙⲱ·ⲧⲛ̄ ⲁⲩⲱ
ⲉⲧⲉⲧⲛ̄·ϣⲁⲛ·ϯ·ⲉⲗⲉⲏⲙⲟⲥⲩⲛⲏ ⲉⲧⲉⲧⲛⲁ·ⲉⲓⲣⲉ
ⲛ̄·ⲟⲩ·ⲕⲁⲕⲟⲛ ⲛ̄·ⲛⲉⲧⲙ̄·ⲡ̄ⲛ̄ⲁ̄ ⲁⲩⲱ ⲉⲧⲉⲧⲛ̄·
·ϣⲁⲛ·ⲃⲱⲕ` ⲉⲍⲟⲩⲛ ⲉ·ⲕⲁⲍ ·ⲛⲓⲙ ⲁⲩⲱ ⲛ̄ⲧⲉⲧⲙ̄·
·ⲙⲟⲟϣⲉ ⲍ̄ⲛ̄·ⲛ̄·ⲭⲱⲣⲁ ⲉⲩ·ϣⲁ·ⲣ̄·ⲡⲁⲣⲁⲇⲉⲭⲉ ⲙ̄·ⲙⲱ·ⲧⲛ̄
         ⲡⲉⲧ·ⲟⲩ·ⲛⲁ·ⲕⲁⲁ·ϥ ⲍⲁⲣⲱ·ⲧⲛ̄ ·ⲟⲩⲟⲙ·ϥ̄
ⲛⲉⲧ·ϣⲱⲛⲉ ⲛ̄·ⲍⲏⲧ·ⲟⲩ ⲉⲣⲓ·ⲑⲉⲣⲁⲡⲉⲩⲉ ⲙ̄·ⲙⲟ·
·ⲟⲩ ⲡⲉⲧ·ⲛⲁ·ⲃⲱⲕ ⲅⲁⲣ` ⲉⲍⲟⲩⲛ ⲍ̄ⲛ̄·ⲧⲉⲧⲛ̄·ⲧⲁⲡⲣⲟ
ϥ·ⲛⲁ·ⲭⲱⲍⲙ̄·ⲧⲏⲩⲧⲛ̄ ⲁⲛ` ⲁⲗⲗⲁ ⲡⲉⲧ·ⲛ̄ⲛⲏⲩ
ⲉⲃⲟⲗ` ⲍ̄ⲛ̄·ⲧⲉⲧⲛ̄·ⲧⲁⲡⲣⲟ ⲛ̄·ⲧⲟ·ϥ ⲡⲉⲧ·ⲛⲁ·ⲭⲁⲍⲙ̄·ⲧⲏⲩⲧⲛ̄

15 ⲡⲉⲭⲉ·ⲓ̅ⲥ̅ ⲭⲉ ⲍⲟⲧⲁⲛ
ⲉⲧⲉⲧⲛ̄·ϣⲁⲛ·ⲛⲁⲩ ⲉ·ⲡⲉⲧⲉ·ⲙ̄ⲡⲟⲩ·ⲭⲡⲟ·ϥ`
ⲉⲃⲟⲗ ⲍ̄ⲛ̄·ⲧ·ⲥⲍⲓⲙⲉ ·ⲡⲉⲍⲧ·``ⲧⲏⲩⲧⲛ̄ ⲉⲭⲙ̄·
·ⲡⲉⲧⲛ̄·ⲍⲟ ⲛ̄ⲧⲉⲧⲛ̄·ⲟⲩⲱϣⲧ ⲛⲁ·ϥ` ⲡⲉⲧ·ⲙ̄·
·ⲙⲁⲩ ⲡⲉ ⲡⲉⲧⲛ̄·ⲉⲓⲱⲧ`

16 ⲡⲉⲭⲉ·ⲓ̅ⲥ̅ ⲭⲉ ⲧⲁⲭⲁ
ⲉⲩ·ⲙⲉⲉⲩⲉ ⲛ̄ϭⲓ·ⲣ̄·ⲣⲱⲙⲉ ⲭⲉ ⲛ̄ⲧⲁⲉⲓ·ⲉⲓ ⲉ·ⲛⲟⲩⲭⲉ
ⲛ̄·ⲟⲩ·ⲉⲓⲣⲏⲛⲏ ⲉⲭⲙ̄·ⲡ·ⲕⲟⲥⲙⲟⲥ ⲁⲩⲱ
ⲥⲉ·ⲥⲟⲟⲩⲛ ⲁⲛ ⲭⲉ ⲛ̄ⲧⲁⲉⲓ·ⲉⲓ ⲁ·ⲛⲟⲩⲭⲉ ⲛ̄·ⲍ̄ⲛ̄·
·ⲡⲱⲣⲭ` ⲉⲭⲛ̄·ⲡ·ⲕⲁⲍ ⲟⲩ·ⲕⲱⲍⲧ ⲟⲩ·ⲥⲛϥⲉ`
ⲟⲩ·ⲡⲟⲗⲉⲙⲟⲥ ⲟⲩⲛ̄·ϯⲟⲩ ⲅⲁⲣ ·ⲛⲁ·ϣⲱ[ⲡⲉ]
ⲍ̄ⲛ̄·ⲟⲩ·ⲏⲉⲓ ⲟⲩⲛ̄·ϣⲟⲙⲧ ·ⲛⲁ·ϣⲱⲡⲉ ⲉⲭⲛ̄·
·ⲥⲛⲁⲩ ⲁⲩⲱ ⲥⲛⲁⲩ ⲉⲭⲛ̄·ϣⲟⲙⲧ` ⲡ·ⲉⲓⲱⲧ`
ⲉⲭⲙ̄·ⲡ·ϣⲏⲣⲉ ⲁⲩⲱ ⲡ·ϣⲏⲣⲉ ⲉⲭⲙ̄·ⲡ·ⲉⲓⲱⲧ`
ⲁⲩⲱ` ⲥⲉ·ⲛⲁ·ⲱⲍⲉ ⲉ·ⲣⲁⲧ·ⲟⲩ ⲉⲩ·ⲟ ⲙ̄·ⲙⲟⲛⲁⲭⲟⲥ

17 ⲡⲉⲭⲉ·ⲓ̅ⲥ̅ ⲭⲉ ϯ·ⲛⲁ·ϯ ⲛⲏ·ⲧⲛ̄ ⲙ̄·ⲡⲉⲧⲉ·
·ⲙ̄ⲡⲉ·ⲃⲁⲗ ·ⲛⲁⲩ ⲉⲣⲟ·ϥ` ⲁⲩⲱ ⲡⲉⲧⲉ·ⲙ̄ⲡⲉ·ⲙⲁⲁⲭⲉ

become drunken, from the same bubbling source from
which I spring.

Then he took him aside, and said three words to him . . .

When Thomas returned to his companions, they questioned
him: "What did Yeshua tell you?"

Thomas answered: "If I told you even one of the things he said
to me, you would pick up stones and throw them at me.
And fire would come out those stones, and consume you."

14   Yeshua said to them:

If you fast, you will be at fault.

If you pray, you will be wrong.

If you give to charity, you will corrupt your mind.

When you go into any land and walk through the countryside,
if they welcome you, eat whatever they offer you.

You can heal their sick.

It is not what goes into your mouth that defiles you,
it is what comes out of your mouth that defiles you.

15   Yeshua said:

When you see someone who was not born from a womb, then
prostrate yourselves and give worship, for this is your
Father.

16   Yeshua said:

People may think that I have come to bring peace to the world.

They do not know that I have come to sow division upon the
earth: fire, sword, war.

When there are five in a house, three will be against two and
two against three; father against son and son against father.

And they will stand, and they will be alone and simple
[*monakhos*].

17   Yeshua said:

I will give you that which no eye has seen,
no ear has heard,

·ⲤⲞⲦⲘ·ⲈⲞ̄` ⲀⲨⲰ ⲠⲈⲦⲈ·Ⲙ̄ⲠⲈ·ϬⲒⲬ` ·ϬⲘ̄ϬⲰⲘ·Ꝙ̄`
ⲀⲨⲰ Ⲙ̄ⲠⲈϤ·`·ⲈⲒ Ⲉ·ⲌⲢⲀⲒ̈ ⲌⲒ·ⲪⲎⲦ`
Ⲣ̄·ⲢⲰⲘⲈ

18 ⲠⲈⲬⲈ·Ⲙ̄·ⲘⲀⲐⲎⲦⲎⲤ Ⲛ̄·ⲒⲤ̄ ⲬⲈ ·ⲬⲞ·
·ⲞⲤ ⲈⲢⲞ·Ⲛ ⲬⲈ ⲦⲚ̄·ⲌⲀⲎ ⲈⲤ·ⲚⲀ·Ⲱ̄ⲰⲠⲈ Ⲛ̄·
·ⲀⲰ Ⲛ̄·ⲌⲈ ⲠⲈⲬⲈ·ⲒⲤ̄ <> ⲀⲦⲈⲦⲚ̄·ϬⲰⲖⲠ` ⲄⲀⲢ ⲈⲂⲞⲖ
Ⲛ̄·Ⲧ·ⲀⲢⲬⲎ ⲬⲈⲔⲀⲀⲤ ⲈⲦⲈⲦⲚⲀ·Ⲱ̄ⲒⲚⲈ Ⲛ̄ⲤⲀ·
·ⲐⲀⲌⲎ ⲬⲈ ⲌⲘ̄·Ⲡ·ⲘⲀ ⲈⲦⲈ Ⲧ·ⲀⲢⲬⲎ Ⲙ̄·ⲘⲀⲨ Ⲉ·
·ⲐⲀⲌⲎ ·ⲚⲀ·Ⲱ̄ⲰⲠⲈ Ⲙ̄·ⲘⲀⲨ ⲞⲨ·ⲘⲀⲔⲀⲢⲒⲞⲤ
ⲠⲈⲦ·ⲚⲀ·Ⲱ̄ⲌⲈ Ⲉ·ⲢⲀⲦ·Ꝙ̄ ⲌⲚ̄·Ⲧ·ⲀⲢⲬⲎ ⲀⲨⲰ
Ꝙ·ⲚⲀ·ⲤⲞⲨⲰⲚ·ⲐⲀⲌⲎ ⲀⲨⲰ Ꝙ·ⲚⲀ·ⲬⲒ·†ⲠⲈ
ⲀⲚ Ⲙ̄·ⲘⲞⲨ

19 ⲠⲈⲬⲈ·ⲒⲤ̄ ⲬⲈ ⲞⲨ·ⲘⲀⲔⲀⲢⲒⲞⲤ
ⲠⲈ Ⲛ̄ⲦⲀⲌ·Ⲱ̄ⲰⲠⲈ ⲌⲀ·Ⲧ·ⲈⲌⲎ ⲈⲘⲠⲀⲦⲈϤ·Ⲱ̄ⲰⲠⲈ
ⲈⲦⲈⲦⲚ̄·Ⲱ̄ⲀⲚ·Ⲱ̄ⲰⲠⲈ ⲚⲀ·ⲈⲒ Ⲙ̄·ⲘⲀⲐⲎⲦⲎⲤ
Ⲛ̄ⲦⲈⲦⲚ̄·ⲤⲰⲦⲘ̄ Ⲁ·ⲚⲀ·Ⲱ̄ⲀⲬⲈ ⲚⲈⲈⲒ·ⲰⲚⲈ
·ⲚⲀ·Ⲣ̄·ⲆⲒⲀⲔⲞⲚⲈⲒ ⲚⲎ·ⲦⲚ̄ ⲞⲨⲚ̄·ⲦⲎ·ⲦⲚ̄
ⲄⲀⲢ` Ⲙ̄·ⲘⲀⲨ Ⲛ̄·†ⲞⲨ Ⲛ̄·Ⲱ̄ⲎⲚ ⲌⲘ̄·ⲠⲀⲢⲀ`
ⲆⲒⲤⲞⲤ Ⲉ·ⲤⲈ·ⲔⲒⲘ ⲀⲚ Ⲛ̄·Ⲱ̄ⲰⲘ` Ⲙ̄·ⲠⲢⲰ
ⲀⲨⲰ ⲘⲀⲢⲈ·ⲚⲞⲨ·ϬⲰⲂⲈ ·ⲌⲈ ⲈⲂⲞⲖ ⲠⲈⲦ·`
·ⲚⲀ·ⲤⲞⲨⲰⲚ·ⲞⲨ Ꝙ·ⲚⲀ·ⲬⲒ·†ⲠⲈ ⲀⲚ` Ⲙ̄·ⲘⲞⲨ

20 ⲠⲈⲬⲈ·Ⲙ̄·ⲘⲀⲐⲎⲦⲎⲤ Ⲛ̄·ⲒⲤ̄ ⲬⲈ ·ⲬⲞ·ⲞⲤ
ⲈⲢⲞ·Ⲛ ⲬⲈ Ⲧ·ⲘⲚ̄ⲦⲈⲢⲞ·Ⲛ·Ⲙ̄·ⲠⲎⲨⲈ ⲈⲤ·
·ⲦⲚ̄ⲦⲰⲚ Ⲉ·ⲚⲒⲘ ⲠⲈⲬⲀ·Ꝙ ⲚⲀ·Ⲩ ⲬⲈ ⲈⲤ·ⲦⲚ̄ⲦⲰⲚ
Ⲁ·Ⲩ·ⲂⲀ̄ⲂⲒⲖⲈ Ⲛ̄·Ⲱ̄ⲖⲦⲀⲘ ⲤⲞⲂⲔ̄ ⲠⲀⲢⲀ·Ⲛ̄·ϬⲢⲞϬ
ⲦⲎⲢ·ⲞⲨ ⲌⲞⲦⲀⲚ ⲆⲈ ⲈⲤ·Ⲱ̄Ⲁ ¯·
·ⲌⲈ ⲈⲬⲘ̄·Ⲡ·ⲔⲀⲌ ⲈⲦ·ⲞⲨ·Ⲣ̄·ⲌⲰⲂ ⲈⲢⲞ·Ꝙ Ⲱ̄ⲀϤ·
·ⲦⲈⲨⲞ ⲈⲂⲞⲖ Ⲛ̄·ⲚⲞⲨ·ⲚⲞϬ Ⲛ̄·ⲦⲀⲢ Ⲛ̄Ꝙ·Ⲱ̄ⲰⲠⲈ
Ⲛ̄·ⲤⲔⲈⲠⲎ Ⲛ̄·ⲌⲀⲖⲀⲦⲈ Ⲛ̄·Ⲧ·ⲠⲈ

21 ⲠⲈⲬⲈ·ⲘⲀⲢⲒⲌⲀⲘ Ⲛ̄·ⲒⲤ̄ ⲬⲈ Ⲉ·ⲚⲈⲔ·ⲘⲀⲐⲎⲦⲎⲤ
·ⲈⲒⲚⲈ Ⲛ̄·ⲚⲒⲘ` ⲠⲈⲬⲀ·Ꝙ` ⲬⲈ ⲈⲨ·ⲈⲒⲚⲈ
Ⲛ̄·ⲌⲚ̄·Ⲱ̄ⲎⲢⲈ·Ⲱ̄ⲎⲘ` ⲈⲨ·[Ϭ]ⲈⲖⲒⲦ` Ⲁ·Ⲩ·ⲤⲰⲰ̄Ⲉ Ⲉ·ⲦⲰ·
·ⲞⲨ ⲀⲚ ⲦⲈ ⲌⲞⲦⲀⲚ ⲈⲨ·Ⲱ̄Ⲁ·ⲈⲒ Ⲛ̄ϬⲒ·Ⲛ̄·ⲬⲞⲈⲒⲤ
Ⲛ̄·Ⲧ·ⲤⲰⲰ̄Ⲉ ⲤⲈ·ⲚⲀ·ⲬⲞ·ⲞⲤ ⲬⲈ ·ⲔⲈ·ⲦⲚ̄·ⲤⲰⲰ̄Ⲉ
ⲈⲂⲞⲖ ⲚⲀ·Ⲛ Ⲛ̄·ⲦⲞ·ⲞⲨ ⲤⲈ·ⲔⲀⲔ Ⲁ·ⲌⲎⲨ Ⲙ̄·ⲠⲞⲨ·Ⲙ̄ⲦⲞ

no hand has touched,
and no human heart has conceived.

18   The disciples asked Yeshua:
"Tell us, what will be our end?"
Yeshua answered:
What do you know of the beginning,
so that you now seek the end?
Where the beginning is, the end will also be.
Blessed are those who abide in the beginning,
for they will know the end and will not taste death.

19   Yeshua said:
Blessed is the one who Is before existing.
If you become my disciples and listen to my words,
these stones will serve you.
In Paradise there are five trees
that do not change from summer to winter.
Their leaves do not fall.
Whoever knows them will not taste death.

20   The disciples asked Yeshua:
"Tell us, what is the Kingdom of Heaven like?"
He answered them:
It is like a grain of mustard,
the tiniest of all seeds.
When it falls upon well-plowed ground,
it becomes a great tree,
where birds of heaven will come to rest.

21   Mary asked Yeshua:
"What are your disciples like?"
He answered:
They are like little children
who have gone into a field that does not belong to them.
When the owners return and say:
"Give us back our field!"
they will remove their clothes, see themselves naked before the
     owners, and leave the field to them.

ЄΒΟλ ЄΤΡΟΥ·ΚΑΑ·С ЄΒΟλ ΝΑ·Υ ΝСЄ·†·ΤΟΥ·
·СѠѠЄ ΝΑ·Υ ΔΙΑ·ΤΟΥΤΟ †·ΧѠ Μ·ΜΟ·С ΧЄ ЄЧ·`
·ѠΑ·ЄΙΜЄ ΝϬΙ·Π·ΧЄС·2Ν·НЄΙ ΧЄ Ч·ΝНΥ ΝϬΙ·
·Π·ΡЄЧ·ΧΙΟΥЄ Ч·ΝΑ·ΡΟЄΙС ЄΜΠΑΤЄЧ·`·ЄΙ ΝЧ·ΤΜ·
·ΚΑΑ·Ч` Є·ѠΟΧΤ` Є2ΟΥΝ Є·ΠЄЧ·НЄΙ ΝΤЄ·ΤЄЧ·`
·ΜΝΤЄΡΟ ЄΤΡЄЧ·ЧΙ Ν·ΝЄЧ·`·СΚЄΥΟС Ν·ΤѠ·ΤΝ
ΔЄ ·ΡΟЄΙС 2Α·Т·Є2Н Μ·Π·ΚΟСΜΟС ·ΜΟΥΡ` Μ·
·ΜѠ·ΤΝ ЄΧΝ·ΝЄΤΝ·†·ΠЄ 2Ν·ΝΟΥ·ΝΟϬ Ν·ΔΥΝΑΜΙС
ѠΙΝΑ ΧЄ ΝЄ·Ν·λНСΤНС ·2Є Є·2ΙН Є·ЄΙ
ѠΑΡѠ·ΤΝ ЄΠЄΙ ΤЄ·ΧΡЄΙΑ ЄΤЄΤΝ·ϬѠѠΤ`
ЄΒΟλ 2НΤ·С̄ СЄ·ΝΑ·2Є ЄΡΟ·С ΜΑΡЄЧ·ѠѠΠЄ
2Ν·ΤЄΤΝ·ΜНТЄ ΝϬΙ·ΟΥ·ΡѠΜЄ Ν·ЄΠΙСΤНΜѠΝ
ΝΤΑΡЄ·Π·ΚΑΡΠΟС ·ΠѠ2 ΑЧ·ЄΙ 2Ν·ΝΟΥ·
·ϬЄΠН Є·ΠЄЧ·ΑС2 2Ν·ΤЄЧ·ϬΙΧ ΑЧ·2ΑС·Ч ΠЄΤЄ·ΟΥΝ·ΜΑΑΧЄ
Μ·ΜΟ·Ч` Є·СѠΤΜ̄ ΜΑΡЄЧ·СѠΤΜ̄

22 Α·Ι͞С ·ΝΑΥ Α·2Ν·ΚΟΥЄΙ ЄΥ·ΧΙ·ЄΡѠΤЄ ΠЄΧΑ·Ч Ν·
·ΝЄЧ·ΜΑΘНΤНС ΧЄ ΝЄЄΙ·ΚΟΥЄΙ ЄΤ·ΧΙ·ЄΡѠΤЄ
ЄΥ·ΤΝΤѠΝ Α·ΝЄΤ·ΒНΚ` Є2ΟΥΝ Α·Τ·ΜΝΤЄΡΟ
ΠЄΧΑ·Υ ΝΑ·Ч` ΧЄ ЄЄΙЄ Ν·Ο Ν·ΚΟΥЄΙ ΤΝ·
·ΝΑ·ΒѠΚ` Є2ΟΥΝ Є·Τ·ΜΝΤЄΡΟ ΠЄΧЄ·Ι͞Н͞С ΝΑ·Υ
ΧЄ 2ΟΤΑΝ ЄΤЄΤΝ·ѠΑ·Ρ̄·Π·СΝΑΥ ΟΥΑ ΑΥѠ
ЄΤЄΤΝ·ѠΑ·Ρ̄·Π·СΑ·Ν·2ΟΥΝ Ν·ΘЄ Μ·Π·СΑ·Ν·ΒΟλ
ΑΥѠ Π·СΑ·Ν·ΒΟλ Ν·ΘЄ Μ·Π·СΑ·Ν·2ΟΥΝ ΑΥѠ Π·СΑ·‾·
·Τ·ΠЄ Ν·ΘЄ Μ·Π·СΑ·Μ·Π·ΙΤΝ̄ ΑΥѠ ѠΙΝΑ ЄΤЄΤΝΑ·ЄΙΡЄ
Μ·ΦΟ·ΟΥΤ` ΜΝ̄·Τ·С2ΙΜЄ Μ·ΠΙ·ΟΥΑ
ΟΥѠΤ` ΧЄΚΑΑС ΝЄ·ΦΟΟΥΤ` ·Ρ̄·2ΟΟΥΤ` ΝΤЄ·
·Τ·С2ΙΜЄ ·Ρ̄·С2ΙΜЄ 2ΟΤΑΝ ЄΤЄΤΝ·ѠΑ·ЄΙΡЄ
Ν·2Ν·ΒΑλ Є·Π·ΜΑ Ν·ΟΥ·ΒΑλ` ΑΥѠ ΟΥ·ϬΙΧ`
Є·Π·ΜΑ Ν·ΝΟΥ·ϬΙΧ` ΑΥѠ ΟΥ·ЄΡНΤЄ Є·Π·ΜΑ
Ν·ΟΥ·ЄΡНΤЄ ΟΥ·2ΙΚѠΝ` Є·Π·ΜΑ Ν·ΟΥ·2ΙΚѠ‾
ΤΟΤЄ ΤЄΤΝΑ·ΒѠΚ` Є2ΟΥΝ [Є·Τ·ΜΝΤЄΡΟ]

23 ΠЄΧЄ·Ι͞С ΧЄ †·ΝΑ·СЄ[Τ]·Π·ТНΝЄ ΟΥΑ ЄΒΟλ
2Ν·ѠΟ ΑΥѠ СΝΑΥ ЄΒΟλ 2Ν·ΤΒΑ ΑΥѠ
СЄ·ΝΑ·Ѡ2Є Є·ΡΑΤ·ΟΥ ЄΥ·Ο ΟΥΑ ΟΥѠΤ`

This is why I say:
If the master of the house knows that a thief is coming,
he will be vigilant and not allow the thief to break into the
   house of his kingdom,
or carry off his goods.
Thus you should be vigilant toward the world.
Strengthen yourselves with great energy
or the robbers will find a way to get to you.
The profit that you are counting on will be found by them.
May there be a wise person among you . . .
When the crop is ripe, he comes immediately
and harvests it with his sickle.
Those who have ears, let them hear!

22 Yeshua saw some infants being nursed at the breast.
He said to his disciples:
These nursing infants are like those who enter the Kingdom.
The disciples asked him:
"Then shall we become as infants to enter into the Kingdom?"
Yeshua answered them:
When you make the two into One,
when you make the inner like the outer
and the high like the low;
when you make male and female into a single One,
so that the male is not male and the female is not female;
when you have eyes in your eyes,
a hand in your hand,
a foot in your foot,
and an icon in your icon,[2]
then you will enter into the Kingdom.

23 Yeshua said:
I will choose one of you from a thousand
and two of you from ten thousand,
and they will stand as one, alone and simple [*monakhos*].

---

2. [The author uses the word *icon*, whereas other translations use *image*. This does not
refer to a physical icon, but rather suggests the deeper meaning of *image*, as evoked by the
original Greek/Coptic term *ikon*. —*Trans.*]

24 ΠΕΧΕ·ΝΕϤ·ΜΑΘΗΤΗC ΧΕ ΜΑ·ΤCΕΒΟ·Ν` Ε·Π·ΤΟΠΟC
ΕΤ·Κ·Μ̄·ΜΑΥ ΕΠΕΙ ΤΑΝΑΓΚΗ ΕΡΟ·Ν ΤΕ
ΕΤΡΝ̄·ϢΙΝΕ Ν̄CΩ·Ϥ` ΠΕΧΑ·Ϥ ΝΑ·Υ ΧΕ ΠΕΤ·ΕΥΝ̄·ΜΑΑΧΕ
Μ̄·ΜΟ·Ϥ ΜΑΡΕϤ·`·CΩΤΜ̄ ΟΥΝ̄·ΟΥΟΕΙΝ`
·ϢΟΟΠ` Μ̄·ΦΟΥΝ Ν̄·ΝΟΥ·ΡΜ̄·ΟΥΟΕΙΝ
ΑΥΩ Ϥ·Ρ̄·ΟΥΟΕΙΝ Ε·Π·ΚΟCΜΟC ΤΗΡ·Ϥ` ΕϤ·ΤΜ̄·
·Ρ̄·ΟΥΟΕΙΝ` ΟΥ·ΚΑΚΕ ΠΕ

25 ΠΕΧΕ·ῙC̄ ·ΜΕΡΕ·
·ΠΕΚ·CΟΝ Ν̄·ΘΕ Ν̄·ΤΕΚ·`ΦΥΧΗ ΕΡΙ·ΤΗΡΕΙ Μ̄·ΜΟ·Ϥ
Ν̄·ΘΕ Ν̄·Τ·ΕΛΟΥ Μ̄·ΠΕΚ·`ΒΑΛ`

26 ΠΕΧΕ·ῙC̄ ΧΕ Π·ΧΗ
ΕΤ·2Μ̄·Π·ΒΑΛ Μ̄·ΠΕΚ·`CΟΝ Κ·ΝΑΥ ΕΡΟ·Ϥ` Π·CΟΕΙ
ΔΕ ΕΤ·2Μ̄·ΠΕΚ·ΒΑΛ` Κ·ΝΑΥ ΑΝ ΕΡΟ·Ϥ` 2ΟΤΑΝ
ΕΚ·ϢΑΝ·ΝΟΥΧΕ Μ̄·Π·CΟΕΙ ΕΒΟΛ 2Μ̄·ΠΕΚ·`
·ΒΑΛ` ΤΟΤΕ Κ·ΝΑ·ΝΑΥ ΕΒΟΛ Ε·ΝΟΥΧΕ Μ̄·Π·ΧΗ
ΕΒΟΛ 2Μ̄·Π·ΒΑΛ Μ̄·ΠΕΚ·CΟΝ

27 ΕΤΕΤΜ̄·Ρ̄·ΝΗCΤΕΥΕ Ε·Π·ΚΟCΜΟC ΤΕΤΝΑ·2Ε ΑΝ` Ε·Τ·ΜΝ̄ΤΕΡΟ
ΕΤΕΤΝ̄·ΤΜ̄·ΕΙΡΕ Μ̄·Π·CΑΜΒΑΤΟΝ Ν̄·CΑΒ`ΒΑΤΟΝ
Ν̄ΤΕΤΝΑ·ΝΑΥ ΑΝ Ε·Π·ΕΙΩΤ`

28 ΠΕΧΕ·ῙC̄ ΧΕ ΑΕΙ·Ω2Ε Ε·ΡΑΤ` 2Ν̄·Τ·ΜΗΤΕ Μ̄·Π·ΚΟCΜΟC
ΑΥΩ ΑΕΙ·ΟΥΩΝ2 ΕΒΟΛ ΝΑ·Υ 2Ν̄·CΑΡ3̄
ΑΕΙ·2Ε ΕΡΟ·ΟΥ ΤΗΡ·ΟΥ ΕΥ·ΤΑ2Ε Μ̄ΠΙ·2Ε Ε·ΛΑΑΥ
Ν̄·2ΗΤ·ΟΥ ΕϤ·ΟΒΕ ΑΥΩ Α·ΤΑ·ΦΥΧΗ †·ΤΚΑC
ΕΧΝ̄·Ν̄·ϢΗΡΕ Ν̄·Ρ̄·ΡΩΜΕ ΧΕ 2Ν̄·ΒΛΛΕΕΥΕ
ΝΕ 2Μ̄·ΠΟΥ·2ΗΤ` ΑΥΩ CΕ·ΝΑΥ ΕΒΟΛ ΑΝ
ΧΕ Ν̄ΤΑΥ·ΕΙ Ε·Π·ΚΟCΜΟC ΕΥ·ϢΟΥΕΙΤ` ΕΥ·
·ϢΙΝΕ ΟΝ ΕΤΡΟΥ·ΕΙ ΕΒΟΛ 2Μ̄·Π·ΚΟCΜΟC
ΕΥ·ϢΟΥΕΙΤ` ΠΛΗΝ ΤΕΝΟΥ CΕ·ΤΟ2Ε 2ΟΤΑΝ
ΕΥ·ϢΑΝ·ΝΕ2·ΠΟΥ·ΗΡΠ` ΤΟΤΕ CΕ·ΝΑ·Ρ̄·ΜΕΤΑΝΟΕΙ

24   His disciples asked:
"Teach us about the place where you dwell,
for we must seek it."
He told them:
Those who have ears, let them hear!
There is light within people of light,
and they shine it upon the whole world.
If they do not shine it,
what darkness!

25   Yeshua said:
Love your brother and sister as your soul;
protect them as you do the pupil of your eye.

26   Yeshua said:
You see the sliver in your brother's eye,
but you do not see the log in your own eye.
When you remove the log from your eye,
then you will see clearly enough to remove the sliver from your
    brother's eye.

27   Yeshua said:
If you do not fast from the world,
you will not find the Kingdom.
If you do not celebrate the Sabbath as a Sabbath,
you will not know the Father.

28   Yeshua said:
I stood in the midst of the world
and revealed myself to them in the flesh.
I found them all intoxicated.
Not one of them was thirsty
and my soul grieved for the children of humanity,
for they are blind in their hearts.
They do not see.
They came naked into the world,
and naked they will leave it.
At this time, they are intoxicated.
When they have vomited their wine,
they will return to themselves.

29 ΠΕΧΕ·ΙC <> ΕϢΧΕ Ν̄ΤΑ·Τ·CΑΡΞ
·ϢΩΠΕ ΕΤΒΕ·Π̄Ν̄Α ΟΥ·ϢΠΗΡΕ ΤΕ ΕϢΧΕ·Π̄Ν̄Α
ΔΕ ΕΤΒΕ·Π·CΩΜΑ ΟΥ·ϢΠΗΡΕ
Ν̄·ϢΠΗΡΕ ΠΕ ΑΛΛΑ ΑΝΟ·Κ' †·Ρ̄·ϢΠΗΡΕ
Μ̄·ΠΑΕΙ ΧΕ ΠΩ[C] Α·[ΤΕΕΙ·]ΝΟϬ Μ̄·ΜΝ̄Τ·ΡΜ̄·ΜΑΟ
ΑC·ΟΥΩϨ ϨΝ̄·ΤΕΕΙ·ΜΝ̄Τ·ϨΗΚΕ

30 ΠΕΧΕ·ΙC ΧΕ Π·ΜΑ ΕΥΝ̄·ϢΟΜΤ Ν̄·ΝΟΥΤΕ Μ̄·ΜΑΥ ϨΝ̄·ΝΟΥΤΕ
ΝΕ Π·ΜΑ ΕΥΝ̄·CΝΑΥ Η ΟΥΑ ΑΝΟ·Κ'
†·ϢΟΟΠ' ΝΜΜΑ·Ϥ'

31 ΠΕΧΕ·ΙC <> ΜΝ̄·ΠΡΟΦΗΤΗC
·ϢΗΠ' ϨΜ̄·ΠΕϤ·†ΜΕΜΑ·ΡΕ·CΟΕΙΝ ·Ρ̄·ΘΕΡΑΠΕΥΕ
Ν̄·ΝΕΤ·'·CΟΟΥΝ Μ̄·ΜΟ·Ϥ'

32 ΠΕΧΕ·ΙC ΧΕ ΟΥ·ΠΟΛΙC ΕΥ·ΚΩΤ Μ̄·ΜΟ·C ϨΙΧΝ̄·ΟΥ·ΤΟΟΥ
ΕϤ·ΧΟCΕ ΕC·ΤΑΧΡΗΥ ΜΝ̄·ϬΟΜ Ν̄C·Ϩ̄Ε
ΟΥΔΕ C·ΝΑϢ·Ϩ̄ΩΠ' ΑΝ

33 ΠΕΧΕ·ΙC <> ΠΕΤ·'·Κ·ΝΑ·
·CΩΤΜ̄ ΕΡΟ·Ϥ ϨΜ̄·ΠΕΚ·'·ΜΑΑΧΕ ϨΜ̄·Π·ΚΕ·ΜΑΑΧΕ
·ΤΑϢΕ·ΟΕΙϢ' Μ̄·ΜΟ·Ϥ ϨΙΧΝ̄·ΝΕΤΝ̄·ΧΕΝΕΠΩΡ'
ΜΑ·ΡΕ·ΛΑΑΥ' ΓΑΡ ·ΧΕΡΕ·ϨΒ̄Β̄C Ν̄Ϥ·'
·ΚΑΑ·Ϥ' ϨΑ·ΜΑΑΧΕ ΟΥΔΕ ΜΑϤ·ΚΑΑ·Ϥ' Ϩ̄Μ·ΜΑ
ΕϤ·Ϩ̄ΗΠ' ΑΛΛΑ Ε·ϢΑΡΕϤ·ΚΑΑ·Ϥ' ϨΙΧΝ̄·Τ·ΛΥΧΝΙΑ
ΧΕΚΑΑC ΟΥΟΝ ·ΝΙΜ' ΕΤ·ΒΗΚ' Ε·ϨΟΥΝ
ΑΥΩ ΕΤ·Ν̄ΝΗΥ ΕΒΟΛ ΕΥ·ΝΑ·ΝΑΥ Α·ΠΕϤ·ΟΥΟΕΙΝ

29   Yeshua said:
If flesh came into being because of spirit,
it is a wonder.
But if spirit came into being because of flesh,
it is a wonder of wonders.
Yet the greatest of wonders is this:
How is it that this Being, which Is,
inhabits this nothingness?

30   Yeshua said:
Where there are three gods,
they are gods.
Where there are two or one,
I am with them.

31   Yeshua said:
No one is a prophet in his own village.
No one is a physician in his own home.

32   Yeshua said:
A strong city built upon a high mountain
cannot be destroyed,
cannot be hidden.

33   Yeshua said:
What you hear with your ears,
tell it to other ears
and proclaim it from the rooftops.
No one lights a lamp
so that it will be put under a basket
or hidden somewhere.
Rather, one puts it upon a stand
so that all who enter and leave
may see the light.

34 ΠΕΧΕ·ΙC ΧΕ ΟΥ·ΒⳖⲖⲈ Ⲉϥ·ϢⲀⲚ·`·CⲰⲔ`
ⳍⲎⲦ·ϥ` Ⲛ̄·ⲚⲞⲨ·ΒⳖⲖⲈ ϢⲀⲨ·ⳍⲈ Ⲙ̄·ⲠⲈ·CⲚⲀⲨ`
Ⲉ·Π·ⲈCⲎⲦ` Ⲉ·Ⲩ·ⳍ¡Ⲉ¡Ⲧ`

35 ΠⲈΧⲈ·ΙC <> ⲘⲚ̄·ⳆⲞⲘ`
Ⲛ̄ⲦⲈ·ⲞΥⲀ ·ΒⲰⲔ` ⲈⳍⲞΥⲚ Ⲉ·Π·ⲎⲈ¡ Ⲙ̄·Π·ΧⲰⲰⲢⲈ
Ⲛ̄ϥ·Χ¡Ⲧ·ϥ` Ⲛ̄·ΧⲚⲀⳍ Ⲉ¡ⲘⲎⲦ¡ Ⲛ̄ϥ·ⲘⲞΥⲢ
Ⲛ̄·ⲚⲈϥ·Ⳇ¡Χ` ⲦⲞⲦⲈ ϥ·ⲚⲀ·ΠⲰⲰⲚⲈ ⲈΒⲞⳖ
Ⲙ̄·ΠⲈϥ·ⲎⲈ¡

36 ΠⲈΧⲈ·ΙC <> ⲘⲚ̄·ϥ¡·ⲢⲞⲞΥϢ Χ¡ ⁻·
·ⳍⲦⲞⲞΥⲈ ϢⲀ·ⲢⲞΥⳍⲈ ⲀΥⲰ Χ¡Ⲛ·ⳍ¡·ⲢⲞΥⳍⲈ
ϢⲀ·ⳍⲦⲞⲞΥⲈ ΧⲈ ⲞΥ ΠⲈ ⲈⲦ·ⲚⲀ·ⲦⲀⲀ·ϥ ⳍ¡ⲰⲦ·`
·ⲦⲎΥⲦⲚ̄

37 ΠⲈΧⲈ·ⲚⲈϥ·ⲘⲀⲐⲎⲦⲎC ΧⲈ ⲀϢ Ⲛ̄·
·ⳍⲞⲞΥ ⲈⲔ·ⲚⲀ·ⲞΥⲰⲚⳍ ⲈΒⲞⳖ ⲚⲀ·Ⲛ ⲀΥⲰ ⲀϢ
Ⲛ̄·ⳍⲞⲞΥ ⲈⲚⲀ·ⲚⲀΥ ⲈⲢⲞ·Ⲕ` ΠⲈΧⲈ·ΙC ΧⲈ ⳍⲞⲦⲀⲚ
ⲈⲦⲈⲦⲚ̄·ϢⲀ·ⲔⲈⲔ·ⲦⲎΥⲦⲚ̄ Ⲉ·ⳍⲎΥ Ⲙ̄·ΠⲈⲦⲚ̄·Ϣ¡ΠⲈ
ⲀΥⲰ Ⲛ̄ⲦⲈⲦⲚ̄·ϥ¡ Ⲛ̄·ⲚⲈⲦⲚ̄·ϢⲦⲎⲚ
Ⲛ̄ⲦⲈⲦⲚ̄·ⲔⲀⲀ·Υ ⳍⲀ·Π·ⲈCⲎⲦ` Ⲛ̄·ⲚⲈⲦⲚ̄·ⲞΥⲈⲢⲎⲦⲈ
Ⲛ̄·ⲐⲈ Ⲛ̄·Ⲛ¡·ⲔⲞΥⲈ¡ Ⲛ̄·ϢⲎⲢⲈ·ϢⲎⲘ` Ⲛ̄ⲦⲈⲦⲚ̄·ΧⲞΠΧⲠ̄`
Ⲙ̄·ⲘⲞ·ⲞΥ ⲦⲞⲦ[Ⲉ ⲦⲈⲦⲚⲀ·ⲚⲀ]Υ
Ⲉ·Π·ϢⲎⲢⲈ Ⲙ̄·ΠⲈⲦ·ⲞⲚⳍ ⲀΥⲰ ⲦⲈⲦⲚⲀ·Ⲣ̄·
·ⳍⲞⲦⲈ ⲀⲚ

38 ΠⲈΧⲈ·ΙC ΧⲈ ⳍⲀⳍ Ⲛ̄·CⲞΠ` ⲀⲦⲈⲦⲚ̄·
·Ⲣ̄·ⲈⲠⲐΥⲘⲈ¡ Ⲉ·CⲰⲦⲘ̄ Ⲁ·ⲚⲈⲈ¡·ϢⲀΧⲈ ⲚⲀⲈ¡`
Ⲉ·Ⲧ†·Χⲱ Ⲙ̄·ⲘⲞ·ⲞΥ ⲚⲎ·ⲦⲚ̄ ⲀΥⲰ ⲘⲚ̄·ⲦⲎ·ⲦⲚ̄·
·ⲔⲈ·ⲞΥⲀ Ⲉ·CⲞⲦⲘ·ⲞΥ Ⲛ̄·ⲦⲞⲞⲦ·ϥ̄ ⲞΥⲚ̄·ⳍⲚ̄·ⳍⲞⲞΥ
·ⲚⲀ·ϢⲰΠⲈ Ⲛ̄ⲦⲈⲦⲚ̄·Ϣ¡ⲚⲈ Ⲛ̄CⲰ·Ⲉ¡ ⲦⲈⲦⲚⲀ·ⳍⲈ
ⲀⲚ` Ⲉ·ⲢⲞ·Ⲉ¡`

39 ΠⲈΧⲈ·ΙC ΧⲈ Ⲙ̄·ⲪⲀⲢ¡CⲀ¡ⲞC
ⲘⲚ̄·Ⲛ̄·ⲄⲢⲀⲘⲘⲀⲦⲈΥC ⲀΥ·Χ¡ Ⲛ̄·ϢⲀϢⲦ`
Ⲛ̄·Ⲧ·ⲄⲚⲰC¡C ⲀΥ·ⳍⲞΠ·ⲞΥ ⲞΥⲦⲈ Ⲙ̄ΠⲞΥ·ΒⲰⲔ`
ⲈⳍⲞΥⲚ ⲀΥⲰ ⲚⲈⲦ·ⲞΥⲰϢ Ⲉ·ΒⲰⲔ` ⲈⳍⲞΥⲚ
Ⲙ̄ΠⲞΥ·ⲔⲀⲀ·Υ Ⲛ̄·Ⲧⲱ·ⲦⲚ̄ ⲆⲈ ·ϢⲰΠⲈ Ⲙ̄·ⲪⲢⲞⲚ¡ⲘⲞC

34 Yeshua said:
When a blind person leads another blind person,
they both fall into a pit.

35 Yeshua said:
One cannot capture the house of the strong
except by tying their hands.
Then everything can be overturned.

36 Yeshua said:
Do not worry from morning to evening,
or from evening to morning,
about having clothes to wear.

37 His disciples asked:
"When will be the day that you appear to us?"
"When will be the day of our vision?"
Yeshua replied:
On the day when you are naked
as newborn infants
who trample their clothing,
then you will see the Son of the Living One
and you will have no more fear.

38 Yeshua said:
Often you have wanted to hear
the words I speak to you now.
No one else can say them to you,
and the days will come
when you seek me
and do not find me.

39 Yeshua said:
The Pharisees and the scribes
have received the keys of knowledge
and hidden them.
They did not go within,
and those who wanted to go there
were prevented by them.

 N·ΘΕ N·N·ϨΟϤ` ΑΥΩ N·ΑΚΕΡΑΙΟС N·ΘΕ N·N·
·ϬΡΟΜΠΕ

40 ΠΕΧΕ·ῙС̄ <> ΟΥ·ΒΕ·N·ΕΛΟΟΛΕ ΑΥ·
·ΤΟϬ·С M̄·Π·СΑ·N·ΒΟΛ M̄·Π·ΕΙΩΤ` ΑΥΩ ΕС·ΤΑΧΡΗΥ
ΑΝ СΕ·ΝΑ·ΠΟΡΚ·С̄ ϨΑ·ΤΕС·ΝΟΥΝΕ N̄С·
·ΤΑΚΟ

41 ΠΕΧΕ·ῙС̄ ΧΕ ΠΕΤ·ΕΥN̄·ΤΑ·Ϥ ϨN̄·ΤΕϤ·`
·ϬΙΧ СΕ·ΝΑ·† ΝΑ·Ϥ` ΑΥΩ ΠΕΤΕ·ΜN̄·ΤΑ·Ϥ Π·ΚΕ·
·ϢΗΜ ΕΤ·ΟΥN̄·ΤΑ·Ϥ СΕ·ΝΑ·ϤΙΤ·ϥ̄ N̄·ΤΟΟΤ·Ϥ`

42 ΠΕΧΕ·ῙС̄ ΧΕ ·ϢΩΠΕ ΕΤΕΤN̄·Ρ̄·ΠΑΡΑΓΕ

43 ΠΕΧΑ·Υ ΝΑ·Ϥ` N̄ϬΙ·ΝΕϤ·`ΜΑΘΗΤΗС ΧΕ N̄·ΤΑ·Κ`
ΝΙΜ` ΕΚ·ΧΩ N̄·ΝΑΪ ΝΑ·Ν` ϨN̄·ΝΕ†·ΧΩ M̄·
·ΜΟ·ΟΥ ΝΗ·ΤN̄ N̄ΤΕΤN̄·ΕΙΜΕ ΑΝ ΧΕ ΑΝΟ·Κ`
ΝΙΜ ΑΛΛΑ N̄·ΤΩ·ΤN̄ ΑΤΕΤN̄·ϢΩΠΕ N̄·ΘΕ N̄·
·ΝΙ·ΪΟΥΔΑΙΟС ΧΕ СΕ·ΜΕ M̄·Π·ϢΗΝ СΕ·ΜΟСΤΕ
M̄·ΠΕϤ·ΚΑΡΠΟС ΑΥΩ СΕ·ΜΕ M̄·Π·ΚΑΡΠΟС
СΕ·ΜΟСΤΕ M̄·Π·ϢΗΝ

44 ΠΕΧΕ·ῙС̄ ΧΕ ΠΕΤΑ·ΧΕ·
·ΟΥΑ Α·Π·ΕΙΩΤ` СΕ·ΝΑ·ΚΩ ΕΒΟΛ ΝΑ·Ϥ` ΑΥΩ
ΠΕΤΑ·ΧΕ·ΟΥΑ Ε·Π·ϢΗΡΕ СΕ·ΝΑ·ΚΩ ΕΒΟΛ
ΝΑ·Ϥ` ΠΕΤΑ·ΧΕ·ΟΥΑ ΔΕ Α·Π·Π̄Ν̄Ᾱ ΕΤ·ΟΥΑΑΒ
СΕ·ΝΑ·ΚΩ ΑΝ ΕΒΟΛ ΝΑ·Ϥ` ΟΥΤΕ ϨM̄·Π·ΚΑϨ
ΟΥΤΕ ϨN̄·Τ·ΠΕ

As for you, be as alert as the serpent
and as simple as the dove.

40   Yeshua said:
A grapevine planted away from the Father
has no vitality.
It will be torn up by its roots
and will perish.

41   Yeshua said:
Whoever has something in hand
will be given more.
Whoever has nothing,
even the little they have
will be taken away.

42   Yeshua said:
Be passersby.

43   The disciples asked him:
"Who are you to say these things to us?"
Yeshua replied:
Do you not know me from what I say to you?
Or have you become like those Judeans:
If they love the tree,
they despise the fruit.
If they love the fruit,
they despise the tree.

44   Yeshua said:
Whoever blasphemes against the Father
will be forgiven,
and whoever blasphemes against the Son
will be forgiven.
But whoever blasphemes against the Holy Spirit
will not be forgiven,
either on earth or in heaven.

45 ПЕХЕ·ĪС <> МАУ·ХЕЛЕ·ЕЛООЛЕ
ЕВОЛ ２Ṉ·ШОΝΤΕ ОУТЕ МАУ·КШТ϶`
·КṈТЕ ЕВОЛ ２Ṉ·СР̄·бАМОУЛ` МАУ·†·КАРПОС
[ГАР ОУ·АГА]ӨОС Р̄·РШМЕ ША϶·ЕΙΝΕ Ṉ·
·ОУ·АГАӨОΝ ЕВОЛ ２[Ṁ·]ПЕ϶·Е２О ОУ·КА[КОС]
Р̄·РШМЕ ША϶·ЕΙΝΕ Ṉ·２Ṉ·ПОΝΗΡОΝ ЕВОЛ
２Ṁ·ПЕ϶·Е２О ЕӨООУ ЕΤ·２Ṉ·ПЕ϶·２ΗΤ` АУШ
Ṉ϶·ХШ Ṉ·２Ṉ·ПОΝΗΡОΝ ЕВОЛ ГАР ２Ṁ·
·ФОУО Ṁ·ФΗΤ` ША϶·`ЕΙΝΕ ЕВОЛ Ṉ·２Ṉ·ПОΝΗΡОΝ

46 ПЕХЕ·ĪС ХЕ ХΙΝ·`АДАМ ШΑ·ЇШ２Α ‾ΝΗС
П·ВАПТΙСТΗС ２Ṉ·Ṉ·ХПО Ṉ·Ṉ·２ΙОМЕ
МṈ·ПЕТ·ХОСЕ Α·ЇШ２АΝΝΗС П·ВАПТΙСТΗС
ШΙΝΑ ХЕ Ν·ОУШбП̄` ṈбΙ·ΝЕ϶·ВАЛ
ΑЕΙ·ХО·ОС ДЕ ХЕ ПЕТ·ΝΑ·ШШПЕ ２Ṉ·ТΗУΤṈ
Е϶·О Ṉ·КОУЕΙ ϶·ΝΑ·СОУШΝ·Τ·МṈΤЕРО
АУШ ϶·ΝΑ·ХΙСЕ Α·ЇШ２АΝΝΗС

47 ПЕХЕ·ĪС ХЕ МṈ·бОМ ṈΤЕ·ОУ·РШМЕ ·ТЕЛО Α·２ТО
СΝΑУ Ṉ϶·ХШЛК` Ṁ·ПΙТЕ ·СṈΤЕ АУШ МṈ·
·бОМ` ṈΤЕ·ОУ·２Ṁ２ÁÁ ·ШṀШЕ·ХОЕΙС ·СΝΑУ
Η ϶·ΝΑ·Р̄·ТΙМΑ Ṁ·П·ОУΑ` АУШ П·КЕ·ОУΑ ϶·ΝΑ·
·Р̄·２УВРΙΖЕ Ṁ·МО·϶·МΑ·РЕ·РШМЕ ·СЕ·РП̄·АС
АУШ Ṉ·Τ·ЕУΝОУ Ṉ϶·`ЕПΙӨУМЕΙ Α·СШ ΗΡП`
В̄·ВРРЕ АУШ МАУ·ΝОУХ·`ΗΡП В̄·ВР̄РЕ Е·АСКОС
Ṉ·АС ХЕКΛΑС Ṉ·ΝОУ·ПШ２ АУШ МАУ·
·ΝЕХ·`ΗΡП` Ṉ·АС Е·АСКОС В̄·ВР̄РЕ ШΙΝΑ ХЕ
ΝЕ϶·ТЕКΑ·϶` МАУ·ХΛб·ТОЕΙС Ṉ·АС Α·ШΤΗ‾
Ṉ·ШΑЕΙ ЕПЕΙ ОУΝ·ОУ·ПШ２ ·ΝΑ·ШШПЕ

48 ПЕХЕ·ĪС ХЕ ЕРШΑ·СΝΑУ ·Р̄·ЕΙΡΗΝΗ МṈ·
·ΝОУ·ЕРΗУ ２Ṁ·ПЕΙ·ΗЕΙ ОУШΤ` СЕ·ΝΑ·ХО·ОС
Ṁ·П·ΤΑУ ХЕ ·ПШШΝЕ ЕВОЛ АУШ ϶·ΝΑ·ПШШΝЕ

45   Yeshua said:
Grapes are not picked from thornbushes
nor figs from thistles,
for they do not give fruit.
The good offer goodness
from the secret of their heart.
The perverse offer perversity
from the secret of their heart.
That which is expressed
is what overflows from the heart.

46   Yeshua said:
From Adam to John the Baptist,
no one born of woman
is higher than John the Baptist.
Thus his eyes will not be destroyed.
But I have said:
Whoever among you becomes small
will know the Kingdom, and be higher than John.

47   Yeshua said:
A man cannot ride two horses
nor bend two bows.
A servant cannot serve two masters,
for he will honor one and disdain the other.
No one drinks an old wine
and then desires a new one.
New wine is not put into old wineskins,
for they will crack.
Old wine is not put into new skins,
for it will spoil.
A patch of old cloth is not sewn
onto a new garment,
for it will tear.

48   Yeshua said:
If two make peace with each other
in a single house,
then they can say to the mountain: "Move!"
And it will move.

49 ΠΕΧΕ·ΙC ΧΕ ϨΕΝ·ΜΑΚΑΡΙΟC ΝΕ Ν·
·ΜΟΝΑΧΟC ΑΥШ ΕΤ·CΟΤΠˋ ΧΕ ΤΕΤΝΑ·
·ϨΕ Α·Τ·ΜΝ̄ΤΕΡΟ ΧΕ Ν̄·ΤШ·ΤΝ̄ ϨΝ̄·ΕΒΟΛ
Ν̄·ϨΗΤ·C̄ ΠΑΛΙΝ ΕΤΕΤΝΑ·ΒШΚˋ Ε·ΜΑΥ

50 ΠΕΧΕ·ΙC̄ ΧΕ ΕΥ·ШΑΝ·ΧΟ·ΟC ΝΗ·ΤΝ̄ ΧΕ Ν̄ΤΑΤΕΤΝ̄·ШШΠΕ
ΕΒΟΛ ΤШΝ ·ΧΟ·ΟC ΝΑ·Υ
ΧΕ Ν̄ΤΑΝ·ΕΙ ΕΒΟΛ ϨΜ̄·Π·ΟΥΟΕΙΝ Π·ΜΑ
ΕΝΤΑ·Π·ΟΥΟΕΙΝ ·ШШΠΕ Μ̄·ΜΑΥ ΕΒΟΛ
ϨΙ·ΤΟΟΤ·qˋ ΟΥΑΑΤ·qˋ Αq·Ш[ϨΕ Ε·ΡΑΤ·q̄]
[Α]ΥШ Αq·ΟΥШ[ΝϨ] [ΕΒ]ΟΛ [Ϩ]Ν̄·ΤΟΥ·ϨΙΚШΝ ΕΥ·
·ШΑ·ΧΟ·ΟC ΝΗ·ΤΝ̄ ΧΕ Ν̄·ΤШ·ΤΝ̄ ΠΕ ·ΧΟ·ΟC
ΧΕ ΑΝΟ·Ν ΝΕq·ШΗΡΕ ΑΥШ ΑΝΟ·Ν Ν̄·CШΤΠˋ
Μ̄·Π·ΕΙШΤˋ ΕΤ·ΟΝϨ ΕΥ·ШΑΝ·ΧΝΕ·ΤΗΥΤΝ̄
ΧΕ ΟΥ ΠΕ Π·ΜΑΕΙΝ Μ̄·ΠΕΤΝ̄·ΕΙШΤˋ ΕΤ·ϨΝ̄·
·ΤΗΥΤΝ̄ ·ΧΟ·ΟC ΕΡΟ·ΟΥ ΧΕ ΟΥ·ΚΙΜ ΠΕ ΜΝ̄·
·ΟΥ·ΑΝΑΠΑΥCΙC

51 ΠΕΧΑ·Υ ΝΑ·q Ν̄ϬΙ·ΝΕq·ΜΑΘΗΤΗC
ΧΕ ΑШ Ν̄·ϨΟΟΥ Ε·Τ·ΑΝΑΠΑΥCΙC Ν̄·
·ΝΕΤ·ΜΟΟΥΤˋ ·ΝΑ·ШШΠΕ ΑΥШ ΑШ Ν̄·ϨΟΟΥ
Ε·Π·ΚΟCΜΟC Β̄·ΒΡ̄ΡΕ ·ΝΗΥ ΠΕΧΑ·q ΝΑ·Υ ΧΕ
ΤΗ ΕΤΕΤΝ̄·ϬШШΤˋ ΕΒΟΛ ϨΗΤ·C̄ ΑC·ΕΙ ΑΛΛΑ
Ν̄·ΤШ·ΤΝ̄ ΤΕΤΝ̄·CΟΟΥΝ ΑΝ Μ̄·ΜΟ·C

52 ΠΕΧΑ·Υ
ΝΑ·q Ν̄ϬΙ·ΝΕq·ΜΑΘΗΤΗC ΧΕ ΧΟΥΤ·ΑqΤΕ
Μ̄·ΠΡΟΦΗΤΗC ΑΥ·ШΑΧΕ ϨΜ̄·Π·ΙCΡΑΗΛˋ
ΑΥШ ΑΥ·ШΑΧΕ ΤΗΡ·ΟΥ ϨΡΑΪ Ν̄·ϨΗΤ·Κˋ ΠΕˋ
ΧΑ·q ΝΑ·Υ ΧΕ ΑΤΕΤΝ̄·ΚШ Μ̄·ΠΕΤ·ΟΝϨ Μ̄·ΠΕ
ΕΒΟΛ ΑΥШ ΑΤΕΤΝ̄·ШΑΧΕ ϨΑ·ΝΕΤ·
·ΜΟΟΥΤˋ

49 Yeshua said:
Blessed are you, the whole ones and the chosen ones.
You will find the Kingdom,
for you came from there,
and you will return.

50 Yeshua said:
If they ask you from where you come,
say:
We were born of the Light,
there where Light is born of Light.
It holds true
and is revealed within their image.
If they ask you who you are,
say:
We are its children,
the beloved of the Father, the Living One.
If they ask you what is the sign of the Father in you,
say:
It is movement and it is repose.

51 His disciples said to him:
"When will the dead be at rest?"
"When will the new world come?"
He answered them:
What you are waiting for has already come,
but you do not see it.

52 His disciples said to him:
"Twenty-four prophets have spoken in Israel,
and they all spoke of you."
He said to them:
You have disregarded the Living One
who is in your presence,
and you have spoken of the dead.

53 ΠΕΧΑ·Υ ΝΑ·Ϥ ΝΟΙ·ΝΕϤ·ΜΑΘΗΤΗΟ
ΧΕ Π·ϹΒΒΕ ·Ρ·ωϤΕλΕΙ Η Μ·ΜΟ·Ν ΠΕΧΑ·Ϥ`
ΝΑ·Υ ΧΕ ΝΕϤ·Ρ·ωϤΕλΕΙ ΝΕ·ΠΟΥ·ΕΙωΤ` ·ΝΑ·
·ΧΠΟ·ΟΥ ΕΒΟλ ΖΝ·ΤΟΥ·ΜΑΑΥ ΕΥ·ϹΒΒΗΥ
ΑλλΑ Π·ϹΒΒΕ Μ·ΜΕ ΖΜ·ΠΝΑ ΑϤ·ΟΝ·ΖΗΥ
ΤΗΡ·Ϥ`

54 ΠΕΧΕ·ΙϹ ΧΕ ΖΝ·ΜΑΚΑΡΙΟϹ ΝΕ Ν·ΖΗΚΕ
ΧΕ ΤωΤΝ ΤΕ Τ·ΜΝΤΕΡΟ·Ν·Μ·ΠΗΥΕ`

55 ΠΕΧΕ·ΙϹ ΧΕ ΠΕΤΑ·ΜΕϹΤΕ·ΠΕϤ·`·ΕΙωΤ`
ΑΝ` ΜΝ·ΤΕϤ·ΜΑΑΥ Ϥ·ΝΑω·Ρ·ΜΑΘΗΤΗϹ ΑΝ
ΝΑ·ΕΙ` ΑΥω ΝϤ·ΜΕϹΤΕ·ΝΕϤ·`·ϹΝΗΥ` ΜΝ·
·ΝΕϤ·ϹωΝΕ ΝϤ·Ϥ·ϤΕΙ Μ·ΠΕϤ·Ϲ·ΡΟϹ Ν·ΤΑ·ΖΕ
Ϥ·ΝΑ·ωωΠΕ ΑΝ ΕϤ·Ο Ν·ΑΖΙΟϹ ΝΑ·ΕΙ

56 ΠΕΧΕ·ΙϹ
ΧΕ ΠΕΤΑΖ·ϹΟΥωΝ·Π·ΚΟϹΜΟϹ ΑϤ·`
·ΖΕ Ε·Υ·ΠΤωΜΑ ΑΥω ΠΕΝΤΑΖ·ΖΕ Ε·Α·ΠΤωΜΑ
Π·ΚΟϹΜΟϹ ·ΜΠωΑ Μ·ΜΟ·Ϥ ΑΝ

57 ΠΕΧΕ·ΙϹ ΧΕ Τ·ΜΝΤΕΡΟ Μ·Π·ΕΙωΤ` ΕϹ·ΤΝΤω ̄
Α·Υ·ΡωΜΕ ΕΥΝ·ΤΑ·Ϥ Μ·ΜΑΥ Ν·ΝΟΥ·ϬΡΟϬ
[Ε·ΝΑΝΟΥ·]Ϥ` Α·ΠΕϤ·ΧΑΧΕ ·ΕΙ Ν·Τ·ΟΥωΗ`
ΑϤ·ϹΙΤΕ Ν·ΟΥ·ΖΙΖΑΝΙ[ΟΝ ΕΧ]Ν·ΠΕ·ϬΡΟ[Ϭ Ε]Τ·ΝΑΝΟΥ·Ϥ`
 Μ·ΠΕ·Π·ΡωΜΕ ·ΚΟΟ·Υ Ε·ΖωλΕ
Μ·Π·ΖΙΖΑΝΙΟΝ ΠΕΧΑ·Ϥ ΝΑ·Υ ΧΕ ΜΗΠωϹ
ΝΤΕΤΝ·ΒωΚ` ΧΕ ΕΝΑ·ΖωλΕ Μ·Π·ΖΙΖΑΝΙΟ ̄
ΝΤΕΤΝ·ΖωλΕ Μ·Π·ϹΟΥΟ ΝΜΜΑ·Ϥ` ΖΜ·ΦΟΟΥ
ΓΑΡ Μ·Π·ωΖϹ ̄ Ν·ΖΙΖΑΝΙΟΝ ·ΝΑ·ΟΥωΝΖ
ΕΒΟλ` ϹΕ·ΖΟλ·ΟΥ ΝϹΕ·ΡΟΚΖ·ΟΥ

58 ΠΕΧΕ·ΙϹ ΧΕ ΟΥ·ΜΑΚΑΡΙΟϹ ΠΕ Π·ΡωΜΕ ΝΤΑΖ·ΖΙϹΕ
ΑϤ·ΖΕ Α·Π·ωΝΖ

53   His disciples asked him:
"Is circumcision useful or not?"
He replied:
If it were useful, fathers would engender sons born circumcised
    from their mothers.
Rather, it is the circumcision in spirit that is truly useful.

54   Blessed are you, the poor,
for yours is the Kingdom of Heaven.

55   Yeshua said:
Whoever cannot free themselves from their father and their
    mother
cannot become my disciple.
Whoever cannot free themselves from their brother and sister
and does not bear their cross as I do
is not worthy of me.

56   Yeshua said:
Whoever knows the world
discovers a corpse.
And whoever discovers a corpse
cannot be contained by the world.

57   Yeshua said:
The Kingdom of the Father is like the man
who had some good seed.
His enemy came at night and sowed weeds
among the good seed.
The man would not allow them to pull up the weeds,
saying, "I fear you might pull up the wheat as well."
Indeed, at harvesttime, the weeds will be conspicuous.
They will be pulled up and burned.

58   Yeshua said:
Blessed are those who have undergone ordeals.
They have entered into life.

59 ΠΕΧΕ·ΙC ΧΕ ϬⲰϢΤ` ⲚCⲀ·ΠΕΤ·ΟⲚϨ
ϨⲰC ΕΤΕΤⲚ·ΟⲚϨ ϨΙⲚⲀ ΧΕ ⲚΕΤⲘ·ⲘΟⲨ
ⲀⲨⲰ ⲚΤΕΤⲚ·ϢΙⲚΕ Ε·ⲚⲀⲨ ΕΡΟ·ϥ ⲀⲨⲰ ΤΕΤⲚⲀϢ·
·ϬⲘ· Ϭ Ο Μ ⲀⲚ

60 Ε·ⲚⲀⲨ Ⲁ·Ⲩ·CⲀⲘⲀΡΕΙΤⲎC Εϥ·ϥΙ Ⲛ·
·ⲚΟⲨ·ϨΙΕΙⲂ` Εϥ·ⲂⲎⲔ` ΕϨΟⲨⲚ Ε·ΤΟⲨⲆⲀΙⲀ ΠΕΧⲀ·ϥ`
Ⲛ·ⲚΕϥ·`·ⲘⲀⲐⲎΤⲎC ΧΕ ΠⲎ Ⲙ·Π·ⲔⲰΤΕ
Ⲙ·ΠΕ·ϨΙΕΙⲂ` ΠΕΧⲀ·Ⲩ ⲚⲀ·ϥ <> ΧΕⲔⲀⲀC Εϥ·ⲚⲀ·
·ΜΟΟⲨΤ·ϥ` Ⲛϥ·ΟⲨΟⲘ·ϥ` ΠΕΧⲀ·ϥ ⲚⲀ·Ⲩ <> ϨⲰC Εϥ·ΟⲚϨ
ϥ·ⲚⲀ·ΟⲨΟⲘ·ϥ` ⲀⲚ ⲀⲖⲖⲀ Εϥ·ϢⲀ·ⲘΟΟⲨΤ·ϥ`
Ⲛϥ·ϢⲰΠΕ Ⲛ·ΟⲨ·ΠΤⲰⲘⲀ ΠΕΧⲀ·Ⲩ
ΧΕ Ⲛ·ⲔΕ·CⲘΟΤ` ϥ·ⲚⲀϢ·Ⲁ·C ⲀⲚ ΠΕΧⲀ·ϥ ⲚⲀ·Ⲩ
ΧΕ Ⲛ·ΤⲰ·ΤⲚ ϨⲰΤ·`·ΤⲎⲨΤⲚ ·ϢΙⲚΕ ⲚCⲀ·ΟⲨ·
·ΤΟΠΟC ⲚⲎ·ΤⲚ ΕϨΟⲨⲚ Ε·Ⲩ·ⲀⲚⲀΠⲀⲨCΙC
ΧΕⲔⲀⲀC ⲚⲚΕΤⲚ·ϢⲰΠΕ Ⲙ·ΠΤⲰⲘⲀ ⲚCΕ·
·ΟⲨⲰⲘ·`·ΤⲎⲨΤⲚ

61 ΠΕΧΕ·ΙC <> ΟⲨⲚ·CⲚⲀⲨ ·ⲚⲀ·ⲘΤΟⲚ`
Ⲙ·ⲘⲀⲨ ϨΙ·ΟⲨ·ϬⲖΟϬ Π·ΟⲨⲀ ·ⲚⲀ·ⲘΟⲨ Π·ΟⲨⲀ
·ⲚⲀ·ⲰⲚϨ ΠΕΧΕ·CⲀⲖⲰⲘⲎ <> ⲚΤⲀ·Ⲕ` ⲚΙⲘ`
Π·ΡⲰⲘΕ ϨⲰC ΕⲂΟⲖ ϨⲚ·ΟⲨⲀ ⲀⲔ·ΤΕⲖΟ ΕΧⲘ·
·ΠⲀ·ϬⲖΟϬ ⲀⲨⲰ ⲀⲔ·`·ΟⲨⲰⲘ ΕⲂΟⲖ ϨⲚ·ΤⲀ·
·ΤΡⲀΠΕⲌⲀ ΠΕΧΕ·ΙC ⲚⲀ·C ΧΕ ⲀⲚΟ·Ⲕ` ΠΕ
ΠΕΤ·ϢΟΟΠ` ΕⲂΟⲖ ϨⲘ·ΠΕΤ·`·ϢⲎϢ ⲀⲨ·†
ⲚⲀ·ΕΙ ΕⲂΟⲖ ϨⲚ·ⲚⲀ·ΠⲀ·ΕΙⲰΤ` ⲀⲚΟ·Ⲕ` ΤΕⲔ·`
ⲘⲀⲐⲎΤⲎC ΕΤⲂΕ·ΠⲀΕΙ †·ΧⲰ Ⲙ·ⲘΟ·C ΧΕ
ϨΟΤⲀⲚ Εϥ·ϢⲀ·ϢⲰΠΕ Εϥ·ϢⲎϥ` ϥ·ⲚⲀ·ⲘΟⲨϨ
ΟⲨΟΕΙⲚ ϨΟΤⲀⲚ ⲆΕ Εϥ·ϢⲀⲚ·ϢⲰΠΕ Εϥ·
·ΠⲎϢ ϥ·ⲚⲀ·ⲘΟⲨϨ Ⲛ·ⲔⲀⲔΕ

59   Yeshua said:
Look to the Living One
while you are alive.
If you wait until you are dead,
you will search in vain for the vision.

60   They saw a Samaritan carrying a lamb,
  entering into Judea.
He said to his disciples:
What will the man do with the lamb?
They answered:
"He will kill it and eat it."
He told them:
As long as it is alive, he will not eat it,
but only if he kills it and it becomes a cadaver.
They said: "He cannot do otherwise."
He told them:
Seek a place in Repose.
Do not become cadavers,
lest you be eaten.

61   Yeshua said:
Two will lie on a single bed.
One will die, the other will live.
Salome asked him:
"Who are you, Sir?
Where do you come from, you who
lie on my bed and eat at my table?"
Yeshua replied:
I come from the One who is Openness.
What comes from my Father has been given to me.
Salome answered:
"I am your disciple."
Yeshua told her:
That is why I say that when disciples are open,
they are filled with light.
When they are divided,
they are filled with darkness.

62 ΠΕΧΕ·ΙС ΧΕ ΕΙ·
·ΧШ Ν̄·ΝΑ·ΜΥСΤΗΡΙΟΝ Ν̄·Ν[ΕΤ·Μ̄ΠШΑ Ν̄·]
[·ΝΑ·Μ]ΥСΤΗΡΙΟΝ ΠΕ[Τ]Ε·ΤΕΚ·‘·ΟΥΝΑΜ ·ΝΑ·Α·Ϥ
ΜΝ̄ΤΡΕ·ΤΕΚ·2ΒΟΥΡ‘ ·ΕΙΜΕ ΧΕ ΕС·Ρ·ΟΥ

63 ΠΕΧΕ·ΙС ΧΕ ΝΕΥΝ̄·ΟΥ·ΡШΜΕ Μ̄·ΠΛΟΥСΙΟС ΕΥΝ̄·ΤΑ·Ϥ Μ̄·
·ΜΑΥ Ν̄·2Α2 Ν̄·ΧΡΗΜΑ ΠΕΧΑ·Ϥ ΧΕ †·ΝΑ·Ρ̄·ΧΡШ Ν̄·
·ΝΑ·ΧΡΗΜΑ ΧΕΚΑΑС Ε·ΕΙ·ΝΑ·ΧΟ Ν̄ΤΑ·ШС2
Ν̄ΤΑ·ΤШ6Ε Ν̄ΤΑ·ΜΟΥ2 Ν̄·ΝΑ·Ε2ШΡ Ν̄·ΚΑΡ‘ΠΟС
ШΙΝΑ ΧΕ Ν·Ι·Ρ̄·6ΡШ2 Λ̄·ΛΑΑΥ ΝΑΕΙ ΝΕ
ΝΕϤ·ΜΕΕΥΕ ΕΡΟ·ΟΥ 2Μ̄·ΠΕϤ·2ΗΤ‘ ΑΥШ 2Ν̄·
·Τ·ΟΥШΗ ΕΤ·Μ̄·ΜΑΥ ΑϤ·ΜΟΥ ΠΕΤ·ΕΥΜ̄·ΜΑΧΕ
Μ̄·ΜΟ·Ϥ‘ ΜΑΡΕϤ·‘·СШΤΜ̄

64 ΠΕΧΕ·ΙС ΧΕ ΟΥ·ΡШΜΕ
ΝΕΥΝ̄·ΤΑ·Ϥ·2Ν̄·ШΜ̄ΜΟ ΑΥШ Ν̄ΤΑΡΕϤ·СΟΒΤΕ
Μ̄·Π·ΔΙΠΝΟΝ ΑϤ·ΧΟΟΥ Μ̄·ΠΕϤ·2Μ̄2ΑΛ̄ ШΙΝΑ
ΕϤ·ΝΑ·ΤШ2Μ̄ Ν̄·Ν̄·ШΜ̄ΜΟΕΙ ΑϤ·ΒШΚ‘ Μ̄·
·Π·ШΟΡΠ‘ ΠΕΧΑ·Ϥ ΝΑ·Ϥ‘ ΧΕ ΠΑ·ΧΟΕΙС ·ΤШ2Μ̄
Μ̄·ΜΟ·Κ‘ ΠΕΧΑ·Ϥ ΧΕ ΟΥΝ̄·ΤΑ·ΕΙ·2Ν̄·2ΟΜΤ‘
Α·2ΕΝ·ΕΜΠΟΡΟС СΕ·Ν̄ΝΗΥ ШΑΡΟ·ΕΙ Ε·ΡΟΥ2Ε
†·ΝΑ·ΒШΚ‘ Ν̄ΤΑ·ΟΥΕ2·СΑ2ΝΕ ΝΑ·Υ †·Ρ̄·ΠΑΡΑΙΤΕΙ
Μ̄·Π·ΔΙΠΝΟΝ ΑϤ·ΒШΚ‘ ШΑ·ΚΕ·ΟΥΑ ΠΕΧΑ·Ϥ
ΝΑ·Ϥ‘ ΧΕ Α·ΠΑ·ΧΟΕΙС ·ΤШ2Μ̄ Μ̄·ΜΟ·Κ‘
ΠΕΧΑ·Ϥ ΝΑ·Ϥ ΧΕ ΑΕΙ·ΤΟΟΥ ΟΥ·ΗΕΙ ΑΥШ СΕ·
·Ρ̄·ΑΙΤΕΙ Μ̄·ΜΟ·ΕΙ Ν̄·ΟΥ·2ΗΜΕΡΑ †·ΝΑ·СΡ̄ϤΕ Α ⎯
ΑϤ·ΕΙ ША·ΚΕ·ΟΥΑ ΠΕΧΑ·Ϥ ΝΑ·Ϥ‘ ΧΕ ΠΑ·ΧΟΕΙС
·ΤШ2Μ̄ Μ̄·ΜΟ·Κ‘ ΠΕΧΑ·Ϥ ΝΑ·Ϥ ΧΕ ΠΑ·ШΒΗΡ
·ΝΑ·Ρ̄·ШΕΛΕΕΤ ΑΥШ ΑΝΟ·Κ‘ ΕΤ·ΝΑ·Ρ̄·ΔΙΠΝΟΝ
†·ΝΑ·Ш·Ι ΑΝ †·Ρ̄·ΠΑΡΑΙΤΕΙ Μ̄·Π·ΔΙΠΝΟΝ‘ ΑϤ·‘
·ΒШΚ‘ ША·ΚΕ·ΟΥΑ ΠΕΧΑ·Ϥ ΝΑ·Ϥ ΧΕ ΠΑ·ΧΟΕΙС
·ΤШ2Μ̄ Μ̄·ΜΟ·Κ‘ ΠΕΧΑ·Ϥ ΝΑ·Ϥ‘ ΧΕ ΑΕΙ·ΤΟΟΥ Ν̄·
·ΟΥ·ΚШΜΗ Ε·ΕΙ·ΒΗΚ‘ Α·ΧΙ Ν̄·ШΟΜ †·ΝΑ·Ш·Ι
ΑΝ †·Ρ̄·ΠΑΡΑΙΤΕΙ ΑϤ·ΕΙ Ν̄6Ι·Π·2Μ̄2ΑΛ̄ ΑϤ·ΧΟ·
·ΟС Α·ΠΕϤ·ΧΟΕΙС ΧΕ ΝΕΝΤΑΚ·‘·ΤΑ2Μ·ΟΥ Α·
·Π·ΔΙΠΝΟΝ ΑΥ·ΠΑΡΑΙΤΕΙ ΠΕΧΕ·Π·ΧΟΕΙС Μ̄·
·ΠΕϤ·2Μ̄2ΑΛ̄ ΧΕ ·ΒШΚ‘ Ε·Π·СΑ·Ν·ΒΟΛ Α·Ν·2ΙΟΟΥΕ
ΝΕΤ·Κ·ΝΑ·2Ε ΕΡΟ·ΟΥ ·ΕΝΙ·ΟΥ ΧΕΚΑΑС
ΕΥ·ΝΑ·Ρ̄·ΔΙΠΝΕΙ Ν̄·ΡΕϤ·ΤΟΟΥ ΜΝ̄·Ν·ΕШΟ[ΤΕ ΕΥ·ΝΑ·ΒШΚ]
ΑΝ‘ Ε2ΟΥΝ‘ Ε·Ν·ΤΟΠΟС Μ̄·ΠΑ·ΙШΤ‘

62 Yeshua said:
I reveal my mysteries
to those who become worthy.
Do not let your left hand know
what your right hand is doing.

63 Yeshua said:
There was once a rich man with a great amount of money
who said: "I will use my money for sowing,
reaping, planting, and filling my silos with grain
so that I will never lack for anything."
Such was the thought of his heart.
Yet that night, he died.
Those who have ears,
Let them hear!

64 Yeshua said:
There was a man who invited some visitors. After preparing
the meal, he sent his servant
to summon the guests.
The servant went to the first one and said "My master invites
you."
The man answered: "I have business with some merchants who
are arriving this evening. Please excuse me from the dinner."
The servant went to the next one and said "My master invites
you."
This man answered: "I have just bought a house and need one
day more, so I cannot come."
The servant went to another guest and said "My master invites
you."
The man answered: "My friend is getting married and I must
prepare the food. Excuse me."
The servant returned to his master and said:
"Those you have invited to dinner cannot come."
His master replied:
"Then go out on the roads and invite whoever you find
to dine with me.
Buyers and merchants will not enter my Father's dwelling."

65 ΠΕΧΑ·Ϥ ΧΕ ΟΥ·ΡΩΜΕ Ν̄·ΧΡΗ[ϹΤΟ]Ϲ ΝΕΥΝ̄·[·ΤΑ·Ϥ]
Ν̄·ΟΥ·ΜΑ Ν̄·ΕΛΟΟΛΕ ΑϤ·ΤΑΑ·Ϥ Ν̄·[Ϩ]Ν̄·ΟΥΟΕΙΕ
ϢΙΝΑ ΕΥ·ΝΑ·Ρ̄·Ϩ ΩΒ` ΕΡΟ·Ϥ` Ν̄Ϥ·ΧΙ [Μ̄·]ΠΕϤ·ΚΑΡ`ΠΟϹ
Ν̄·ΤΟΟΤ·ΟΥ ΑϤ·ΧΟΟΥ Μ̄·ΠΕϤ·ϨΜϨᾹΛ ΧΕΚΑΑϹ
Ε·Ν·ΟΥΟΕΙΕ ·ΝΑ·† ΝΑ·Ϥ` Μ̄·Π·ΚΑΡΠΟϹ Μ̄·
·Π·ΜΑ Ν̄·ΕΛΟΟΛΕ ΑΥ·ΕΜΑϨΤΕ Μ̄·ΠΕϤ·ϨΜϨᾹΛ
ΑΥ·ϨΙΟΥΕ ΕΡΟ·Ϥ` ΝΕ·ΚΕ·ΚΟΥΕΙ ΠΕ Ν̄ϹΕ·ΜΟΟΥΤ·Ϥ`
Α·Π·ϨΜϨᾹΛ ·ΒΩΚ` ΑϤ·ΧΟ·ΟϹ Ε·ΠΕϤ·ΧΟΕΙϹ
ΠΕΧΕ·ΠΕϤ·ΧΟΕΙϹ ΧΕ ΜΕϢΑΚ` Μ̄ΠΕϤ·`·ϹΟΥΩΝ·ΟΥ
ΑϤ·ΧΟΟΥ Ν̄·ΚΕ·ϨΜϨᾹΛ Α·Ν·ΟΥΟΕΙΕ ·ϨΙΟΥΕ
Ε·Π·ΚΕ·ΟΥΑ ΤΟΤΕ Α·Π·ΧΟΕΙϹ ·ΧΟΟΥ Μ̄·
·ΠΕϤ·ϢΗΡΕ ΠΕΧΑ·Ϥ` ΧΕ ΜΕϢΑΚ` ϹΕ·ΝΑ·ϢΙΠΕ
ϨΗΤ·Ϥ` Μ̄·ΠΑ·ϢΗΡΕ Α·Ν·`·ΟΥΟΕΙΕ ΕΤ·Μ̄·ΜΑΥ ΕΠΕΙ
ϹΕ·ϹΟΟΥΝ ΧΕ Ν̄·ΤΟ·Ϥ ΠΕ ΠΕ·ΚΛΗΡΟΝΟΜΟϹ
Μ̄·Π·ΜΑ Ν̄·ΕΛΟΟΛΕ ΑΥ·ϬΟΠ·Ϥ` ΑΥ·ΜΟΟΥΤ·Ϥ`
ΠΕΤ·ΕΥΜ̄·ΜΑΑΧΕ Μ̄·ΜΟ·Ϥ` ΜΑΡΕϤ·`·ϹΩΤΜ̄

66 ΠΕΧΕ·ῙϹ ΧΕ ΜΑ·ΤϹΕΒΟ·ΕΙ Ε·Π·ΩΝΕ ΠΑΕΙ Ν̄ΤΑΥ·
·ϹΤΟ·Ϥ` ΕΒΟΛ` Ν̄Ϭ·ΝΕΤ·`·ΚΩΤ` Ν̄·ΤΟ·Ϥ ΠΕ Π·ΩΝΕ
Ν̄·ΚΩϨ

67 ΠΕΧΕ·ῙϹ ΧΕ ΠΕΤ·ϹΟΟΥΝ Μ̄·Π·ΤΗΡ·Ϥ
ΕϤ·Ρ̄·ϬΡΩϨ ΟΥΑΑ·Ϥ ·Ρ̄·ϬΡΩϨ Μ̄·Π·ΜΑ ΤΗΡ·Ϥ`

68 ΠΕΧΕ·ῙϹ ΧΕ Ν̄·ΤΩ·ΤΝ̄ Ϩ Μ̄·ΜΑΚΑΡΙΟϹ ϨΟΤΑ
ΕΥ·ϢΑΝ·ΜΕϹΤΕ·ΤΗΥΤΝ̄ Ν̄ϹΕ·Ρ̄·ΔΙΩΚΕ Μ̄·
·ΜΩ·ΤΝ̄ ΑΥΩ ϹΕ·ΝΑ·Ϩ Ε ΑΝ Ε·ΤΟΠΟϹ Ϩ Μ̄·Π·ΜΑ
ΕΝΤΑΥ·ΔΙΩΚΕ Μ̄·ΜΩ·ΤΝ̄ ϨΡΑΪ Ν̄·ϨΗΤ·Ϥ`

69 ΠΕΧΕ·ῙϹ <> Ϩ Μ̄·ΜΑΚΑΡΙΟϹ ΝΕ ΝΑΕΙ Ν̄ΤΑΥ·ΔΙΩΚΕ
Μ̄·ΜΟ·ΟΥ ϨΡΑΪ Ϩ Μ̄·ΠΟΥ·ϨΗΤ` ΝΕΤ·Μ̄·ΜΑΥ`
ΝΕΝΤΑϨ·ϹΟΥΩΝ·ΠΕΙΩΤ` Ϩ Ν̄·ΟΥ·ΜΕ Ϩ Μ̄·
·ΜΑΚΑΡΙΟϹ ΝΕΤ·ϨΚΑΕΙΤ` ϢΙΝΑ ΕΥ·ΝΑ·
·ΤϹΙΟ Ν̄·ΘΗ Μ̄·ΠΕΤ·ΟΥΩϢ

65   Yeshua said:

A good man had a vineyard,
which he gave to tenants to work
and harvest the fruit for him.
He sent his servant to collect the fruit of the vine.
But the tenants seized the servant
and beat him nearly to death.
The servant reported this to his master, who thought:
"Perhaps they didn't recognize him."
And he sent another servant, who was also beaten.
Then the master sent his own son,
thinking: "Perhaps they will treat him with respect."
When the tenants realized that he was the inheritor of the
    vineyard,
they seized him and killed him.
Those who have ears,
Let them hear!

66   Yeshua said:

Show me the stone rejected by the builders.
That is the cornerstone.

67   Yeshua said:

Those who know the All
yet do not know themselves
are deprived of everything.

68   Yeshua said:

Blessed are you when they hate you
and persecute you.
There is a place where you are not persecuted
that they will never find.

69   Yeshua said:

Blessed are those
who have been persecuted in their hearts,
for they have known the Father in Truth.
Blessed are those who are hungry,
for they will be fulfilled.

70 ⲡⲉϫⲉ·ⲓ̅ⲥ̅ <> ϩⲟⲧⲁⲛ
ⲉⲧⲉⲧⲛ̅·ϣⲁ·ϫⲡⲉ·ⲡⲏ ϩⲛ̅·ⲧⲏⲩⲧⲛ̅ ⲡⲁⲓ̈
ⲉⲧ·ⲉⲩⲛ̅·ⲧⲏ·ⲧⲛ̅·ϥ̅ ϥ·ⲛⲁ·ⲧⲟⲩϫⲉ·ⲧⲏⲩⲧⲛ̅ ⲉϣⲱⲡⲉ
ⲙⲛ̅·ⲧⲏ·ⲧⲛ̅·ⲡⲏ ϩⲛ̅[·ⲧⲏⲩⲧ]ⲛ̅ ⲡⲁⲉⲓ ⲉⲧⲉ
ⲙⲛ̅·ⲧⲏ·ⲧⲛ̅·ϥ̅ ϩⲛ̅·ⲧⲏⲛⲉ ϥ[·ⲛⲁ·ⲙ]ⲟⲩⲧ·`·ⲧⲏⲛⲉ

71 ⲡⲉϫⲉ·ⲓ̅ⲥ̅ ϫⲉ ϯ·ⲛⲁ·ϣⲟⲣ[ϣⲣ̅ ⲙ̅·ⲡⲉⲉⲓ·ⲏ]ⲉⲓ
ⲁⲩⲱ ⲙⲛ̅·ⲗⲁⲁⲩ ·ⲛⲁϣ·ⲕⲟⲧ·ϥ [ⲁⲛ ⲛ̅·ⲕⲉ·ⲥⲟⲡ]

72 [ⲡⲉϫⲉ·ⲟⲩ·ⲣⲱⲙⲉ ⲛⲁ·ϥ`] ϫⲉ ·ϫⲟ·ⲟⲥ ⲛ̅·ⲛⲁ·ⲥⲛⲏⲩ
ϣⲓⲛⲁ ⲉⲩ·ⲛ[ⲁ·ⲡ]ⲱϣⲉ ⲛ̅·ⲛ̅·ϩⲛⲁⲁⲩ ⲙ̅·ⲡⲁ·ⲉⲓⲱⲧ`
ⲛⲙ̅ⲙⲁ·ⲉⲓ ⲡⲉϫⲁ·ϥ ⲛⲁ·ϥ` ϫⲉ ⲱ ⲡ·ⲣⲱⲙⲉ ⲛⲓⲙ
ⲡⲉ ⲛ̅ⲧⲁϩ·ⲁ·ⲁⲧ` ⲛ̅·ⲣⲉϥ·ⲡⲱϣⲉ ⲁϥ·ⲕⲟⲧ·ϥ̅ ⲁ·`
·ⲛⲉϥ·ⲙⲁⲑⲏⲧⲏⲥ ⲡⲉϫⲁ·ϥ ⲛⲁ·ⲩ ϫⲉ ⲙⲏ ⲉ·ⲉⲓ·
·ϣⲟⲟⲡ` ⲛ̅·ⲣⲉϥ·`·ⲡⲱϣⲉ

73 ⲡⲉϫⲉ·ⲓ̅ⲥ̅ ϫⲉ ⲡ·ⲱϩⲥ
ⲙⲉⲛ ·ⲛⲁϣⲱ·ϥ` ⲛ̅·ⲉⲣⲅⲁⲧⲏⲥ ⲇⲉ ⲥⲟⲃⲕ` ·ⲥⲟⲡⲥ̅
ⲇⲉ ⲙ̅·ⲡ·ϫⲟⲉⲓⲥ ϣⲓⲛⲁ ⲉϥ·ⲛⲁ·ⲛⲉϫ·`·ⲉⲣⲅⲁⲧⲏⲥ
ⲉⲃⲟⲗ` ⲉ·ⲡ·ⲱϩ̅ⲥ̅

74 ⲡⲉϫⲁ·ϥ ϫⲉ ⲡ·ϫⲟⲉⲓⲥ ⲟⲩⲛ̅·
·ϩⲁϩ ⲙ̅·ⲡ·ⲕⲱⲧⲉ ⲛ̅·ⲧ·ϫⲱⲧⲉ ⲙⲛ̅·ⲗⲁⲁⲩ ⲇⲉ ϩⲛ̅·
·ⲧ·ϣⲱⲛⲉ`

75 ⲡⲉϫⲉ·ⲓ̅ⲥ̅ <> ⲟⲩⲛ·ϩⲁϩ ·ⲁϩⲉⲣⲁⲧ·ⲟⲩ
ϩⲓⲣⲙ̅·ⲡ·ⲣⲟ ⲁⲗⲗⲁ ⲙ̅·ⲙⲟⲛⲁⲭⲟⲥ ⲛⲉⲧ·ⲛⲁ·ⲃⲱⲕ`
ⲉϩⲟⲩⲛ ⲉ·ⲡ·ⲙⲁ ⲛ̅·ϣⲉⲗⲉⲉⲧ`

76 ⲡⲉϫⲉ·ⲓ̅ⲥ̅ ϫⲉ
ⲧ·ⲙⲛ̅ⲧⲉⲣⲟ ⲙ̅·ⲡ·ⲉⲓⲱⲧ` ⲉⲥ·ⲧⲛ̅ⲧⲱⲛ ⲁ·ⲩ·ⲣⲱⲙⲉ
ⲛ̅·ⲉϣⲱⲱⲧ` ⲉⲩⲛ̅·ⲧⲁ·ϥ` ⲙ̅·ⲙⲁⲩ ⲛ̅·ⲟⲩ·ⲫⲟⲣⲧⲓⲟⲛ
ⲉ·ⲁϥ·ϩⲉ ⲁ·ⲩ·ⲙⲁⲣⲅⲁⲣⲓⲧⲏⲥ ⲡ·ⲉϣⲱⲧ`
ⲉⲧ·ⲙ̅·ⲙⲁⲩ ⲟⲩ·ⲥⲁⲃⲉ ⲡⲉ ⲁϥ·ϯ·ⲡⲉ·ⲫⲟⲣⲧⲓⲟⲛ

70   Yeshua said:
When you bring forth *that* within you,
then *that* will save you.
If you do not,
then *that* will kill you.

71   Yeshua said:
I will overturn this house
and none will be able to rebuild it.

72   A man said to him:
"Speak to my brothers,
that they may share with me
my father's property."
Yeshua answered him:
Who made me into a divider?
Turning to his disciples,
he said:
Who am I, to divide?

73   Yeshua said:
The harvest is abundant
but the workers are few.
Pray the Master to send
more workers to the harvest.

74   The Master said:
There are many who stand round the well,
but no one to go down into it.

75   Yeshua said:
Many are standing by the door,
but only those who are alone and simple [*monakhos*]
can enter the bridal chamber.

76   The Kingdom of the Father
is like the merchant
who had a load of goods to sell.
Then he saw a pearl.

ЄΒΟΛ ΑϤ·ΤΟΟΥ ΝΑ·Ϥ` Μ̄·ΠΙ·ΜΑΡΓΑΡΙΤΗС
ΟΥΩΤ` Ν̄·ΤΩ·ΤΝ̄ ϨΩΤ·`·ΤΗΥΤΝ̄ ·ϢΙΝЄ
Ν̄СΑ·ΠЄϤ·ЄϨΟ Є·ΜΑϤ·ΩΧΝ̄ ЄϤ·ΜΗΝ` ЄΒΟΛ
Π·ΜΑ Є·ΜΑ·ΡЄ·ΧΟΟΛЄС ·ΤϨΝΟ ЄϨΟΥΝ` Є·ΜΑΥ
Є·ΟΥΩΜ` ΟΥΔЄ ΜΑ·ΡЄϤ·ϤΝ̄Τ ·ΤΑΚΟ

77 ΠЄΧЄ·ῙС̄ ΧЄ ΑΝΟ·Κ ΠЄ Π·ΟΥΟЄΙΝ ΠΑЄΙ ЄΤ·ϨΙΧΩ·ΟΥ
ΤΗΡ·ΟΥ ΑΝΟ·Κ` ΠЄ Π·ΤΗΡ·Ϥ` Ν̄ΤΑ·
·Π·ΤΗΡ·Ϥ` ·ЄΙ ЄΒΟΛ Ν̄·ϨΗΤ·` ΑΥΩ Ν̄ΤΑ·Π·ΤΗΡ·Ϥ`
·ΠΩϨ ϢΑΡΟ·ЄΙ ·ΠΩϨ Ν̄·ΝΟΥ·ϢЄ ΑΝΟ·Κ`
†·Μ̄·ΜΑΥ ·ϤΙ Μ̄·Π·ΩΝЄ Є·ϨΡΑΪ ΑΥΩ ΤЄΤΝΑ·
·ϨЄ ЄΡΟ·ЄΙ Μ̄·ΜΑΥ

78 ΠЄΧЄ·ῙС̄ ΧЄ ЄΤΒЄ·ΟΥ
ΑΤЄΤΝ̄·ЄΙ ЄΒΟΛ Є·Τ·СΩϢЄ Є·ΝΑΥ Є·Υ·ΚΑϢ
ЄϤ·ΚΙΜ [ЄΒΟΛ] ϨΙΤΜ̄·Π·ΤΗΥ ΑΥΩ Є·ΝΑΥ
Є·Υ·Ρ[ΩΜЄ ЄΥ]Ν̄·ϢΤΗΝ ЄΥ·ϬΗΝ ϨΙΩ·ΩΒ
[Ν̄·ΘЄ Ν̄·ΝЄΤΝ̄·]Ρ̄ΡΩΟΥ ΜΝ̄·ΝЄΤΜ̄·ΜЄΓΙСΤΑΝΟС
ΝΑЄΙ Є·Ν[Є·ϢΤΗ]Ν Є[Τ·]
·ϬΗΝ ϨΙΩ·ΟΥ ΑΥΩ СЄ·[ΝΑ]·Ϣ·С̄СΟΥΝ·
·Τ·ΜЄ ΑΝ

79 ΠЄΧЄ·ΟΥ·СϨΙΜ[Є] ΝΑ·Ϥ ϨΜ̄·
·Π·ΜΗϢЄ ΧЄ ΝЄЄΙΑΤ[·С̄ Ν̄·]ΘϨΗ
Ν̄ΤΑϨ·ϤΙ ϨΑΡΟ·Κ ΑΥΩ Ν̄·ΚΙΒЄ ЄΝΤΑϨ·
·САΝΟΥϢ·Κ ΠЄΧΑ·Ϥ ΝΑ·[С] ΧЄ
ΝЄЄΙΑΤ·ΟΥ Ν̄·ΝЄΝΤΑϨ·СΩΤΜ̄ Α·`
·Π·ΛΟΓΟС Μ̄·Π·ЄΙΩΤ ΑΥ·ΑΡЄϨ ЄΡΟ·Ϥ
ϨΝ̄·ΟΥ·ΜЄ ΟΥΝ̄·ϨΝ̄·ϨΟΟΥ ΓΑΡ ·ΝΑ·ϢΩΠЄ
Ν̄ΤЄΤΝ̄·ΧΟ·ΟС ΧЄ ΝЄЄΙΑΤ·С̄ Ν̄·ΘΗ ΤΑЄΙ
ЄΤЄ Μ̄ΠС̄·Ω ΑΥΩ Ν̄·ΚΙΒЄ ΝΑЄΙ Є·ΜΠΟΥ·
·†·ЄΡΩΤЄ

The merchant was wise
and sold his goods to buy the pearl.
You too should pursue
that treasure which is everlasting,
there where moths never go
nor worms devour.

77 Yeshua said:
I am the Light
that shines on everyone.
I am the All.
The All came forth from me
and the All came into me.
Split the wood, and I am there.
Turn over the stone,
and there you will find me.

78 Yeshua said:
Why do you roam the countryside?
To see some reeds shaken by the wind?
To see people like your kings and courtiers
in elegant clothes?
They wear fine clothes,
but they cannot know the truth.

79 A woman in the crowd said to him:
"Blessed are the womb that bore you
and the breasts that nursed you!"
He answered:
Blessed are those who listen
to the Word of the Father
and truly follow it,
for the day will come
when you will say:
Blessed are the womb that has never borne
and the breasts that have never nursed.

80 ΠΕΧΕ·Ι͢C ΧΕ ΠΕΝΤΑ2·CΟΥШΝ·
·Π·ΚΟCΜΟC ΑϤ·2Ε Ε·Π·CШΜΑ ΠΕΝΤΑ2·2Ε
ΔΕ Ε·Π·CШΜΑ Π·ΚΟCΜΟC ·ΜΠШΑ Μ·ΜΟ·Ϥ`
ΑΝ`

81 ΠΕΧΕ·Ι͢C ΧΕ ΠΕΝΤΑ2·Ρ̄·ΡΜ̄·ΜΑΟ
ΜΑΡΕϤ·Ρ̄·ΡΡΟ ΑΥШ ΠΕΤ·ΕΥΝ̄·ΤΑ·Ϥ` Ν̄·ΟΥ·ΔΥΝΑΜΙC
ΜΑΡΕϤ·ΑΡΝΑ

82 ΠΕΧΕ·Ι͢C ΧΕ ΠΕΤ·2ΗΝ
ΕΡΟ·ΕΙ ΕϤ·2ΗΝ Ε·Τ·CΑΤΕ ΑΥШ ΠΕΤ·ΟΥΗΥ`
Μ̄·ΜΟ·ΕΙ Ϥ·ΟΥΗΥ Ν̄·Τ·ΜΝ̄ΤΕΡΟ

83 ΠΕΧΕ·Ι͢C ΧΕ Ν·2ΙΚШΝ CΕ·ΟΥΟΝ2 ΕΒΟΛ Μ̄·Π·ΡШΜΕ
ΑΥШ Π·ΟΥΟΕΙΝ ΕΤ·Ν̄·2ΗΤ·ΟΥ Ϥ·2ΗΠ`
2Ν̄·ΘΙΚШΝ Μ̄·Π·ΟΥΟΕΙΝ Μ̄·Π·ΕΙШΤ` Ϥ·ΝΑ·
·6ШΛΠ` ΕΒΟΛ ΑΥШ ΤΕϤ·2ΙΚШΝ ·2ΗΠ`
ΕΒΟΛ 2ΙΤΝ̄·ΠΕϤ·`·ΟΥΟΕΙΝ

84 ΠΕΧΕ·Ι͢C <> Ν̄·2ΟΟΥ
ΕΤΕΤΝ̄·ΝΑΥ Ε·ΠΕΤΝ̄·ΕΙΝΕ ШΑΡΕΤΝ̄·
·ΡΑШΕ 2ΟΤΑΝ ΔΕ ΕΤΕΤΝ̄·ШΑΝ·ΝΑΥ`
Α·ΝΕΤΝ̄·2ΙΚШΝ` Ν̄ΤΑ2·ШШΠΕ 2Ι·ΤΕΤΝ·Ε2Η
ΟΥΤΕ ΜΑΥ·ΜΟΥ ΟΥΤΕ ΜΑΥ·ΟΥШΝ2
ΕΒΟΛ ΤΕΤΝΑ·ϤΙ 2Α·ΟΥΗΡ`

85 ΠΕΧΕ·Ι͢C ΧΕ
Ν̄ΤΑ·ΑΔΑΜ ·ШШΠΕ ΕΒΟΛ 2Ν̄·ΝΟΥ·ΝΟ6
Ν̄·ΔΥΝΑΜΙC ΜΝ̄·ΟΥ·ΝΟ6 Μ̄·ΜΝ̄Τ·ΡΜ̄·ΜΑΟ
ΑΥШ Μ̄ΠΕϤ·ШШΠΕ Ε·[Ϥ·Μ̄Π]ШΑ Μ̄·ΜШ·
·ΤΝ̄ ΝΕ·Υ·ΑΞΙΟC ΓΑΡ ΠΕ [ΝΕϤ·ΝΑ·ΧΙ·†ΠΕ]
ΑΝ Μ̄·Π·ΜΟΥ

80 Yeshua said:
Whoever knows the world
discovers the body.
But the world is unworthy
of whoever discovers the body.

81 Yeshua said:
Whoever has become rich,
may he become king;
Whoever has power,
may he renounce it.

82 Yeshua said:
Whoever is near to me
is near to the fire.
Whoever is far from me
is far from the Kingdom.

83 Yeshua said:
When images become visible to people,
the light that is in them is hidden.
In the icon of the light of the Father
it will be manifest
and the icon veiled by the light.

84 Yeshua said:
When you see
your true likeness,
you rejoice.
But when you see your icons,
those that were before you existed,
and that never die and never manifest,
what grandeur!

85 Yeshua said:
Adam was produced by a great power
and a great wealth,
yet he was not worthy of you.
If he had been worthy,
he would not have known death.

86 ΠΕΧΕ·ΙC Χ[Ε Ν·ΒΑϢΟΡ
ΟΥ][Ν·ΤΑ·]Υ·Ν[ΟΥ·ΒΗΒ] ΑΥⲰ Ν·ΖΑΛΑΤΕ ΟΥΝ·ΤΑ·Υ
Μ·ΜΑΥ Μ·[ΠΟ]Υ·ΜΑΖ Π·ϢΗΡΕ ΔΕ Μ·Π·ΡⲰΜΕ
ΜΝ·ΤΑ·Ϥ` Ν·[ΝΟΥ]ΜΑ Ε·ΡΙΚΕ Ν·ΤΕϤ·`·ΑΠΕ Νϥ·`
·ΜΤΟΝ` Μ[ΜΟ]·ϥ`

87 ΠΕΧΑ·ϥ Ν6Ι·ΙC ΧΕ ΟΥ·ΤΑΛΑΙΠⲰΡΟΝ`
Π[Ε] Π·CⲰΜΑ ΕΤ·ΑϢΕ Ν·ΟΥ·CⲰΜΑ`
ΑΥⲰ ΟΥ·Τ[Α]ΛΑΙΠⲰΡΟC ΤΕ Τ·`·ΨΥΧΗ ΕΤ·ΑϢΕ
Ν·ΝΑΕΙ Μ·Π·CΝΑΥ

88 ΠΕΧΕ·ΙC ΧΕ Ν·ΑΓΓΕΛΟC
·ΝΗΥ ϢΑΡⲰ·ΤΝ ΜΝ·Ν·ΠΡΟΦΗΤΗC ΑΥⲰ CΕ·
·ΝΑ·† ΝΗ·ΤΝ Ν·ΝΕΤ·ΕΥΝ·ΤΗ·ΤΝ·CΕ ΑΥⲰ`
Ν·ΤⲰ·ΤΝ ΖⲰΤ·`·ΤΗΥΤΝ ΝΕΤ·ΝΤΟΤ·`·ΤΗΝΕ
·ΤΑΛ·Υ ΝΑ·Υ ΝΤΕΤΝ·ΧΟ·ΟC ΝΗ·ΤΝ ΧΕ ΑϢ Ν·
·ΖΟΟΥ ΠΕΤ·ΟΥ·ΝΝΗΥ ΝCΕ·ΧΙ·ΠΕΤΕ·ΠⲰ·ΟΥ

89 ΠΕΧΕ·ΙC ΧΕ ΕΤΒΕ·ΟΥ ΤΕΤΝ·ΕΙϢΕ Μ·Π·CΑ·Ν·
·ΒΟΛ` Μ·Π·ΠΟΤΗΡΙΟΝ ΤΕΤΝ·Ρ·ΝΟΕΙ ΑΝ ΧΕ
ΠΕΝΤΑΖ·ΤΑΜΙΟ Μ·Π·CΑ·Ν·ΖΟΥΝ Ν·ΤΟ·ϥ ΟΝ
ΠΕΝΤΑϥ·ΤΑΜΙΟ Μ·Π·CΑ·Ν·ΒΟΛ`

90 ΠΕΧΕ·ΙΗC ΧΕ ·ΑΜΗΕΙΤΝ ϢΑΡΟ·ΕΙ` ΧΕ ΟΥ·ΧΡΗCΤΟC
ΠΕ ΠΑ·ΝΑΖΒ` ΑΥⲰ ΤΑ·ΜΝΤ·ΧΟΕΙC ΟΥ·ΡΜ·
·ΡΑϢ ΤΕ ΑΥⲰ ΤΕΤΝΑ·ΖΕ Α·Υ·ΑΝΑΠΑCΙC ΝΗ·ΤΝ

91 ΠΕΧΑ·Υ ΝΑ·ϥ` ΧΕ ·ΧΟ·ΟC ΕΡΟ·Ν ΧΕ
ΝΤΚ·ΝΙΜ` ϢΙΝΑ ΕΝΑ·Ρ·ΠΙCΤΕΥΕ ΕΡΟ·Κ`
ΠΕΧΑ·ϥ ΝΑ·Υ ΧΕ ΤΕΤΝ·Ρ·ΠΙΡΑΖΕ Μ·Π·ΖΟ Ν·Τ·ΠΕ
ΜΝ·Π·ΚΑΖ ΑΥⲰ ΠΕΤ·Ν·ΠΕΤΝ·ΜΤΟ ΕΒΟΛ`

86 Yeshua said:
Foxes have their holes
and birds have their nests.
The Son of Man has no place
to lay his head and rest.

87 Yeshua said:
Wretched is the body
that depends on another body.
Wretched is the soul
that depends on both.

88 Yeshua said:
Angels and prophets
will come to you
and give you what is yours.
And you, too, should give what you have
and ask yourselves:
When will the time come
for them to take what is theirs?

89 Yeshua said:
Why do you wash the outside of the cup?
Do you not understand
that the one who made the outside
also made the inside?

90 Yeshua said:
Come to me;
my yoke is good,
my command is gentle,
and you will find repose within you.

91 They said to him:
"Tell us who you are
so that we may believe in you."
He answered them:
You search the face
of heaven and earth,

ⲘⲠⲈⲧⲚ·ⲤⲞⲨⲰⲚ·ϥ` ⲀⲨⲰ ⲠⲈⲈⲒ·ⲔⲀⲒⲢⲞⲤ
ⲦⲈⲦⲚ·ⲤⲞⲞⲨⲚ ⲀⲚ Ⲛ·Ⲣ·ⲠⲒⲢⲀⲌⲈ Ⲙ·ⲘⲞ·ϥ`

92   ⲠⲈⲬⲈ·Ⲓ̅Ⲥ̅ ⲬⲈ
·ϢⲒⲚⲈ ⲀⲨⲰ ⲦⲈⲦⲚⲀ·ϬⲒⲚⲈ ⲀⲖⲖⲀ
ⲚⲈⲦ·ⲀⲦⲈⲦⲚ·ⲬⲚⲞⲨ·ⲈⲒ ⲈⲢⲞ·ⲞⲨ Ⲛ·ⲚⲒ·ⲢⲞⲞⲨ Ⲉ·ⲘⲠⲒ·
·ⲬⲞ·ⲞⲨ ⲚⲎ·ⲦⲚ Ⲙ·ⲪⲞⲞⲨ ⲈⲦ·Ⲙ·ⲘⲀⲨ ⲦⲈⲚⲞⲨ
Ⲉ·ⲢⲚⲀ·Ⲓ̈ Ⲉ·ⲬⲞ·ⲞⲨ ⲀⲨⲰ ⲦⲈⲦⲚ·ϢⲒⲚⲈ ⲀⲚ` Ⲛ̄ⲤⲰ·ⲞⲨ

93   Ⲙ̄Ⲡ̄Ⲣ̄·ⲧ·ⲠⲈⲦ·ⲞⲨⲀⲀⲂ Ⲛ·Ⲛ·ⲞⲨⲢⲞⲞⲢ` ⲬⲈⲔⲀⲤ
ⲚⲞⲨ·ⲚⲞⲬ·ⲞⲨ Ⲉ·Ⲧ·ⲔⲞⲠⲢⲒⲀ Ⲙ̄Ⲡ̄Ⲣ̄·ⲚⲞⲨⲬⲈ Ⲛ·Ⲙ̄·
·ⲘⲀⲢⲄⲀⲢⲒⲦⲎ[Ⲥ Ⲛ·]Ⲛ·ⲈϢⲀⲨ ϢⲒⲚⲀ ⲬⲈ ⲚⲞⲨ·Ⲁ·Ⲁϥ`
[-]·Ⲗ[---]

94   [ⲠⲈⲬⲈ·]Ⲓ̅Ⲥ̅ <> ⲠⲈⲦ·ϢⲒⲚⲈ ϥ·ⲚⲀ·ϬⲒⲚⲈ
[ⲀⲨⲰ ⲠⲈⲦ·ⲦⲀⲢⲘ` Ⲉ·]ⲢⲞⲨⲚ ⲤⲈ·ⲚⲀ·ⲞⲨⲰⲚ ⲚⲀ·ϥ`

95   [ⲠⲈⲬⲈ·Ⲓ̅Ⲥ̅ ⲬⲈ] ⲈϢⲰⲠⲈ ⲞⲨⲚ·ⲦⲎ·ⲦⲚ·ⲢⲞⲘⲦ`
Ⲙ̄Ⲡ̄Ⲣ̄·ⲧ Ⲉ·Ⲧ·ⲘⲎⲤⲈ ⲀⲖⲖⲀ ⲧ [Ⲙ̄ⲘⲞϥ Ⲙ̄·]ⲠⲈ[ⲦⲈ]ⲦⲚⲀ·ⲬⲒⲦ·ⲞⲨ
ⲀⲚ Ⲛ̄·ⲦⲞⲞⲦ·ϥ`

96   [ⲠⲈⲬⲈ·]Ⲓ̅Ⲥ̅ ⲬⲈ Ⲧ·ⲘⲚ̄ⲦⲈⲢⲞ
Ⲙ̄·Ⲡ·ⲈⲒⲰⲦ` ⲈⲤ·ⲦⲚ̄ⲦⲰ[Ⲛ Ⲉ·Ⲩ·]Ⲥ̄ⲢⲒⲘⲈ
ⲀⲤ·ⲬⲒ Ⲛ̄·ⲞⲨ·ⲔⲞⲨⲈⲒ Ⲛ̄·ⲤⲀⲈⲒⲢ [ⲀⲤ·ⲢⲞ]Ⲡ·ϥ` ⲢⲚ̄·
·ⲞⲨ·ϢⲰⲦⲈ ⲀⲤ·Ⲁ·Ⲁϥ Ⲛ̄·ⲢⲚ̄·ⲚⲞ[Ϭ Ⲛ̄]Ⲛ·ⲞⲈⲒⲔ`
ⲠⲈⲦ·ⲈⲨⲘ̄·ⲘⲀⲀⲬⲈ Ⲙ̄·ⲘⲞ·ϥ ⲘⲀ[ⲢⲈϥ·]ⲤⲰⲦⲘ̄`

97   ⲠⲈⲬⲈ·Ⲓ̅Ⲥ̅ ⲬⲈ Ⲧ·ⲘⲚ̄ⲦⲈⲢⲞ Ⲙ̄·Ⲡ·Ⲉ[ⲒⲰⲦ` ⲈⲤ·]ⲦⲚ̄ ⲦⲰⲚ
Ⲁ·Ⲩ·Ⲥ̄ⲢⲒⲘⲈ ⲈⲤ·ϥⲒ ⲢⲀ·ⲞⲨ·Ϭⲁ̄[ⲘⲈⲈⲒ] Ⲉϥ·`
·ⲘⲈⲢ Ⲛ̄·ⲚⲞⲈⲒⲦ` ⲈⲤ·ⲘⲞⲞϢⲈ Ⲣ[Ⲓ·ⲞⲨ·]ⲢⲒⲎ`
ⲈⲤ·ⲞⲨⲚⲞⲨ Ⲁ·Ⲡ·ⲘⲀⲀⲬⲈ Ⲙ̄·Ⲡ·Ϭⲁ̄Ⲙ[ⲈⲈⲒ] ·ⲞⲨⲰϬⲠ`
Ⲁ·Ⲡ·ⲚⲞⲈⲒⲦ` ·ϢⲞⲨⲞ Ⲛ̄ⲤⲰ·[Ⲥ Ⲣ̄·]ⲦⲈ·ⲢⲒⲎ

but you do not recognize
the one who is in your presence
and you do not know how to experience
the present moment.

92 Yeshua said:
Seek and you shall find.
Yet those things
you asked me about before
and which I did not tell you
I am willing to reveal now,
but you no longer ask.

93 Do not give sacred things to dogs,
for they may treat them as dung.
Do not throw pearls to swine,
for they may treat them as rubbish.

94 Yeshua said:
Whoever seeks will find;
whoever knocks from inside, it will open to them.

95 Yeshua said:
If you have money,
do not lend it with interest,
but give it to the one
who will never pay you back.

96 Yeshua said:
The Kingdom of the Father
is like the dough in which a woman
has hidden some yeast.
It becomes transformed into good bread.
Those who have ears,
let them hear!

97 Yeshua said:
The Kingdom of the Father
is like the woman who carried a jar of flour.

ⲛⲉ·ⲥ·ⲥⲟⲟⲩⲛ ⲁⲛ ⲡⲉ ⲛⲉ·ⲙ̅ⲡⲉⲥ·ⲉⲓⲙⲉ
ⲉ·ϩⲓⲥⲉ ⲛ̅ⲧⲁⲣⲉⲥ·ⲡⲱϩ ⲉϩⲟⲩⲛ ⲉ·ⲡⲉⲥ·ⲏⲉⲓ
ⲁⲥ·ⲕⲁ·ⲡ·ϭⲗ̅ⲙⲉⲉⲓ ⲁ·ⲡ·ⲉⲥⲏⲧ` ⲁⲥ·ϩⲉ ⲉⲣⲟ·ϥ ⲉϥ·` ·ϣⲟⲩⲉⲓⲧ`

98 ⲡⲉϫⲉ·ⲓ̅ⲥ̅ <> ⲧ·ⲙⲛ̅ⲧⲉⲣⲟ ⲙ̅·ⲡ·ⲉⲓⲱⲧ`
ⲉⲥ·ⲧⲛ̅ⲧⲱⲛ ⲉ·ⲩ·ⲣⲱⲙⲉ ⲉϥ·ⲟⲩⲱϣ ⲉ·ⲙⲟⲩⲧ·
·ⲟⲩ·ⲣⲱⲙⲉ ⲙ̅·ⲙⲉⲅⲓⲥⲧⲁⲛⲟⲥ ⲁϥ·ϣⲱⲗⲙ` ⲛ̅·
·ⲧ·ⲥⲏϥⲉ ϩⲙ̅·ⲡⲉϥ·ⲏⲉⲓ ⲁϥ·ϫⲟⲧ·ⲥ̅ ⲛ̅·ⲧ·ϫⲟ ϫⲉⲕⲁⲁⲥ
ⲉϥ·ⲛⲁ·ⲉⲓⲙⲉ ϫⲉ ⲧⲉϥ·ϭⲓϫ` ·ⲛⲁ·ⲧⲱⲕ`
ⲉϩⲟⲩⲛ ⲧⲟⲧⲉ ⲁϥ·ϩⲱⲧⲃ̅ ⲙ̅·ⲡ·ⲙⲉⲅⲓⲥⲧⲁⲛⲟⲥ

99 ⲡⲉϫⲉ·ⲙ̅·ⲙⲁⲑⲏⲧⲏⲥ ⲛⲁ·ϥ ϫⲉ ⲛⲉⲕ·`·ⲥⲛⲏⲩ
ⲙⲛ̅·ⲧⲉⲕ·ⲙⲁⲁⲩ ⲥⲉ·ⲁϩⲉⲣⲁⲧ·ⲟⲩ ϩⲓ·ⲡ·ⲥⲁ·ⲛ·
·ⲃⲟⲗ ⲡⲉϫⲁ·ϥ ⲛⲁ·ⲩ ϫⲉ ⲛⲉⲧ·ⲛ̅·ⲛⲉⲉⲓ·ⲙⲁ
ⲉϯⲣⲉ ⲙ̅·ⲡ·ⲟⲩⲱϣ ⲙ̅·ⲡⲁ·ⲉⲓⲱⲧ` ⲛⲁⲉⲓ ⲛⲉ
ⲛⲁ·ⲥⲛⲏⲩ ⲙⲛ̅·ⲧⲁ·ⲙⲁⲁⲩ ⲛ̅·ⲧⲟ·ⲟⲩ ⲡⲉ ⲉⲧ·ⲛⲁ·
·ⲃⲱⲕ` ⲉϩⲟⲩⲛ ⲉ·ⲧ·ⲙⲛ̅ⲧⲉⲣⲟ ⲙ̅·ⲡⲁ·ⲉⲓⲱⲧ`

100 ⲁⲩ·ⲧⲥⲉⲃⲉ·ⲓ̅ⲥ̅ ⲁ·ⲩ·ⲛⲟⲩⲃ ⲁⲩⲱ ⲡⲉϫⲁ·ⲩ ⲛⲁ·ϥ`
ϫⲉ ⲛⲉⲧ·ⲏⲡ` ⲁ·ⲕⲁⲓⲥⲁⲣ` ⲥⲉ·ϣⲓⲧⲉ ⲙ̅·ⲙⲟ·ⲛ ⲛ̅·
·ⲛ̅·ϣⲱⲙ` ⲡⲉϫⲁ·ϥ ⲛⲁ·ⲩ ϫⲉ ·ϯ·ⲛⲁ·ⲕⲁⲓⲥⲁⲣ`
ⲛ̅·ⲕⲁⲓⲥⲁⲣ ·ϯ·ⲛⲁ·ⲡ·ⲛⲟⲩⲧⲉ ⲙ̅·ⲡ·ⲛⲟⲩⲧⲉ
ⲁⲩⲱ ⲡⲉⲧⲉ·ⲡⲱ·ⲉⲓ ⲡⲉ ⲙⲁ·ⲧⲛ̅ⲛⲁ·ⲉⲓ·ϥ

101 ⲡⲉⲧⲁ·ⲙⲉⲥⲧⲉ·ⲡⲉϥ·ⲉ[ⲓⲱⲧ` ⲁ]ⲛ ⲙⲛ̅·ⲧⲉϥ·`
·ⲙⲁⲁⲩ ⲛ̅·ⲧⲁ·ϩⲉ ϥ·ⲛⲁϣ·ⲣ̅·ⲙ[ⲁⲑⲏⲧⲏ]ⲥ [ⲛⲁ·]ⲉⲓ ⲁ ̄
ⲁⲩⲱ ⲡⲉⲧⲁ·ⲙⲣ̅ⲣⲉ·ⲡⲉ[ϥ·ⲉⲓⲱⲧ` ⲁⲛ ⲙⲛ̅·ⲧ]ⲉϥ·`
·ⲙⲁⲁⲩ ⲛ̅·ⲧⲁ·ϩⲉ ϥ·ⲛⲁϣ·ⲣ̅·ⲙ[ⲁⲑⲏⲧⲏⲥ ⲛⲁ·]
·ⲉⲓ ⲁⲛ ⲧⲁ·ⲙⲁⲁⲩ ⲅⲁⲣ ⲛ̅ⲧⲁ[ⲥ·ϫⲡⲉ·ⲡⲁ·ⲥⲱⲙⲁ]
[ⲉⲃ]ⲟⲗ [ⲧⲁ·ⲙⲁⲁⲩ] ⲇⲉ ⲙ̅·ⲙⲉ ⲁⲥ·ϯ ⲛⲁ·ⲉⲓ ·ⲡ·ⲱⲛϩ

After she walked a long way,
the handle of the jar broke
and the flour began to spill behind her along the road.
Heedless, she noticed nothing.
When she arrived, she set down the jar
and found it empty.

98 Yeshua said:
The Kingdom of the Father
is like the man who wanted to kill
a man of power.
First, he unsheathed his sword at home
and thrust it into the wall to test his strength.
Then he was able to kill the man of power.

99 His disciples said to him:
"Your brothers and your mother are waiting outside."
He replied:
Those who do my Father's will
are my brothers and my mother.
It is they who will enter the Kingdom of God.

100 They showed Yeshua a gold coin
and said to him:
"Caesar's agents demand that we pay taxes."
He answered them:
Give to Caesar what is Caesar's,
give to God what is God's,
and give to me what is mine.

101 Yeshua said:
Whoever does not hate their father and mother
as I do
cannot become my disciple.
And whoever does not love their father and mother
as I do
cannot become my disciple.
For my mother made me to die,
but my true mother gave me Life.

102 ΠΕΧΕ·ΙC [ΧΕ Ο]ΥΟΕΙ ΝΑ·Υ Μ·ΦΑΡΙCΑΙΟC ΧΕ
ΕΥ·ΕΙΝ[Ε Ν·Ν]ΟΥ·ΟΥ2ΟΡ ΕϤ·ΝΚΟΤΚ` 2ΙΧΝ·Π·ΟΥΟΝΕϤ`
Ν·[2ΕΝ]·Ε2ΟΟΥ ΧΕ ΟΥΤΕ Ϥ·ΟΥWΜ ΑΝ
ΟΥΤΕ Ϥ·[ΚW Α]Ν Ν·Ν·Ε2ΟΟΥ Ε·ΟΥWΜ

103 ΠΕΧΕ·ΙC ΧΕ
ΟΥ·Μ[ΑΚΑ]ΡΙΟC ΠΕ Π·ΡWΜΕ ΠΑΕΙ ΕΤ·CΟΟΥ‾
ΧΕ 2[Ν·ΑϢ] Μ·ΜΕΡΟC Ε·Ν·ΛΗCΤΗC ·ΝΗΥ Ε2ΟΥ‾
ϢΙΝΑ [ΕϤ·Ν]Α·ΤWΟΥΝ` ΝϤ·CWΟΥ2 Ν·ΤΕϤ·
·ΜΝΤ[ΕΡΟ] ΑΥW ΝϤ·ΜΟΥΡ Μ·ΜΟ·Ϥ` ΕΧΝ·ΤΕϤ·
·†ΠΕ [2Α]·Τ·Ε2Η ΕΜ·ΠΑΤΟΥ·ΕΙ Ε2ΟΥΝ

104 ΠΕΧΑ·Υ Ν·[ΙC] ΧΕ ·ΑΜΟΥ ΝΤΝ·ϢΛΗΛ` Μ·ΠΟΟΥ
ΑΥW ΝΤΝ·Ρ·ΝΗCΤΕΥΕ ΠΕΧΕ·ΙC ΧΕ ΟΥ ΓΑΡ
ΠΕ Π·ΝΟΒΕ ΝΤΑΕΙ·Α·ΑϤ` Η ΝΤΑΥ·ΧΡΟ ΕΡΟ·ΕΙ
2Ν·ΟΥ ΑΛΛΑ 2ΟΤΑΝ ΕΡϢΑΝ·Π·ΝΥΜΦΙΟC ·ΕΙ
ΕΒΟΛ 2Μ·Π·ΝΥΜΦWΝ ΤΟΤΕ ΜΑΡΟΥ·ΝΗ`
CΤΕΥΕ ΑΥW ΜΑΡΟΥ·ϢΛΗΛ`

105 ΠΕΧΕ·ΙC ΧΕ
ΠΕΤ·ΝΑ·CΟΥWΝ·Π·ΕΙWΤ` ΜΝ·Τ·ΜΑΑΥ CΕ·ΝΑ·ΜΟΥΤΕ
ΕΡΟ·Ϥ` ΧΕ Π·ϢΗΡΕ Μ·ΠΟΡΝΗ

106 ΠΕΧΕ·ΙC ΧΕ
2ΟΤΑΝ ΕΤΕΤΝ·ϢΑ·Ρ·Π·CΝΑΥ ΟΥΑ ΤΕΤΝΑ·ϢWΠΕ
Ν·ϢΗΡΕ Μ·Π·ΡWΜΕ ΑΥW ΕΤΕΤΝ·ϢΑΝ·
·ΧΟ·ΟC ΧΕ Π·ΤΟΟΥ ·ΠWWΝΕ ΕΒΟΛ` Ϥ·ΝΑ·
·ΠWWΝΕ

107 ΠΕΧΕ·ΙC ΧΕ Τ·ΜΝΤΕΡΟ ΕC·ΤΝΤW‾
Ε·Υ·ΡWΜΕ Ν·ϢWC ΕΥΝ·ΤΑ·Ϥ` Μ·ΜΑΥ Ν·ϢΕ Ν·
·ΕCΟΟΥ Α·ΟΥΑ Ν·2ΗΤ·ΟΥ ·CWΡΜ` Ε·Π·ΝΟ6 ΠΕ
ΑϤ·ΚW Μ·ΠCΤΕ·ΦΙΤ ΑϤ·ϢΙΝΕ ΝCΑ·ΠΙ·ΟΥΑ

102 Yeshua said:
Wretched are the Pharisees.
They are like the dog
lying in the cow's manger.
He cannot eat,
and will not let the cows eat.

103 Yeshua said:
Blessed are they who know
at what time of night the thieves will come.
They will be awake,
gathering their strength
and strapping on their belts
before the thieves arrive.

104 They said to him:
"Come, let us pray and fast today."
Yeshua answered:
What wrong have I done?
How have I been defeated?
When the bridegroom leaves the bridal chamber,
that will be the time to fast and pray.

105 Yeshua said:
He who knows his father and his mother,
will they call him the son of a whore?

106 Yeshua said:
When you make the two into One,
you will be a Son of Man.
And when you say:
Mountain, move!
It will move.

107 Yeshua said:
The Kingdom is like the shepherd
with a hundred sheep.
One of them disappeared—

ϢΑΝΤΕϤ·2Ε ΕΡΟ·Ϥˋ Ν̄ΤΑΡΕϤ·2ΙϹΕ ΠΕΧΑ·Ϥˋ
Μ̄·Π·ΕϹΟΟΥ ΧΕ †·ΟΥΟϢ·Κˋ ΠΑΡΑ·ΠϹΤΕ·ΦΙΤˋ

108 ΠΕΧΕ·Ι͞Ϲ ΧΕ ΠΕΤΑ·ϹⲰ ΕΒΟⲖ 2Ν̄·ΤΑ·ΤΑΠΡΟ
Ϥ·ΝΑ·ϢⲰΠΕ Ν̄·ΤΑ·2Ε ΑΝΟ·Κ 2Ⲱ· †·ΝΑ·ϢⲰΠΕ
Ε·ΝΤΟ·Ϥ ΠΕ ΑΥⲰ ΝΕΘΗΠˋ ·ΝΑ·ΟΥⲰΝ2 ΕΡΟ·Ϥˋ

109 ΠΕΧΕ·Ι͞Ϲ ΧΕ Τ·Μ̄Ν̄ΤΕΡΟ ΕϹ·ΤΝ̄ΤⲰΝ Ε·Υ·ΡⲰΜΕ
ΕΥΝ̄·ΤΑ·Ϥ [Μ̄]ΜΑΥ 2Ν̄·ΤΕϤ·ˋ·ϹⲰ ϢΕ Ν̄·ΝΟΥ·
·Ε2Ο ΕϤ·2[ΗΠˋ ΕϤ·]Ο Ν̄·ΑΤ·ϹΟΟΥΝˋ ΕΡΟ·Ϥ ΑΥⲰ
Μ̄[Μ̄Ν̄Ν̄ϹΑ·Τ]ΡΕϤ·ΜΟΥ ΑϤ·ΚΑΑ·Ϥ Μ̄·ΠΕϤ·ˋ
[·ϢΗΡΕ ΝΕ·Π]ϢΗΡΕ ·ϹΟΟΥΝ ΑΝˋ ΑϤ·ϤΙ·ˋ
·Τ·ϹⲰϢΕ ΕΤ·Μ̄·ΜΑΥ ΑϤ·ΤΑΑ·[Ϲ ΕΒΟⲖ ΑΥⲰ
ΠΕΝ]ΤΑ2·ΤΟΟΥ·Ϲ ΑϤ·ΕΙ ΕϤ·ϹΚΑΕΙ Α[Ϥ·2Ε] Α·Π·Ε2Ο ΑϤ·
·ΑΡΧΕΙ Ν̄·†·2ΟΜΤˋ Ε·Τ·ΜΗϹΕ Ν̄[·ΝΕΤ]·Ϥ̄·ΟΥΟϢ·ΟΥ

110 ΠΕΧΕ·Ι͞Ϲ ΧΕ ΠΕΝΤΑ2·6ΙΝΕ [Μ̄·]Π·ΚΟϹΜΟϹ
Ν̄Ϥ·Ρ̄·ΡΜ̄·ΜΑΟ ΜΑΡΕϤ·ΑΡΝΑ Μ̄·Π·ΚΟϹΜΟϹ

111 ΠΕΧΕ·Ι͞Ϲ ΧΕ Μ̄·ΠΗΥΕ ·ΝΑ·6ⲰⲖˋ ΑΥⲰ Π·ΚΑ2
Μ̄·ΠΕΤΝ̄·Μ̄ΤΟ ΕΒΟⲖˋ ΑΥⲰ ΠΕΤ·ΟΝ2 ΕΒΟⲖ 2Ν̄·
·ΠΕΤ·ΟΝ2 Ϥ·ΝΑ·ΝΑΥ ΑΝ Ε·ΜΟΥ ΟΥΧ·2ΟΤΙ Ε·Ι͞Ϲ
·ΧⲰ Μ̄·ΜΟ·Ϲ ΧΕ ΠΕΤΑ·2Ε ΕΡΟ·Ϥˋ ΟΥΑΑ·Ϥ Π·ΚΟϹΜΟϹ
·Μ̄ΠϢΑ Μ̄·ΜΟ·Ϥˋ ΑΝ

it was the most beautiful.
The shepherd left the other ninety-nine sheep
and looked only for that one
until he found it.
After his great effort he said to the lamb:
I love you more than the other ninety-nine.

108 Yeshua said:
Whoever drinks from my mouth
will become like me,
and I will become them,
and what was hidden from them will be revealed.

109 Yeshua said:
The Kingdom is like the man
who had a hidden treasure in his field.
He did not know it was there.
When he died, he left the field to his son,
who knew nothing and sold the field.
The buyer came to plow the field
and found the treasure while working.
He began to lend money with interest
to all who wanted it.

110 Yeshua said:
Whoever has found the world
and become wealthy,
may they renounce the world.

111 Yeshua said:
The heavens and the earth will roll up before you.
The living who come from the Living
will know neither fear nor death,
for it is said:
Whoever has self-knowledge,
the world cannot contain them.

112 ΠΕΧΕ·ΙC̄ ΧΕ ΟΥΟΕΙ

Ⲛ̄·Τ·ϹⲀⲢⳄ` ⲦⲀⲈⲒ ⲈⲦ·ⲞϢⲈ Ⲛ̄·Ⲧ·ⲪⲨⲬⲎ ⲞⲨⲞⲈⲒ

Ⲛ̄·Ⲧ·ⲪⲨⲬⲎ ⲦⲀⲈⲒ ⲈⲦ·ⲞϢⲈ Ⲛ̄·Ⲧ·ϹⲀⲢⳄ

113 ΠⲈⳊⲀ·Ⲩ

ⲚⲀ·Ϥ Ⲛ̄ϬⲒ·ⲚⲈϤ·ⲘⲀⲐⲎⲦⲎⲤ ⳊⲈ Ⲧ·Ⲙ̄Ⲛ̄ⲦⲈⲢⲞ

ⲈϹ·Ⲛ̄ⲚⲎⲨ Ⲛ̄·ⲀϢ Ⲛ̄·ⳊⲞⲞⲨ ⲈϹ·Ⲛ̄ⲚⲎⲨ ⲀⲚ Ⳅ̄Ⲛ̄·ⲞⲨ·

·ϬⲰϢⲦ` ⲈⲂⲞⲖ` ⲈⲨ·ⲚⲀ·ⳊⲞ·ⲞϹ ⲀⲚ ⳊⲈ ⲈⲒϹ·ⳄⲎⲎⲦⲈ

Ⲙ̄·ⲠⲒ·ϹⲀ Ⲏ ⲈⲒϹ·ⳄⲎⲎⲦⲈ ⲦⲎ ⲀⲖⲖⲀ Ⲧ·Ⲙ̄Ⲛ̄ⲦⲈⲢⲞ

Ⲙ̄·Ⲡ·ⲈⲒⲰⲦ` ⲈϹ·ⲠⲞⲢϢ` ⲈⲂⲞⲖ ⳄⲒⳊⲘ̄·Ⲡ·ⲔⲀⳄ ⲀⲨⲰ

Ⲣ̄·ⲢⲰⲘⲈ ·ⲚⲀⲨ ⲀⲚ ⲈⲢⲞ·Ϲ

114 ΠⲈⳊⲈ·ⲤⲒⲘⲰⲚ·ⲠⲈⲦⲢⲞⲤ

ⲚⲀ·Ⲩ ⳊⲈ ⲘⲀⲢⲈ·ⲘⲀⲢⲒⳄⲀⲘ ·ⲈⲒ ⲈⲂⲞⲖ Ⲛ̄·ⳄⲎⲦ·Ⲛ̄

ⳊⲈ Ⲛ̄·ϹⳄⲒⲞⲘⲈ ·Ⲙ̄·ⲠⲰⲀ ⲀⲚ` Ⲙ̄·Ⲡ·ⲰⲚⳄ ⲠⲈⳊⲈ·ⲒⲤ̄

ⳊⲈ ⲈⲒϹ·ⳄⲎⲎⲦⲈ ⲀⲚⲞ·Ⲕ` †·ⲚⲀ·ⲤⲰⲔ` Ⲙ̄·ⲘⲞ·Ϲ

ⳊⲈⲔⲀⲀϹ Ⲉ·ⲈⲒ·ⲚⲀ·Ⲁ·Ϲ Ⲛ̄·ⳄⲞⲞⲨⲦ` ϢⲒⲚⲀ Ϲ·ⲚⲀ·ϢⲰⲠⲈ

ⳄⲰ·ⲰϹ Ⲛ̄·ⲞⲨ·Ⲡ̄Ⲛ̄Ⲁ̄ ⲈϤ·ⲞⲚⳄ ⲈϤ·ⲈⲒⲚⲈ Ⲙ̄·

·ⲘⲰ·ⲦⲚ̄ Ⲛ̄·ⳄⲞⲞⲨⲦ` ⳊⲈ ϹⳄⲒⲘⲈ ·ⲚⲒⲘ` ⲈϹ·ⲚⲀ·Ⲁ·Ϲ

Ⲛ̄·ⳄⲞⲞⲨⲦ` Ϲ·ⲚⲀ·ⲂⲰⲔ` ⲈⳄⲞⲨⲚ Ⲉ·Ⲧ·Ⲙ̄Ⲛ̄ⲦⲈⲢⲞ·

·Ⲛ̄·Ⲙ̄·ⲠⲎⲨⲈ

112 Yeshua said:
Wretched is the flesh
that depends on the soul;
wretched is the soul
that depends on the flesh.

113 The disciples asked him:
"When will the Kingdom come?"
Yeshua answered:
It will not come by watching for it.
No one will be saying, Look, here it is!
or, Look, there it is!
The Kingdom of the Father
is spread out over the whole earth,
and people do not see it.

114 Simon Peter said to him:
Mary should leave us,
for women are not worthy of the Life.
Yeshua answered:
This is how I will guide her
so that she becomes Man.
She, too, will become a living breath like you Men.
Any woman who makes herself a Man
will enter into the Kingdom of God.

COMMENTARY

PROLOGUE

> These are the words of the Secret.
> They were revealed by the Living Yeshua.
> Didymus Judas Thomas wrote them down.

> (CF. JER 36:1, 37:4; BARUCH I; I COR 24:44; REV 4:9, 10:6.)

Some would translate "apocryphal words" in the literal sense of the Greek word *apokruphos*, which simply means "hidden." But this prologue implies much more that: Yeshua has come to reveal to us the Words of the Secret, of the Human and of the Divine: God in Human and Human in God . . . the secret of Being and of Love. In the Gospel of Matthew he invites us to "pray to the Father who is there, in secret," and not to be rigid in our justice, like the Pharisees and hypocrites. The God of Love who dwells in the depths of human beingness is a secret, and it is from these hidden depths that we can act, think, and speak in true freedom.

Yeshua, the Living, the Awakened One, reveals through his words, his life, and his acts the secret that all human beings can realize and manifest. He fully incarnates life and love, which is why he is given the name the Living One, the revealer of that which we can attain if we allow ourselves to be and live in the Presence of God.

Didymus Judas Thomas, the "twin" (*didymos*, in Greek), is Jesus' intimate friend who has compiled these words. They were written down by Thomas, which could mean the apostle himself during the time of Yeshua or perhaps another author who represented the lineage of Thomas. (According to later tradition, Thomas died in Madras, India, and his tomb is still venerated there today.) But what is important for us is to read these scriptures so as to come closer to the Word: to hear the voice and the secret of the Living One within us.

LOGION 1

> Yeshua said:
> Whoever lives the interpretation of these words
> will no longer taste death.

(CF. JOHN 5:24, 8:51–52; MATT 13:10–15.)

Hermeneutics, or the art of interpretation, implies something more than exegesis, which often limits itself to reconstructing the context of a scripture in order to explain its structure and meaning—and forgets to look for deeper Meaning. It is like measuring the structure and thickness of the shell and forgetting to taste the almond inside it.

Hermeneutists[1] are thirsty for Meaning and are not as interested in the color and form of the water jug as they are in drinking at the Source that is accessible through the words. To be a hermeneutist in this sense means to live the interpretation of the logia of Yeshua. It means to become One—if only for a moment—with that Meaning. This moment of unity awakens in us the Presence of the Uncreated and the taste of something beyond that which is composite and is therefore subject to decomposition—in other words, the taste of something beyond death.

There are different ways of interpreting a piece of music. Players sometimes do a disservice to the composer through their lack of inspiration or by using a badly tuned instrument, for instance. But the highest priority in the hermeneutical art is an awareness of the spirit in which we are interpreting the word in question. Is this spirit in harmony, in resonance, with the Life that breathes in the text that we are trying to translate? Of course, we must also have a good instrument, knowledge, and a cultivated intelligence and feeling so as to perceive all the harmonics of this subtle text.

The greatest musicians are those who—after long practice—are able to forget that they are interpreting. They become One with the inspiration

---

1. [Here, as in the prologue, the author uses the French word *herméneute* in a special sense. Because the English equivalent, *hermeneutist,* is so laden with academic connotations, I have avoided it in the gospel itself and chosen the phrase "lives the interpretation" instead of the more literal "becomes a hermeneutist." —*Trans.*]

that moved the composer, and the music is played through them as through an instrument.

Yeshua has become the interpreter who lives the meaning of Love and Life through deeds as well as words. His exegesis was written not only through his teaching, but also with his flesh, his blood, his laughter, and his tears. Those who had eyes to see saw in him the Living One.

LOGION 2

> Yeshua said:
> Whoever searches
> must continue to search
> until they find.
> When they find,
> they will be disturbed;
> and being disturbed, they will marvel
> and will reign over All.
>
> (CF. MATT 7:7–8; LUKE 11:9–10.)

This logion describes the major stages in gnosis, which constitute a true initiatory process.

The first stage is the quest; the second is the discovery; the third is the shock and disturbance of this discovery; the fourth is wonder and amazement; and the fifth is the presence and reign over All.

The last of these stages is spoken of in the Oxyrhynchus[2] manuscript (654, no. 1), where this reign over the All is further described as the great Repose. This is also echoed in the Gospel of Philip and in Clement of Alexandria (*Stromata*, Book II).

Some further elaboration on each of these stages may be useful.

1. SEEKING

The seeker must always be on the quest. The truth is hidden so as to be found. As the prophet said, it is a "hidden God" who invites us to participate in this great game of the quest.

An old rabbi explained it to his grandson in this way: "When you play hide-and-seek with your friend, imagine his disappointment and pain if he hides and you simply stop looking for him."

When we stop looking for the hidden God, we resign from the divine game. Yet this game, this quest, is what gives our life meaning.

---

2. [The manuscript found in 1898 at Oxyrhynchus, in Egypt, contains fragments of the Gospel of Thomas in the original Greek, predating the Coptic version. Many scholars now believe that the original Thomas Gospel, from which this Greek copy was made, predates the earliest canonical gospels. —*Trans.*]

Is not the whole history of Israel that of a game of hide-and-seek between a people and their God?

Thus the first stage on the path of initiation consists of rediscovering the thirst and taste for the game, the quest. It consists of becoming a seeker and remaining a seeker even after we have found, so as to experience the new and endless depths in what we have discovered.

2. FINDING

In a sense, to seek is already to find. Otherwise, how could we ever have the idea to search, how could we be propelled by this desire, unless it were for something that we somehow already know? Surely we have all had moments in our lives that testify to this, moments of discovering the light (if only from a distant star) that had always been there, in the darkest of nights.

"You would not seek me if you had not already found me." Thus the essential movement of the quest is a greater opening to what is already here. But we do not know it enough: "In your very center, there is someone you do not recognize," said John the Baptist to his disciples. In our very core there is a Presence that needs to be recognized and affirmed. Seeking/finding means being more and more open to the gift that has always been ours.

3. BEING TROUBLED AND UPSET

The recognition of Being troubles us and upsets us, for awakening to this dimension forces us to question our ordinary, so-called normal view of the world.

When quantum physics showed that an object could be both wave and particle, both present and absent, many of the best minds were greatly troubled, for ordinary logic could not deal with this phenomenon.

The experience of Being is a radical questioning of our view of reality, a view conditioned by the conceptual means with which we think we understand reality. This discovery that our habitual ways of conceiving the world are no more than that—habits—cannot occur without trouble and upset. The more we accept this trouble as a necessary stage in the evolution of our consciousness, however, the more we are led, little by little, toward wonder and marveling.

4. MARVELING

In the fourth century C.E., Gregory of Nyssa said: "Concepts create idols of God of whom only wonder can tell us anything."

The Greek philosophical tradition also saw wonder and astonishment as the beginning of wisdom. In our own time, Einstein remarked that only idiots are incapable of wonder—and we might define *idiots* as those who forsake their quest, thinking that they know.

The more we discover, the more we *marvel* and *wonder.* But these two are not some kind of romantic imagination or fantasy. For Einstein, wonder lay in the fact that at certain moments the world becomes intelligible, that there is a possibility of *resonance* between our intelligence and the Cosmos, as if they were both animated by the same consciousness. Only after experiencing this wonder can we enter into the mystery of that which reigns over All.

5. REIGNING OVER ALL

At this stage we perceive ourselves no longer as separate from the world, but instead as a space where it is possible for the Universe to become conscious of itself. I am One with that which reigns over All. The same Spirit, the same Breath, the same Energy that moves mountains and stars, moves me. The Psalmist speaks of "Mountains leaping like rams, and hills like lambs," an image that would make a modern geologist feel at home. The life that surges in the veins of a child is akin to the sap that makes trees grow.

Here, I see myself only as a particular expression among others of the same All that is One. Here, in the living interconnectedness of all things, I know the immensity of Repose.

6. IN REPOSE

The meaning of the Sabbath is extremely important to Jews. After the time of work, of doing, of possessing, we must take the time to sit before God, to simply *be.*

The theme of repose is just as important to gnostics. At last, thinking and feeling are united in this consciousness that animates all things, and we can find true repose. What previously appeared as contradictory or in opposition now appears complementary, for a passage beyond duality has opened up. In the myriad reflections scattered upon all the ponds of the world, we discover a single moon.

This living nonduality is the peace and repose that is endlessly sought during all stages of the initiatory path. But the spiritual path requires us to live the quest fully and not harbor fear or aversion toward trouble and upset, so that we find our home in this wonder and repose.

LOGION 3

Yeshua said:
If those who guide you say: Look,
the Kingdom is in the sky,
then the birds are closer than you.
If they say: Look,
it is in the sea,
then the fish already know it.
The Kingdom is inside you,
and it is outside you.
When you know yourself, then you will be known,
and you will know that you are the child of the Living Father;
but if you do not know yourself,
you will live in vain
and you will be vanity.

(CF. MATT 24:26–27; MARK 13:5–7; LUKE 17:21; DEUT 30:11–14;
ROM 10:6–8.)

Before attempting to define the meaning of the Kingdom, it is better to ask the question "What is it that rules me? Is it my past, my unconscious, my environment, or perhaps some idea or passion?"

The Kingdom is the reign of Spirit in us, permeating all our faculties. It is no longer just ego that rules us, with its memories, fears, and desires—it is the beginning of the reign of the Living One within us.

This logion tells us that the Kingdom is the presence of the Spirit of God within us. It is not to be sought exclusively in the outer, and it is not to be sought exclusively in the inner. It invites us to move out of the dualism that forms the climate of our ordinary consciousness.

This climate is one of oppositions, antagonisms, and exclusions. For example, we know the harm that is created by phrases such as "no salvation outside the Church." When the term *church* is understood in merely an institutional sense, then there are those inside it, and those outside it—which means that most of humanity is excluded from salvation. Augustine, however, sensed the obstruction of such dualistic language when he said: "There are many people who claim to be inside the Church, but they are really outside it, for they do not practice the love and the life of Christ; and there are many who are apparently outside the Church, but who are really inside it, for they do practice the love and life of Christ."

Also, every outside is an inside from another point of view. Everything outside us is inside a vaster space of "us." A house is inside a city, which itself is inside a country, and so forth. Thus every interior is shaped by an outside reality, including our breathing, our thoughts (shaped by the words and thoughts of others), and our most intimate desires (a human being is the desire of the desire of the other).

We begin to see the wisdom of the nondualist language in the Gospel of Thomas. If it had simply said, "The Kingdom is within you," it would give one-sided privilege to inner experiences and meditations. This would encourage us to flee the world, to disregard what is going on around us. Happiness would be only spiritual and we would be separate from our carnal half. The world, others, and matter itself would be reduced to temptations and threats prowling around our inner being.

If the gospel had said, "The Kingdom is outside you," then we would be encouraged to transform the world and convert others at all costs, and it would be selfishness to sit in silence and listen to the song of the Living One in our heart.

This gospel is a cure for our schizophrenia of outside vs. inside, for it tells us that the Kingdom includes both. There is no opposition, because outer and inner realities come together in the Kingdom. This can transform our way of seeing things. Henceforth, we may *see* both outer and inner aspects of everything that we meet. First, we respect the outer skin, the form, the details of our surroundings, for the Presence of Being is there too. We no longer close our eyes to "mere appearances"; but we also do not allow ourselves to become stuck in them. We endeavor to sense the inner dimensions of all that exists, the inner depths of the invisible within the visible, the meaningful silence within the words we hear, the intangible in everything we touch. This attitude cultivates a special kind of wakefulness in everyday life. "Our asceticism is our surrender, our miracle is our daily bread," say the gnostics.

When we listen to great music and a certain quality of silence settles in us, then silence and sound are not opposed or contradictory. On the contrary, they rejoice in a wedding with each other. This is a glimpse of the Kingdom, of total Presence.

To touch someone with love, with inward attention, is something that is sensuous and yet open to the presence of an invisible dimension. As Augustine said, "The carnal person is carnal even in spiritual things; and the spiritual person is spiritual even in carnal things." To love others as ourselves and as if they were within us, yet without reducing another to ourselves—these are the conditions of true relationship.

Love is respect for otherness and for identity: for unity and for difference. If only otherness and external objects were real, then no communion would be possible. We would be marooned in separation and in ultimate incommunicability. And if the only reality were that of identity-sameness, then no relationship would be possible, only a kind of fusion-mixture. Difference, otherness, is the very space that makes relationship possible. If I were not other than you, how could I ever love you, and go beyond myself in this love?

So we see that to work for the coming of the Kingdom implies a twofold movement: toward the inwardness of all things, spiritualizing matter; and toward the outwardness of things, manifesting the Spirit, incarnating it fully within the space, time, society, and situations that are ours. The Kingdom is not above us, not below us, not to the right or to the left, not inside or outside . . . It is at once height and depth, width and thickness, inside and outside. It is the totality of what is and what we are.

Gnostics are whole human beings who do not exclude any part of themselves. True self-knowledge cannot be limited to knowledge of the soul, nor to knowledge of the "little me," the one wrapped up in a bag of skin. Self-knowledge is consciousness of all the dimensions of our being.

In this consciousness, as the second part of this logion tells us, we discover that we are also known. In our most intimate core, in the very movement of integration of all that we are, we discover the Other who is our ground. Again, we discover the metaphysical outer in the ultimate depths of the inner.

Thus, to know ourselves is to discover that we are known. It is to discover that in every act of true knowledge there is participation by an

Intelligence that communicates through us and that offers us participation in its Light.

To love is to discover that we are loved. In every act of love there is a participation in a Love that is given to us and which offers us participation in its Life. This is what the apostle John means when he says, "Whoever loves, dwells in God, and God dwells in them, for God is Love." To be able to truly love—even a dog or a flower—is always a grace. Hell is the absence of love, the loss of the power to love.

To know ourselves, to know that we are known, is also to discover ourselves reborn, each of us child of the Living One, flame of the Fire, child of the Wind. Not to know ourselves is to fall short of ourselves, to live in vain, to arise and disappear like fog from breath on a glass, to be vanity.

LOGION 4

> Yeshua said:
>
> An aged person will not hesitate to ask a seven-day-old infant about the Place of Life, and that person will live.
>
> Many of the first will make themselves last, and they will become One.
>
> (CF. MATT 19:30, 20:16; MARK 10:31; LUKE 13:30; JOHN 17:20–23.)

We are very old beings. Scientists say that we are billions of years old on a cellular level, and the old parts of our brain remember the beginnings of humankind. Here the Gospel of Thomas reminds those who are old that they must ask the child, for true knowledge consists not in accumulating more information, but in a new and fresh way of looking—an innocence of the heart.

The child is close to the Place of Life, not yet confined by duality, not yet separate from its mother and from the world. Thus one may fruitfully inquire of the child as to the beginning.

Those who are aged sense that their end will be like their beginning. What was our face before we were born? This is the same question as "What will be our face after death?" The infant still retains something of its face of eternity, of the serene Source. It is not yet fully one sex or the other, recalling the myth of the primordial androgyne. We begin to sense, then, that the seven-day-old infant symbolizes the initiate, the one who has received the seven gifts of Spirit and who has realized in itself the union of opposites: the beginning and the end. Seven days also symbolizes the time allowed for the return to the unconditioned state. This is why the eighth day is chosen for the circumcision ceremony, when a male child acquires his first sign of membership in a sex, a religion, and a society.

But no matter what our age is, no matter how heavy the weight of memories, this gospel invites us to remember the Divine Child within us, our unconditioned core. By letting this Child live, we see the world through the fresh and joyous eyes of the Source.

Many of the first will make themselves last . . .

This line is akin to the teaching of Lao-tzu, who advocated the art of being "useless" (i.e., not used). Masters of this art have no pretense of knowing anything; they simply look, content to be the calm witness of what is. True gnosis consists largely of a vast removal, ridding ourselves of encumbrances. We get rid of vain words and concepts so that the mind becomes like a clear mirror, like the look of a child, like the forgotten lake lost in the wilderness, where no one swims, its water reflecting the moon impeccably, without a ripple.

LOGION 5

Yeshua said:
Recognize what is in front of you,
and what is hidden from you will be revealed.
There is nothing hidden that will not be revealed.

(CF. MATT 4:22, 10:26; LUKE 8:17, 12:2.)

Speaking for the canonical tradition of Matthew (Mattias), Clement of Alexandria said: "Admire the things that are in front of you!" (*Stromata*, Book II, IX:45)

Gnosis is not a system, not another ideology through which we are to interpret and understand the world. On the contrary, it means opening our eyes to what we are already looking at, right in front of us, not searching somewhere else. Heaven, the Kingdom, God are there where *I am*. As Meister Eckhart said, "The eye with which I see God is the eye with which God sees me: one eye, one vision, one knowledge, one love." Things are not hidden in themselves; they are open—the veils hiding them are in the habits of our own vision, so crude, so overloaded with memories and assumptions about reality, distorting what is before us.

We know the story of Paul, of the day when the scales fell from his eyes and he saw the living Christ in the very people he had been persecuting. And on Mount Thabor, as the Byzantine tradition teaches, it was not Christ who was transformed, but rather the eyes of the disciples, who were finally able to see him truly.

Gnosis is a long-term work of recognition, of purity of attention so as really to see what is in front of us. The consequence of this attention is that we become what we see and what we love. This is why it is important to look deeply in order to perceive what is truest in all beings: seeing the face within, deeper than the surface grins and frowns. "Mankind is a free mirror," according to the patristic tradition. If we look at chaos, we will reflect chaos. If we look at light, we will reflect light.

Consider this logion from the Gospel of Philip, also found at Nag Hammadi, which develops this theme further:

It is impossible for anyone to see the everlasting reality and not
    become like it.
The Truth is not realized like truth in the world:
Those who see the sun do not become the sun;
those who see the sky, the earth, or anything that exists, do not
    become what they see.
But when you see something in this other space,
you become it.
If you know the Breath, you are the Breath.
If you know the Christ, you become the Christ.
If you see the Father, you are the Father.[3]

---

3. [See Jean-Yves Leloup, *The Gospel of Philip* (Rochester, Vt.: Inner Traditions, 2004). Cf. also the famous Sanskrit proverb, from the Advaita tradition, *Tat tvam asi*, "Thou art That." —*Trans.*]

LOGION 6

> His disciples questioned him:
> "Should we fast? How should we pray? How should we give
>   alms? What rules of diet should we follow?"
> Yeshua said:
> Stop lying.
> Do not do that which is against your love.
> You are naked before heaven.
> What you hide will be revealed,
> whatever is veiled will be unveiled.
>
> (Cf. Matt 6:2,7,16; Luke 6:31; Rom 7:15; II Cor 5:10; Eph 4:25;
> Col 3:9; James 3:14; Gal 4:10.)

These questions of the disciples concern the three classic obligations of religious asceticism: praying, fasting, and almsgiving. Any earnest seeker might have asked such a question regarding this subject: "What must I do?" Yeshua seems to be saying that this is not the right question. Before doing this or that, we must *be*. What is important is not so much what we do as the spirit in which we do it: the quality and sincerity of our being. This is a warning against our tendency to assume that we are justified by our works and practices.

There exists a form of "spiritual materialism," denounced by sages from all traditions. The ego is an extremely clever monkey indeed—it can make use of fasting, prayer, and alms in such a way as to feed and inflate itself and to confirm itself in its vanity.

This is what is meant by the usage of the term *Pharisee* in the Gospel of Thomas, as well as in the canonical gospels. It is the desire to appear righteous in the eyes of others while something is rotten inside. In the canonical gospels, Yeshua seems even more severely against this pseudo-spirituality: "You clean the outside of the cup, but inside it is full of rapine and slander" (Matt 23:25).

But in the Gospel according to Thomas, Yeshua contents himself with exhorting his disciples to stop lying: Stop telling your old stories, stop your role-playing of pure, saintly, holy ones. Be who you are, stop the pretense, and stop feeding the separation between Being and appearance.

Do not do that which is against your love.

In other words, do not do unto others what you would not have them do unto you. This sums up the Law and the prophets.

You are naked before heaven.

We cannot lie to ourselves eternally. Sooner or later the day will come when what we are is revealed. All our secret agendas are exposed in the light of day—a blessed day! In the crucifying clarity that exposes our nullity, essential Being may finally manifest. The ego has dropped its spiritual disguises. The Self, naked at last, is revealed.

Meanwhile, this logion reminds us that our acts have value only through the love and quality of Presence that informs them. Anything that we do without love is time lost. Everything we do with love is Eternity rediscovered. As the apostle says elsewhere, "All will disappear . . . only Love will never pass."

LOGION 7

> Yeshua said:
> Fortunate is the lion eaten by a human,
> for lion becomes human.
> Unfortunate is the human eaten by a lion,
> for human becomes lion.
>
> (CF. EX 22:30 ; I PETER 5:8; REV 4:7.)

Some would interpret this lion, which a human may eat but which must not eat a human, as a symbol of the libido, the life force within us. "Eating" the libido means taming and mastering it so that it becomes humanized and ultimately transformed into a force of love. On the other hand, when we are "eaten"—that is, manipulated—by it, we are conditioned by this libido and become its slave.

In gnostic thought, the lion is more the ego or mental activity that stalks us, devouring our attention and our true identity, which is the Self.

Fortunate is the "little me" integrated into the Self, for it has found its true place. Unfortunate is the person so devoured by ego (that "bundle of memories," as Krishnamurti called it) that he forgets the Self. Then human becomes lion (egocentric): the ego-persona co-opts and devours everything in sight.

LOGION 8

> Yeshua said:
> A human being is like a good fisherman
> who casts his net into the sea.
> When he pulls it out, he finds a multitude of little fish.
> Among them there is one fine, large fish.
> Without hesitation, he keeps it and throws all the small fish
>   back into the sea.
> Those who have ears, let them hear!
>
> (CF. MATT 4:9, 5:13, 8:32, 11:15, 13:9, 13:45–50; LUKE 4:9, 5:10;
> JOHN 25:8; ROM 3:28.)

Our intellect is more or less a finely woven net with which we "capture" myriad things. The small fish symbolize the specialized knowledge of the arts and sciences. The big fish is the knowledge of Being.

Sooner or later on the gnostic path, a moment comes when we must throw back all the small fish. We must let go of all that vast array of information, for though it is not bad in itself, it often distracts us and, in any case, can teach us nothing about what is essential. What good is it to know the natures of all the universes if we do not know ourselves and if we do not know That through which all is known?

To keep the big fish is to deepen our self-knowledge, our knowledge of Being. It is to maintain the Presence of the One in the midst of multiplicity.

LOGION 9

Yeshua said:
Once a sower went out
and sowed a handful of seeds.
Some fell on the road,
and were eaten by birds.
Some fell among the thorns,
which smothered their growth,
and the worms devoured them.
Some fell among the rocks,
and could not take root.
Others fell on fertile ground,
and their fruits grew up toward heaven.
They produced sixty and one hundred-twenty units per measure.

(CF. GEN 26; EX 9:8; DEUT 28:39; MATT 13:3–9; MARK 4:3–9;
LUKE 8:58; ACTS 12:23.)

This logion recalls the importance of the ground that receives the seed. The growth of the divine seed, which has been planted in each of us, depends on how we receive it. The word is different according to the ear that hears it. The divine seed—in other words, the creative code—is the same for all. Variation in the fruits is dependent upon the type of ground in which the seed grows.

The road symbolizes the typical, ordinary way of mankind, with all its distractions. When the creative seed is received by a dispersed, distracted consciousness, it cannot grow and thrive. It cannot sink its roots deeply into our depths. This is how the gospel becomes reduced to a topic of salon conversation or a consumer product or a form of entertainment: It becomes like a handful of seed thrown to the birds.

When the seed falls among the thorns, it is received by the one-sidedly analytical, critical consciousness so characteristic of many contemporary minds, which chokes and smothers the spontaneity of life. Here, too, the creative code cannot express and incarnate itself.

The self-knowledge of which the Gospel of Thomas speaks is not some form of introspection, some endless process of self-analysis that finally renders us sterile and inhibited. It is a state of nonjudgmental attention, without a "why?" as Meister Eckhart said.

The worm that lives in the thorns and devours whatever manages to grow there is our narcissism. A consciousness that is constantly turning around its own reflected image blocks the essential movement of the Logos in its unfolding.

Rocks, where the seed cannot take root, often symbolize hardness of heart in the Bible. The closed heart, or "heart of stone," is impervious to the creative code. We often become hard-hearted out of fear. The body itself becomes more rigid, adopting an attitude of defense. Over time this produces a strange kind of armoring in the muscles. But we should never confuse such hardness with strength. Outer hardness, like the shell of a shrimp, hides an inner weakness or softness. Those who have inner strength—people of "backbone"—have no need to present a hard facade to the world. On the contrary, they have the confidence to show themselves as vulnerable and sensitive. They welcome the creative code without fear, thus providing good soil for the seed.

Good soil must also be worked and plowed, which amounts to work on our own heart. This theme recurs in the Gospel of Thomas. Whether this work on ourselves happens through ascetic practices or through the hardships of life, it makes the heart less hard, less egocentric, and less distracted. It is a long labor involving clearing away the rocks and thorns. The heart then becomes open to the essential and capable of hearing and contemplating the Word of God and the creative code that circulates in our veins. It is then that the fruit of Awakening begins to appear.

LOGION 10

Yeshua said:
I have sown fire upon the world,
and now I tend it to a blaze.

(CF. LUKE 12:49.)

On the day of Pentecost the Spirit descended upon the disciples like flames. They caught fire and were illuminated by its Presence. Like the burning bush, they burned without being consumed. These flames symbolize the conscious love taught and revealed by Yeshua Christ. This union of intellect and heart renders us both loving and luminous. This fire is in us, smoldering beneath the ashes of our mediocrity, a hidden glow that awaits the Ruah,[4] the divine Breath, to burst into flame.

In the Gospel of Luke, Yeshua expresses his impatience to see the fire lit. But in the Gospel of Thomas it would seem that he is preserving the fire, tending it. It is as if he must tend it, like a spirited and unruly horse that must be controlled, so that it does not get out of hand.

It is true that the whole of the Good News can be summed up in a phrase such as this one, from Augustine: "Love. And do as you wish." Yet this can be dangerous when heard by a mind that has not been purified, for such a mind would use it for all sorts of self-indulgence. The fire of love and freedom sown by the Christ can be a dangerous fire.

We human beings have this boundless freedom: that no one and no law can prevent us from loving. This is a truth that is perhaps best contained and preserved and allowed to take root deeply in ourselves. Then we can let it live and act— first of all, in all our cells, then in our acts. Then the fire can spread from us to those around us, until that ultimate day when the world will become like the burning bush, saturated with Presence.

---

4. *Ruah* (pronounced *RUE-akh*) is Hebrew for "spirit" or "breath."

LOGION 11

Yeshua said:
This sky will pass away,
and the one above it will also pass away.
The dead have no life,
and the living have no death.
On days when you ate what was dead,
you made it alive.
When you are in the light, what will you do?
When you were One, you created two.
But now that you are two, what will you do?

(CF. MATT 5:18, 19:16, 24:25; LUKE 3:10, 16:17, 16:21–33; MARK 13:31; JOHN 2:17; I COR 7:31; GEN 2:14–17.)

Everything passes. All the material and celestial worlds must pass. All that is composed shall be decomposed, everything that has a beginning must have an end. With this implacable reminder of impermanence, Yeshua invites us to look for what does not pass, what is truly alive and cannot die: the Uncreated. It is not composed and cannot be decomposed. Yet one of the tasks of the gnostic is to consume what is mortal in order to make it truly alive, to assimilate what has no life in itself—our body, the world, matter—so that it may become the very place where Being manifests.

There is a proverb that states: "All is pure to the pure one." And as H.-Ch. Puech points out,[5] some gnostic traditions work to free the sparks of light contained in matter—for example, in food. Yet light absorbs darkness and life must also integrate death.

The All reunited in light—what is there to "do" except, much as we take the lamp from where it has been hidden under the basket and place it on its stand, allow it to shine?

The second part of the logion reminds us that we have come from Unity and it is we who have brought about duality. This duality is not wrong it itself. It is a step in our process of individuation—we cannot

---

5. Puech, *Le Manichéisme* (Paris: Édition du Musée Guimet, 1949), 191–92.

remain in the undifferentiated unity of an infant and its mother. The passage through duality, or separation, is one of the necessary stages of growth and maturity. But having become two, we must seek to rediscover the One. The Unity we discover will no longer be that of undifferentiated fusion, but rather of Union, of integration. Then our existential being will become transparent to essential Being.

LOGION 12

> The disciples said to Yeshua:
> "We know that you will leave us.
> Who will be great among us then?"
> Yeshua told them:
> When you find yourselves at that point,
> go to James the Just:
> All that concerns heaven and earth is his domain.
>
> (CF. MATT 18:1; MARK 9:34; LUKE 9:46; JOHN 1:3; ACTS 1:11;
> I COR 8:6; HEB 2:10.)

The high standing of Yeshua's brother, James, among the earliest Christians is well known. It even seems that the role the Matthew tradition accords to Peter originally belonged to James. In any case, it is clear that the Thomas tradition designates James as Yeshua's public representative.

In Jewish circles there had been a long debate as to whom the world was created for: the Torah, Moses, Abraham, or the Messiah.[6] In the Babylonian Talmud, the world was considered as being made for Moses and Aaron together. It is possible that James might have been considered as having the same relation to Yeshua as Aaron did to Moses-Joshua (Epiphanius, Panarion 29:3–4).[7]

All that concerns heaven and earth is his domain.

This may be read in an ironic sense: "If you are unable to follow the inner Master, and still need an external Master, a leader, then go to James. He will take care of all that. Building a church or a structured community is his domain."

---

6. Cf. G. L. Ginzberg, *The Legends of the Jews*, vol. 5, reprint edition (Baltimore: Johns Hopkins University Press, 1998), 67.

7. [This thesis is further strengthened by the fact that the name Yehoshua, the Hebrew original of the gentile rendering Jesus, is also the origin of the variant Gentile transliteration Joshua. Also, Yehoshua was often shortened, particularly by Aramaic-speaking Jews, to Yeshua. —*Trans.*]

LOGION 13

> Yeshua said to his disciples:
> What am I like, for you?
> To what would you compare me?
> Simon Peter said: "You are like a righteous angel."
> Matthew said: "You are like a wise philosopher."
> Thomas said: "Master, my mouth could never utter what you are
> like."
> Yeshua told him:
> I am no longer your Master, because you have drunk, and become
> drunken, from the same bubbling source from which I spring.
> Then he took him aside, and said three words to him . . .
> When Thomas returned to his companions, they questioned
> him: "What did Yeshua tell you?"
> Thomas answered: "If I told you even one of the things he said
> to me, you would pick up stones and throw them at me. And
> fire would come out those stones, and consume you."
>
> (CF. MATT 3:12, 16:13–20; MARK 8:27–30; LUKE 3:17, 9:18–21;
> JOHN 8:58, 10:6; LEV 9:24; NUM 16:35; JUDGES 9:15.)

"For you, who am I?" This question is also asked in the synoptic gospels. Here, it is not the Messiah that Peter sees in Yeshua, but instead an angel, a "divine messenger." Thus we perceive Yeshua according to our level of consciousness. For some, he is Elijah; for others, a wise philosopher (and in those days this meant someone who lived and incarnated the word, not merely one who spoke it, like a messenger or prophet). Centuries later the Koran would call Yeshua "the seal of sainthood."

But it is Thomas who seems closest to the mystery of his Being. Through self-knowledge he has plumbed the depths of *homo absconditus* in the image of *Deus absconditus*. He has experienced and recognized the Ineffable, the Unknowable in himself, and thus can recognize it in the Other.

> Thomas said: "Master, my mouth could never utter what you
> are like."

Here, Thomas exemplifies what is known as the apophatic tradition, which refuses to name or qualify God. As Thomas Aquinas said: "Of

God, one can only say what he is not, not what he is." Thus the traditional use of negative terms for him: the Infinite, the Uncreated, the Unnamable, the Ineffable, and so forth.

> I am no longer your Master, because you have drunk, and become
>   drunken, from the same bubbling source from which I spring.

In this reply, Yeshua recognizes Thomas as one who has experienced their common origin, the Father. Later, he tells Mary Magdalene: "My Father is your Father." Henceforth, Thomas may be considered the brother, or twin, of Yeshua.

Then Yeshua takes him aside and tells him "three words." We could speculate endlessly about what they were. Perhaps it was a revelation of the Trinity, one that does not break the Unity but is rather the Revelation of an inner fecundity. (Surely the meaning of God as Trinity does not refer to a "sublime bachelor," as Chateaubriand put it.) God is One and Three as Lover, Beloved, and Love. God is relation. According to the Naasenes, these three explosive words were Kaulakau, Saulasau, and Zesar.[8] In the Pistis Sophia, Yeshua cries three words, the same word repeated three times—IAW (in Greek, IAΩ), pronounced "yah-HOO-wah": I, or iota, because everything comes from him; alpha, because everything must return to him; and omega, because the consummation of all consummations is in him.

But what we overlook in these speculations is that the roots of the spoken word are in sound, in a particular vibration. When initiates speak to each other, there is a triple vibration: from the vital center in the loins, to the heart center, to the noetic or intellectual center in the head. It is only in this communion that the initiates can verify that their "resonance" is perfect at all these levels of their being.

However this may be, Thomas speaks here of the special intimacy that he shares with Yeshua. The other disciples might throw stones out of jealousy—thus the fire of love can degenerate into the fire of jealousy. Then, instead of warming and illuminating, it burns and destroys.

---

8. [The Naasenes were a gnostic sect described in Hippolytus's *Refutation of Heresies* v.8.4. These words would appear to be a kind of Hebrew wordplay. Another speculation is that the three words were those God spoke to Moses in Ex 3:14: Ehye Asher Ehye, I am what I am. —*Trans.*]

LOGION 14

Yeshua said to them:
If you fast, you will be at fault.
If you pray, you will be wrong.
If you give to charity, you will corrupt your mind.
When you go into any land and walk through the countryside,
if they welcome you, eat whatever they offer you.
You can heal their sick.
It is not what goes into your mouth that defiles you,
it is what comes out of your mouth that defiles you.

(CF. MATT 6:2,7,16,17 AND 10:11–14; MARK 7:15; LUKE 10:8–11;
JOHN 3:18; ACTS 9:13; COL 10:27.)

The Gospel of Thomas is addressed to people who are aware of certain religious practices but are in danger of complacency with regard to them, thinking that merely observing the practice is enough.

If we feel righteous when we fast, it will inflate our ego instead of freeing us. The true fast comes spontaneously, when we are absorbed in the presence of God. Then we forget about eating. This was Yeshua's state when the disciples found that he had not eaten and were surprised. He told them: "I have something to eat, a food that you do not know . . . My food is doing the will of my Father . . . Do not work for perishable food, but for the food of eternal life." (Cf. John 4:32.)

If you feel righteous when you give to charity, you do harm to your mind. You are giving to gain approval or to create a clear conscience. But we must go further than this, so that you do "not let your left hand know what your right hand is doing."

If your brother is hungry and you have some food, what is more natural than sharing it? This is not "giving to charity"; it is rediscovering the spontaneity of love.

The same applies to prayer. "As long as you pray while seeing yourself as praying, you are not truly praying," said Jean Cassien. Prayer must also become more and more spontaneous—a simple movement of the heart, so that it becomes like the perfume of the rose or the song of a bird.

Yeshua is warning us against practices that are good in themselves, but that can become a hook for "phariseeism," or spiritual narcissism. We must allow the Presence of the Spirit to make us more and more simple, more and more spontaneous. A religion that produces complex people who feel guilty and make others feel guilty is at great risk of being a false religion. It no longer "re-links" (the original meaning of *re-ligio*) us with the vitality of the Living One; it instead separates us from it.

This logion encourages us in this attitude of simplicity: When we are offered hospitality, we must eat what is before us. It is not what goes into our mouth that defiles us, but what comes out of it. In general, Yeshua emphasizes that what make us impure, what defile us, are our acts that defile others, such as useless remarks and hasty judgments. It is calumny and blame that corrupts our hearts and minds and makes our breath nauseating. What good is it to fast, give alms, and pray, if the heart is not fully engaged in these acts, if the mind harbors hate or bitterness?

You can heal their sick.

This is an equally important line of the logion. The Greek word *therapein* refers to more than simply healing the body. The therapists of whom Philo of Alexandria writes were indeed far more than healers—they were also initiators. Thus we might read this as: "You can heal those who are sick or suffering and you can also initiate them into the meaning of life and suffering."

Sickness itself may be only a symptom of a deeper malaise, a forgetfulness of Being. The role of the therapist, then, is to give those who suffer the opportunity to regain their health in the sense of physical, psychic, and spiritual wholeness.

The Gospel of Thomas reminds us that every human being has the power to heal. There is a therapist within each of us. It is the Living One who wants life in abundance for us in all the dimensions of our being. It is attitude that is important, and an openness that allows Life to act in and through us.

LOGION 15

Yeshua said:

When you see someone who was not born from a womb, then prostrate yourselves and give worship, for this is your Father.

(CF. MATT 11:11; MARK 3:11; LUKE 7:28; JOHN 3:9; I COR 14:25; COL 3:4; II THESS 1:10.)

This logion invites us to discover the Unborn within us: that which was not born of woman, flesh, reason, or emotion. It directs our attention to our true origin, unborn and uncreated. There is our true Father. When we discover it, we can only prostrate ourselves and worship it, for we are before the divine abyss of uncreated Being and Love.

LOGION 16

Yeshua said:

People may think that I have come to bring peace to the world.

They do not know that I have come to sow division upon the
earth: fire, sword, war.

When there are five in a house, three will be against two and
two against three; father against son and son against father.

And they will stand, and they will be alone and simple
[*monakhos*].

(CF. MATT 10:34–36; LUKE 12:49, 12:51–53.)

The Peace that Christ offers us is neither euphoria nor some kind of tran-
quilizer. It is the essential Peace of Being, which does not depend upon
favorable outer circumstances. In order to discover this Peace, which
nothing and no one can take from us, it is necessary to be willing to
undergo the fire, the sword, and war—in other words, to experience the
purification, the discrimination, and the polemics (*polemos* is "war" in
Greek) that can shake us out of our false sense of security.

One day Cardinal Newman began to puzzle over a biblical passage
that speaks of God testing souls as silver is tested when it is melted in the
furnace. He visited a silver forge and asked the artisan how he knew when
the silver was free of impurities. The smith replied: "I know the silver is
ready when I can see the features of my face reflected in it."

When we are undergoing such a trial by fire, it may help to remember this metaphor of the Father leaning over us, to see whether his features are reflected . . . as the Son. (Cf. page 132, footnote 19.)

The blade or sword represents discrimination, as indicated in the letters of Paul. The sword enables us to cut through what is ensnaring and
alienating us. This cannot help but cause some kind of conflict (polemos)
and may sometimes lead to confrontation with family members in order
for each of us to attain autonomy. Just as the umbilical cord is cut, so we
must sometimes cut into the flesh of our most legitimate attachments so
as to truly become who we are. When Yeshua says that he comes to bring
us fire, sword, and conflict, he is also offering us the tools of our own liberation. He is teaching us how to break free of the false identifications or

self-images to which we are so attached, but that prevent us from attaining our naked reality, free of illusions.

Whoever has been through liberating trials is able to stand, *alone* and *simplified*—here, we have used two words for one word that is difficult to translate: *monakhos,* which is often poorly translated as "monk." *Monakhos* does not necessarily imply celibacy; it refers to those who move toward the One *(monos),* toward the integration of all their aspects—body, soul, and spirit—so as to become "monogenetic," like the Son, one entire river flowing toward the Father. (Cf. the *Logos pros ton Theon* in the prologue of the Gospel of John.)

This unification happens through solitude and simplification of our life. In the gnostic way, we find ourselves alone, not through any lack of love or friendship, but because the mountain heights are not where the crowds like to roam. At a certain depth of truth, we come face-to-face with ourselves and with God. This solitude is not a separation from others. On the contrary, it allows a deeper meeting with others, meeting them in their own essential solitude.

Gnostics are not fond of crowds. The gregarious, extroverted life is not for them. But it is not pride that compels them to avoid the masses—it is a refusal of superficiality. It is also well known that the deepest and most intimate meetings are those between people who truly live in solitude.

Enduring solitude also leads us to a state beyond ego, for in solitude there can be no dependence on the reflection of the other, the opinion of the other, to confirm us in our existence (and it matters little whether this confirmation is pleasant or unpleasant). This is why so many people fear solitude.

But being alone is not enough. We are also called to be *simple.* It is significant that etymologically this word means "without wrinkles, folds, or convolutions"—in other words, without turning back upon ourselves. The whole work of fire and sword is to unwrinkle us, right down to our most secret folds, so as to rediscover our original simplicity or true identity. This is the pure silver, the pure "I am" freed of the dross of illusory fantasies. It is the "nobleman," the "son of God" of which Meister Eckhart speaks.

LOGION 17

Yeshua said:
I will give you that which no eye has seen,
no ear has heard,
no hand has touched,
and no human heart has conceived.

(CF. MATT 4:9; LUKE 1:77; JOHN 7:39; ACTS 7:23; I COR 2:9;
ISAIAH 64:3; JER 3:16.)

What Yeshua offers here is not something that can be thought, felt, seen, or imagined. Thus he affirms the transcendence of uncreated Being. To say "I know God" can be only presumption and falsehood. While making himself known, God still remains unknowable.

Here, the Gospel of Thomas shows itself as the source of traditions such as Hesychism, which simultaneously affirm the inaccessible character of God and the reality of participation in his Being. From this, Gregory Palamas, the fourteenth-century Greek Orthodox saint, made the distinction between energy and essence. We can never experience the core of the sun, yet we can warm ourselves in its rays. This is also the paradox of union with the divine: It is neither fusion nor separation.

LOGION 18

The disciples asked Yeshua:
"Tell us, what will be our end?"
Yeshua answered:
What do you know of the beginning,
so that you now seek the end?
Where the beginning is, the end will also be.
Blessed are those who abide in the beginning,
for they will know the end and will not taste death.

(CF. MATT 24:3–6; JOHN 20:15; I PETER 4:17.)

Some questions are vain. Why seek to know where we are going and what will become of us when we don't know where we really come from? What we are today is the result of what we have been yesterday; what we will be tomorrow will be the consequence of what we are today.

Questions about origins and endings bring us right back to the present, for it is in this "today," this here and now, that we can reach the beginning and the end.

Heraclitus emphasized that in the circle, beginning and end meet. Every point of the circle could be considered a beginning or an end. Every present moment, in its greatest depths, reveals the alpha and the omega. Instead of asking questions about the end, we would do better to attend to the ever-present Source, where all life, thought, movement, and being are born.

LOGION 19

Yeshua said:
Blessed is the one who Is before existing.
If you become my disciples and listen to my words,
these stones will serve you.
In Paradise there are five trees
that do not change from summer to winter.
Their leaves do not fall.
Whoever knows them will not taste death.

(CF. JOHN 5:24, 8:58; MATT 3:9; MARK 1:13; LUKE 3:8; JAMES
1:11; I PETER 24; REV 2:7; ISAIAH 40:7; ZACH 14:8.)

How can we be before existing? Yet even the etymology of the word *exist*
shows that existence is secondary to essence, that it ex-presses and manifests it. We can also relate this logion to the famous statement of Yeshua
for which it is said he was crucified: "Before Abraham was, I Am." This
means that before entering into the space-time continuum, which
includes the historical Abraham, before any existence, I Am. And this
evokes the Divine Name, the Uncreated.

Meister Eckhart paraphrases this word of Yeshua: "Before I was born,
I Am, for all eternity." Blessed are those who, while still in space-time,
become conscious of their Being in eternity, for they are in this world but
not of it, and even stones will serve them.

When you are in harmony with the uncreated principle of all that is,
then indeed all things seem to "serve" you. There is a real support from all
elements of nature. This is the gnostic view of Paradise.

Kafka said: "Paradise is still here, it is we who were thrown out of it."
In order to rediscover it, we must know the "five trees that do not change
from summer to winter."

According to the Gospel of Philip, these five trees are the five sacra-
ments. Jean Doresse, after citing a Manichean psaltery, mentions the treatise by Chavannes Pelliot on Chinese Manicheism, with a long passage
devoted to the planting of five precious trees by the Messenger of Light.
These are: the Tree of Thought, the Tree of Feeling, the Tree of
Reflection, the Tree of Intellect, and the Tree of Reasoning. Still others

may see in them a symbol of the five spiritual senses as developed by Origen and the patristic tradition.

But most important is that we have ears to hear the song of silence within sound and eyes to see the invisible through the visible. This is the sense of Paradise. Some believe that the gnostics had a practice known as "application of the five senses," an exercise that methodically focuses the sensory organs on an object, which ultimately leads us to a "sensation of the Divine." This is the prelude to the greater apocalypse (*apokalupsis* means unveiling) or revelation of Being in the human microcosm.

LOGION 20

> The disciples asked Yeshua:
> "Tell us, what is the Kingdom of Heaven like?"
> He answered them:
> It is like a grain of mustard,
> the tiniest of all seeds.
> When it falls upon well-plowed ground,
> it becomes a great tree,
> where birds of heaven will come to rest.
>
> (CF. MATT 13:31–32; MARK 4:30–32; LUKE 13:18–19.)

The smallest of seeds can engender the greatest of trees. One human may awaken, and a new humanity can be born.

This is a principle of all beginnings, and of human beginnings in particular. Something that is unnoticed, infinitesimal in size, contains the coded information for growth. The oak is contained within the acorn.

But as this gospel has already pointed out, the ground must be favorable and the soil well plowed. Otherwise, the seed of divine life *(sperma theou)* planted in each of us will not be able to grow and make us into a great tree that can shelter the birds of heaven.

LOGION 21

Mary asked Yeshua:

"What are your disciples like?"

He answered:

They are like little children

who have gone into a field that does not belong to them.

When the owners return and say:

"Give us back our field!"

they will remove their clothes, see themselves naked before the
  owners, and leave the field to them.

This is why I say:

If the master of the house knows that a thief is coming,

he will be vigilant and not allow the thief to break into the
  house of his kingdom

or carry off his goods.

Thus you should be vigilant toward the world.

Strengthen yourselves with great energy

or the thieves will find a way to get to you.

The profit that you are counting on will be found by them.

May there be a wise person among you . . .

When the crop is ripe, he comes immediately

and harvests it with his sickle.

Those who have ears, let them hear!

(CF. MATT 11:16; LUKE 7:32; II COR 5:3.)

Here, Mary Magdalene plays the role of the initiate who asks Yeshua about the stage of development of his disciples. What he confides to her applies not to his closest disciples, but rather to people who follow him from a certain distance. "They are like little children," Yeshua answers. They are not yet "clothed" in the garments of the Christ. Their nudity here is not just innocence; it is also a lack of manifestation of *pneuma*, Spirit.

Yeshua reaffirms the importance of vigilance. Not only spiritual masters may come into possession of the field of gnosis. It may also be taken over by robbers and invaders: hasty judgments, cravings, twisted thoughts. These are the diseases of the mind that can block or destroy true knowledge.

Through vigilance and attention, these children can mature and become wise. It is then that they will harvest the promised fruit. They will no longer be naked strangers in the field of knowledge. They will be masters along with the Master, sons and daughters along with the Son.

LOGION 22

Yeshua saw some infants being nursed at the breast.

He said to his disciples:

These nursing infants are like those who enter the Kingdom.

The disciples asked him:

"Then shall we become as infants to enter into the Kingdom?"

Yeshua answered them:

When you make the two into One,

when you make the inner like the outer

and the high like the low;

when you make male and female into a single One,

so that the male is not male and the female is not female;

when you have eyes in your eyes,

a hand in your hand,

a foot in your foot,

and an icon in your icon,

then you will enter into the Kingdom.

(CF. MATT 18:1–3; MARK 9:36; LUKE 9:47–48; JOHN 17:11; ROM 12:4–5; I COR 12:24; GAL 3:28; EPH 2:14–18; EX 21:24; LEV 24:20.)

Here, too, Yeshua speaks of those of the Kingdom as children who receive milk directly from the breast of their mother, but this time they are innocents in a state of total receptivity, near to that which is considered to be the very source of their life. Later, the Gospel of John speaks of the Breast of the Father on which Yeshua's head rests, and John himself much later rests his head on Yeshua's breast.[9]

In any case, all these images symbolize the attitude of repose and receptivity that is necessary for the contemplative life. The disciples conclude that to become like an infant is sufficient in order to enter into the Kingdom. But Yeshua reminds them that the infant is also a symbol of

9. [Cf. the author's related observation in his commentary on the Gospel of Philip: "Whereas Yeshua has often been depicted with a young man resting his head on his breast (and such images have not been without effect on the behavior of the clergy), it is practically unimaginable to paint him in a pose of intimacy with a woman." Jean-Yves Leloup, *The Gospel of Philip* (Rochester, Vt.: Inner Traditions, 2004). —*Trans.*]

nonduality, and that it is delusive to attempt literally to be like a child, harboring childish behavior or attitudes in ourselves. Rather, we should work to integrate all the dimensions of our being: high, low, masculine, feminine, and so forth.

This is not a mere truism, but an injunction to work on ourselves. The high must be in touch with the low. Many people have their heads in the clouds, but their dreams are often in conflict with their physical drives. The high and the low may even become totally separated. The work of the gnostic is the integration of heaven and earth, the nonopposition of flesh and spirit. This also includes the integration of masculine and feminine, of *anima* and *animus*. We must realize the marriage of man and woman within ourselves—otherwise we will always be searching outside to cure the lack we feel inside. This prevents us from discovering ourselves as realized beings, whole and undivided.

The theme of the androgyne recurs often in gnostic literature. It symbolizes this integration of masculine and feminine polarities: rigor and tenderness, intellect and feeling, strength and gentleness. Yet this is not some wholeness that is closed upon itself. On the contrary, it empowers us to realize our capacity for loving others from wholeness instead of from lack. Then our loves are not merely thirsts—they are also overflowing fountains.

It was Paul who said: "In Christ there is neither male nor female." Indeed, there are only individuals. Their relations are determined by animal attraction not between male and female, but between man and woman, recalling the image of the yin-yang circle, which draws the whole universe into the rhythm of its wedding.

In this rediscovered unity all things appear as transfigured:

You will have eyes in your eyes, for they will see at last.

You will have a hand in your hand, for now you truly will be able to give and receive.

You will have a foot in your foot, for now your feet will know the way.

All is renewed in the image and likeness of God—indeed, you will become God's icon.

Simon the New Theologian, a great Byzantine mystic, said after having communed with the Mysteries (his way of referring to the Eucharist): "Henceforth, I am his foot, his hand, his eyesight. I am his image and his presence . . ." Thus he felt himself permeated by what the Orthodox Fathers called "divine philanthropy." No longer able to accept passively the suffering of even a single being, he prayed for the whole world and cared for both the young woman in misery and her fatherless child.

There are numerous parallels to this logion in apocryphal New Testament literature: Agraphon 71, for example.[10] Asked by someone when the Kingdom would come, the Lord himself replies "When the two become One, the outside like the inside, and the male with the female, neither male nor female. Now, the two are One when each speaks the truth mutually and when, without any hypocrisy, there are two bodies and one unique soul."

Similarly, the Naasenes said that "above, there is neither male nor female, but a new creature, a new human androgyne."[11]

Let us conclude by quoting from the Acts of Thomas,[12] in which the intense human yearning of the gnostic quest is evoked:

"May all my hours become like one single hour. May I be allowed to leave this life all the sooner to contemplate the Living One, who gives Life to those who believe in him, in that place where there is neither night nor day, light nor darkness, good nor evil, rich nor poor, male nor female, liberty nor captivity. What was inner, I shall make outer and what was outer, inner, so that all his abundance is realized in me. I have ceased to look behind me, and have gone forward, into the things that are forward . . ."

---

10. In A. Resch, *Neutestamentlichen Apokryphen.*

11. Cf. Hippolytus, *Elenchos* V, 7, 13–15.

12. [Verses 129–45. The Acts of Thomas are dated much later than the Gospel of Thomas and are considered to be from a different source. —*Trans.*]

LOGION 23

> Yeshua said:
> I will choose one of you from a thousand
> and two of you from ten thousand,
> and they will stand as one, alone and simple [*monakhos*].
>
> (CF. MATT 22:14; JOHN 6:70, 13–18.)

This logion is attributed by Iraneus and Ephiphanius to the Basilidean gnostic sect. These two present it as an example of the "elitism" to which, they claim, gnosticism leads. By the same logic we might say that the words "Many are called, but few are chosen" (from Matthew) could be censured as an example of the doctrine of predestination of souls.

Another reply might be that we are all chosen, for we are all created— that is, "called" into existence.

It is our own response to the creative Intelligence that elects us. One in a thousand respond and two in ten thousand make themselves *capax Dei,* a pure capacity of God, which is one of the names given to the Virgin Mary in Catholic tradition.

These few who do not resist grace are members of one unique response, that of the Son. They arise simplified and without convolutions, "turned toward the Father," as in the beginning—evoking that beginning spoken of in the prologue to the Gospel of John.

LOGION 24

> His disciples asked:
> "Teach us about the place where you dwell,
> for we must seek it."
> He told them:
> Those who have ears, let them hear!
> There is light within people of light,
> and they shine it upon the whole world.
> If they do not shine it,
> what darkness!
>
> (CF. MATT 6:22–23; LUKE 11:1, 33–36; JOHN 1:9, 7:34–36, 12, 36, 38.)

In the Gospel of John, the theme of light is especially important. "The Word is the Light which shines upon all people who come into this world." This means *all* people, not just Christians or gnostics. Yeshua declares himself as the Light incarnate: "I am the Light of the world. Whoever follows me walks not in darkness, but shall have the light of life."

This theme of the "man of light" is present in all the great traditions. It has been studied with the greatest profundity in our time by Henry Corbin.[13]

The "place" where Yeshua dwells, and where all those who walk in his footsteps dwell, is the light. Light fills space and is invisible in itself, yet allows all things to be seen. To be in the light is to be no longer hypnotized by the objects it reveals, but instead to see them through the infinite space that contains them.

In the Gospel of Matthew, Yeshua says: "The eye is the lamp of the body—if the eye is simple, the whole body is luminous, but if the eye is bad[14] [presents an unclear image], the whole body is darkness." The necessary condition for perceiving the light is therefore purity, or simplicity of regard.

---

13. Henry Corbin, *The Man of Light in Iranian Sufism* (Boulder, Colo.: Shambhala, 1978).

14. ["if the eye is bad" = if the eye presents an unclear or distorted image. —*Trans.*]

What else could be meant by a luminous regard, if not that which awakens in each of us, piercing through our shadows, the light that we bear within us? Fortunate are those who have encountered such a regard! Not only does it show them that they are dust and will return to dust, but it also shows them that they are Light and will return to Light.

LOGION 25

Yeshua said:
Love your brother and sister as your soul;
protect them as you do the pupils of your eyes.

(Cf. Lev 19:18; Deut 32:10; Prov 7:2; Matt 5:43–44,19:19,
22:39; Mark 12:31–33; John 2:10, 3:10, 4:21; Rom 13:9; Gal
5:14; James 2:8, 3:10, 4:21.)

The first Letter of John is a good example of the link between the themes
of light and of love: "Whoever pretends to be in the light, yet hates their
neighbor, is still in darkness. Whoever loves their neighbor dwells in the
light, and they are not fallen. But whoever hates their neighbor is in darkness. They walk in darkness, and they know not where they go, for the
darkness has blinded their eyes."

Thus love and light, *gnosis* and *agape,* cannot be separated. Hatred
makes us blind and unhappy. "Whoever does not love, dwells in death,"
as John says elsewhere. They dwell already in hell, closed upon themselves, with no desire for the desire of Other. This is a spiritual autism that
is surely even more painful than psychological autism. For those who love,
everything exists more vividly; the Other is seen in the light, and thus our
fellow human beings can be revealed as precious, like the pupil of our own
eye, a mirror that allows us to see and know ourselves.

Yet it is also true that we cannot reach the ultimate depth of the
"pupil" of our being except through the gift of ourselves. This openness is
like a black hole into which our harmony with the Light is immersed and
reborn.

Logion 26

Yeshua said:
You see the sliver in your brother's eye,
but you do not see the log in your own eye.
When you remove the log from your eye,
then you will see clearly enough to remove the sliver from your
brother's eye.

(Cf. Matt 7:3–5; Luke 6:41–42.)

In this logion Yeshua once more manifests his therapeutic dimension. He unmasks the mechanisms of projection and transference.

What we criticize most harshly in others is often a projection of something that we dislike in ourselves but are afraid to admit. The faults we find most intolerable in others are our own faults.

Listening to certain conversations, we may learn more about those who are speaking than about the person of whom they are speaking. For example, we hear someone say "She is intelligent," but what is really being said is: "She thinks as I do." We might hear the converse as well: Someone is "stupid" because "he does not think as I do."

To judge others is to judge ourselves. The sliver we see in the other's eye is but our own repressed log. If we simply pay attention to the spontaneous judgments that are constantly arising in us, we can learn much about ourselves and our own unconscious. When more light comes to shine in this unconsciousness, we can see others more clearly. We see that what they need is not so much to be judged as to be loved. And this unconditional love may even spark their own transformation toward the light.

LOGION 27

> Yeshua said:
> If you do not fast from the world,
> you will not find the Kingdom.
> If you do not celebrate the Sabbath as a Sabbath,
> you will not know the Father.

> (CF. MATT 5:8–20, 6:33, 18:3; LUKE 12:31, 13:5, 18:17; JOHN 3:5, 6:46, 14:9.)

To be in the world but not of it: This is a strongly recurrent theme in the gospels.

To fast from the world is to manifest our freedom in relation to it. We must leave the city in order to see its real skyline. A time of retreat is necessary for a truly human life. This is the deep meaning of *shabbat,* a word which literally means "a stopping." (When contemporary Israelis needed a word for a labor strike, they coined the word *chevita,* a derivative of *shabbat.*)

The importance of Shabbat to the Jewish people is well known. Each week, individuals stop doing and thereby wrest away the world and human life from the iron, mechanical grip of production. People take the time to be, to sit before God.

This is also a day when humans are equal. They drop their social and professional roles and are simply human beings. Their universal family, all members of which are descendants from God, allows them also to discover this same movement as a kinship with all creatures.

To bring Shabbat into our life is to introduce a time of stopping and of returning—even in the midst of our agitated state—to our essential being. It means taking the time to ask the great questions, such as "What is the real motive of my action? Who is it who thinks? Who am I?"

The Shabbat is also a moment of halting our churning mental apparatus, when time is suspended . . . Then it is possible for a flame to burn from the heart of humanity, an echo of the pure and simple I AM.

LOGION 28

Yeshua said:
I stood in the midst of the world
and revealed myself to them in the flesh.
I found them all intoxicated.
Not one of them was thirsty
and my soul grieved for the children of humanity,
for they are blind in their hearts.
They do not see.
They came naked into the world,
and naked they will leave it.
At this time, they are intoxicated.
When they have vomited their wine,
they will return to themselves.

(CF. MATT 11:17; LUKE 7:32; JOHN 4:13–15, 6:35; I TIM 3:66;
I THESS 5:7; II COR 6:1; GAL 2:2; PHIL 2:16.)

The theme of the "intoxicated" man in gnostic literature is opposed to that of the "man of light," set here as the opposite of "divine drunkenness," for it is a condition in which mind and heart are blurred, dense, and intoxicated by the world of appearances.

The aim here is to break free of an intoxication that produces self-satisfaction and dullness and perpetuates thought processes that are mostly obstinate and obscure. This requires that we let go of our "given truths," all those useless concepts that diminish the Real. Only then can we discover the truth of I AM, the luminous, ungraspable Presence of the One who Is—or, as the Areopagite school would say, the infinitely more than Being.

We came naked into the world and naked we will leave it. It is important to remember this—not to be overwhelmed by it, but to refer to it to maintain a minimum of lucidity. It is not we who gave ourselves Being—by ourselves we are but "pure nullity." The lucidity that comes from facing this hard truth will help us to vomit up our wine, to escape the illusion and inflation of ego. Then we can rediscover our true nature with a new mind and a new heart.

The Gospel of Truth (22:13–19) adds: "Whoever has *gnosis* knows from where they come, and to where they are going. They know this as those who, having been intoxicated, then become sober and return to themselves, regaining what is proper to them."

LOGION 29

Yeshua said:
If flesh came into being because of spirit,
it is a wonder.
But if spirit came into being because of flesh,
it is a wonder of wonders.
Yet the greatest of wonders is this:
How is it that this Being, which Is,
inhabits this nothingness?

(CF. MATT 21:42; MARK 12:11; JOHN 1:14; I TIM 3:16; ROM 8:13;
I COL 5:3.)

The world seems divided by two major views about mind and matter: the spiritualist view and the materialist view.

For spiritualists, matter is a devolved, frozen form of spirit. Spirit is the fundamental reality vibrating at different frequencies, one of the slowest of which produces the phenomenon of matter.

For materialists, on the contrary, spirit and mind are merely products of the increasing complexity of matter. Only chance and necessity rule the behavior of our synapses and the dance of particles that compose us.

There are two opposite ways of framing the question: "How does matter arise from spirit?" and "How does spirit arise from matter?" In either case, it is a wonder of wonders! Each of these approaches has its own reason, its own logic. But logic and reason are insufficient, for—as this logion tells us—the real marvel is that there is something instead of nothing!

Yeshua does not ask why, for that would be to descend to the level of explanation. He simply notes, wonders, and admires, drawing us into a nondualistic vision in which matter and spirit are not opposed but embraced together. Might it be that *matter* and *spirit* are empty words, mere mental concepts? In the moment of sheer wonder, perhaps are we closer to a single Reality whose subtle and gross polarities are revealed as complementary?

The really interesting question is: "How is it that this Being, which Is, inhabits this nothingness?" Some have paraphrased this as "How can this wealth inhabit this poverty?" Within us we contain both the uncreated and the created, the divine and the human. Where does one begin and the other end?

The question is not "Why?" but "How?" How can we live so that they are One, as in "I and the Father are One"? How can we realize this union of God and human, as manifested in Yeshua the Christ, with neither separation nor confusion? How can we live fully the consequences of the theanthropic wedding of created and uncreated?

LOGION 30

> Yeshua said:
> Where there are three gods,
> they are gods.
> Where there are two or one,
> I am with them.
>
> (CF. MATT 18:20; JOHN 5:7–8, 10:34.)

The Gospel of Matthew attributes words to Yeshua that recall this logion: "Wherever two or three are gathered in my name, I am with them." Where love is present, God is present. Where two or three hold together in the One, which is their source, the Mystery of the total interconnectedness of all things reveals itself to them.[15] The Pantokrator, that which holds all things together, is present.

The Egyptian hermit monks had a different way of understanding this teaching. For them, the "two or three" means the body, the soul (or heart), and the spirit. When these three levels of our being, each with its own mode of consciousness, are all present together in unity, then the Christ is truly present.

This is in fact one of the leitmotifs of the Hesychast system of prayer. Through deep breathing and invocation of the Name, the different components of human beingness are brought together so that the light of Spirit can descend into us and transform our being.

---

15. Cf. the nonlocal connectedness of the universe as described by quantum physics.

LOGION 31

> Yeshua said:
> No one is a prophet in his own village.
> No one is a physician in his own home.
>
> (CF. MATT 13:57; MARK 6:4; LUKE 4:23–24; JOHN 4:44.)

Why are prophets so rarely accepted in their own country? Undoubtedly because people *think* they know the prophet. The sound of their voice is already labeled and judged before they speak. It is more effective if they come from elsewhere so that their novelty makes people pay serious attention to what they are saying.

Perhaps this is for the best, after all. It can also help the prophet and the healer to remember that the grace that passes through their voice or their hands comes not from them or from their lineage or from their entourage, but from God. And God can use the jawbone of an ass to prophesy and a lump of clay to heal.

This attitude of humility and love is characteristic of the true gnostic. As the Mandukya Upanishad says, "After realization of nonduality, live in this world as if you were an ordinary being"; to which Shankara adds: " . . . to the point that others do not even suspect who you are and what you have become."

LOGION 32

Yeshua said:
A strong city built upon a high mountain
cannot be destroyed,
cannot be hidden.

(CF. ISAIAH 2:2; MATT 5:14, 7:24–25; REV 14:8, 21:10; LUKE
6:47–49.)

We know the parable of the house built on sand that crumbles and the house built on rock that weathers the storm. Foundations are important. We must ask ourselves whether they are deeply rooted enough, and in what kind of ground.

We must know that the basis of our life is solid. It is like a strong city that symbolizes the efforts of organizing and harmonizing our different modes of being. It is a city that is built upon a high mountain, which imparts not only strength and solidity, but also a visibility that makes it a beacon across the plains.

Those who found their life in love of God have nothing to fear. Their house is built upon the very source of the life force. Nothing can destroy it, nothing can overwhelm it. "Light shines in darkness, and the darkness cannot reach it" (John 1:5).

LOGION 33

Yeshua said:
What you hear with your ears,
tell it to other ears
and proclaim it from the rooftops.
No one lights a lamp
so that it will be put under a basket
or hidden somewhere.
Rather, one puts it upon a stand
so that all who enter and leave
may see the light.

(CF. MATT 5:15, 10:23–27; LUKE 8:16, 11:33, 12:3; JOHN 10:9.)

You cannot steal the perfume from the rose. The rose is not grudging of those who breathe its fragrance. The mission of light is to shine, but the concern of the gnostic is not so much the desire to shine as it is the desire to *be* light.

In order to transmit the word, we must first embody it. The sun does not proselytize; it offers its light freely. Nor are fully human beings proselytes. They simply transmit what they have truly received. They give of themselves—not because they are virtuous, but because it is their nature to do so. "He loves not as I love, but as the emerald is green, for he *is* 'I love.'"

The temptation is to hide this lamp under a basket. The ordinary mind wants to reduce this radiance to something that can be understood within its own limits. But this light cannot remain hidden indefinitely. Even the body yearns to become a transparent beacon of light. And according to the tradition of St. Seraphim of Sarov and other human beings transfigured by this love, it can, so that outside is like inside and all is light.

LOGION 34

> Yeshua said:
> When a blind person leads another blind person,
> they both fall into a pit.
>
> (CF. MATT 15:14; LUKE 6:39; JOHN 9:39–41.)

We cannot guide someone unless we truly see. If we have not awakened, then we will share only our sleep with another, and we will both fall into a pit together.

As John the Baptist said, "One can give only what one has received." Nothing more, nothing less.

Do not let yourself be guided by those who do not have the experience of which they speak. Intuitively, we know to beware of those who eagerly offer "good advice." As the Indian sage Nisargadatta said, "Those who know what is good for others are dangerous people."

You can bear witness to your faith, but never graft it on another. When this is seen as the luminous truth it is, it becomes an awakening force in itself. All that you can say is: "That which is alive in me is also alive in you."

The true master is not someone who speaks eloquently of the Light, but rather one who helps us to see it with our own eyes. As an old proverb says, "Give a man a fish, and he will not hunger for a day. Teach him how to fish, and he will never hunger again."

LOGION 35

Yeshua said:
One cannot capture the house of the strong
except by tying their hands.
Then everything can be overturned.

(CF. MATT 12:29; MARK 3:27; LUKE 11:21–22.)

The Gospel of Thomas teaches that true strength resides in those who have become who they are. The strongest are those who have found their place in which they fulfill God's design for them. For gnostics, weakness always means not knowing who we are, ignorance of our essential being. The true strength of human beings lies in their union with God, who is both their citadel and their liberator, the source of their only real security and freedom. Nothing can conquer them in their depths. But they can be prevented from expressing and giving themselves. The hands of love can be tied and everything overthrown.

The mission of love is to give. If this is prevented, its force can wane. Yet there is no standing still on this path—whoever does not continue to advance, retreats. The fire of love grows only hotter when confronted with obstacles. The only other choice it has is to die down and become ashes.

So the hands of love can be tied, but the radiance of its heart can never be extinguished. Those who have their hands cut off still transmit directly from the heart. Other hands will be raised to accomplish their work.

LOGION 36

Yeshua said:
Do not worry from morning to evening,
or from evening to morning,
about having clothes to wear.

(CF. MATT 6:25–33; LUKE 12:22–31; EX 27:21; LEV 24:3; NUM
9:21.)

This is a major recurrent theme in the gospels: Stop worrying! Stop worrying about food, about clothes, and about "what we will say when they take us before the judges." First seek the Kingdom, the Reign of Spirit within you. Only then will come true clarity, with all things given and resolved beyond belief.

Generally, worry and care are based on fear. They are signs of a lack of inner peace and confidence. Being anxiously concerned, even about noble causes, is also a symptom of pride. We take ourselves too seriously; we believe we can ultimately control what will happen to us. But the truth is that only the One is acting: "In Him we have our Life, our Movement, and our Being."

It is interesting to recall an anecdote from Pope John XXIII concerning an evening when he was deeply distressed about the state of the Church for a number of good reasons. Christ appeared to him and said: "John, is it you or I who directs this Church? Is it you or I who pilots this boat? . . . Then simply do your best and stop worrying."

Letting go of worry does not mean becoming indifferent or irresponsible. We continue to do the best we possibly can—but now we know that the fruit of our actions does not depend on us. As the Bhagavad Gita says: "You have a right to act, but no right to the results of your action."

Ignatius of Loyola put it this way: "In all things, perform your act as if everything depends on it alone; and in all things, act as if the outcome of everything you do depends on God alone."

To relinquish worry is also to live in the Present. "Do not worry from morning to evening, or from evening to morning." In Matthew 6:34, Yeshua says: "Let the day's own trouble be sufficient for the day." And from Luke 6:27: "Who among you can add one cubit to his span of life by being anxious?"

Love naturally lives in the Present. Those who think "I will love," mean that they do not love.

Living in the Present, moment after moment, unveils the secret of the Presence. This demands a great power of attention and a high quality of soul, but it is the greatest source of happiness. Our energy ceases to be dispersed to yesterday and tomorrow. We begin to live intensely with "what is in front of [us]" (logion 5). We are then no longer separate from the spontaneity of Life, which passes through one form to another, from one set of clothes to another, without losing our identity.

Not worrying about our clothes thus also means not worrying about what form life will take for us. Our asceticism consists in being faithful and true in the present moment.

LOGION 37

> His disciples asked:
> "When will be the day that you appear to us?"
> "When will be the day of our vision?"
> Yeshua replied:
> On the day when you are naked
> as newborn infants
> who trample their clothing,
> then you will see the Son of the Living One
> and you will have no more fear.
>
> (CF. GEN 2:25, 3:7; MATT 14:26–27, 16:16, 18:3; MARK 6:10–15,
> 6:48–50; JOHN 3:3, 6:14–22; HEB 4:13; I JOHN 3:2.)

Here, clothes symbolize all the suppositions and impositions with which we have veiled our essential being. They represent all our identifications with roles and situations, all the ideas that make us forget our nakedness.

This gospel invites us to be naked, to be nothing, to be empty as a newborn child without clothes, without prejudices, so as to rediscover that innocence which allows us to see the Living One. When we cease to project the past and the future onto the present, how can we still be afraid?

Another connotation of nakedness is preparation for the Sacred Embrace. Being naked requires an act of faith in the Love that awaits us. Thus the Priscillians removed all their garments when they prayed.[16]

In the Acts of Thomas, humanity is symbolized by a young wife who says: "Henceforth I shall no more veil myself, for the mirror of shame has been removed from me . . . No more shall I feel ashamed and frightened." And what is this mirror of shame if not the unnatural stare of the voyeur?

In the *Liber Graduum* (col. 341:1)[17] Adam and Eve appear without shame as naked as babies at the breast. This is seen as an invitation to become naked and innocent again.

---

16. [For more on the Sacred Embrace, see Leloup, *The Gospel of Philip* (Rochester, Vt.: Inner Traditions, 2004). The Priscillians, or Priscillans, were a fourth-century gnostic Christian group in Spain and southern Gaul. —*Trans.*]

17. [The *Liber Graduum* (Book of Steps) is a fourth-century Syrian Christian text. —*Trans.*]

But in some forms of gnosticism, nakedness goes still further to signify a dis-identification with the physical body. To be naked is to remember that our essence is uncreated and that all pathological attachment to existence in space-time is a form of idolatry. "I will cast off this earthly body! I will discard the Cosmos and the appearance of the five stars: I will destroy the trap laid in me by the Archons, and I will shine resplendent in remembrance of the Paraclete! . . . You have cast down the clothes of infirmity; you have trampled down cruel and deceitful pride . . . I have overthrown the vanity of this fleshly dress" (from the Manichean Psalms).

One of the most beautiful echoes of logion 37 is this poem[18] by the contemporary author Jacques Lacarrière, from his *Surat of Emptiness:*

Unlearning. Deconditioning your birth.
Forgetting your name. Going naked.

Sloughing away your last remains. Disrobing your memory.
Melting down your masks.

Ripping up your duties. Dismantling your certainties.
Disconnecting your doubts. Losing control of your being.

Unbaptizing your springs. Unmapping your roads.
Shearing your desires. Gutting your passions.

Desacralizing the prophets. Discrediting the future.
Overturning the past. Discouraging Time.

Unknotting unreason. Deflowering delirium.
Defrocking the sacred. Sobering up from vertigo.

Defacing Narcissus. Delivering Gilead.
Deposing Moloch. Dethroning Leviathan.

Demystifying blood. Dissecting the monkey.
Disinheriting the ancestor.

---

18. [Translated here from Jacques Lacarrière, *Sourates* (Paris: Albin Michel, 1997). — *Trans.*]

Unburdening your soul. Unfailing your failures.
Disenchanting your despair. Unchaining your hope.

Delivering your madness. Defusing your fears.
Disencumbering your heart. Disappointing your Death.

Debasing your basis. Shredding your acquisitions.

Unlearn. Become naked.

LOGION 38

Yeshua said:
Often you have wanted to hear
the words I speak to you now.
No one else can say them to you,
and the days will come
when you seek me
and do not find me.

(CF. MATT 9:15, 13:17, 23:29; MARK 2:20; LUKE 5:35, 10:24; JOHN
7:33–34, 8:21, 13:33, 16:16.)

The beginning of this logion is echoed in the Acts of John. At the
moment of the crucifixion, the Savior appears to John in a vision on the
Mount of Olives, telling him that he will reveal the cross of light: " . . .
John, it is needful that one should hear these things from me, for I have
need of one that will hear."

According to the Manichean Psalms, the Savior transmitted this
logion so that the eleven disciples would recognize later that it was the
Christ who was calling them. Mary Magdalene would also evoke these
words from Yeshua: "Remember what I revealed of myself to you on the
Mount of Olives: I have something to say, and no one to say it to."

The logion continues, with Yeshua speaking of the day when they will
seek but not find him. But why seek the Christ, the Living One, among
the dead? The right moment is now. Every day is the day of salvation and
every instant the time of Encounter. Tomorrow will be too late. Never put
off love and joy until tomorrow. The Kingdom is here and now. Where
but in the Present will you search for the Living One?

As Angelus Silesius said, "What does it matter that Christ was born
long ago in Bethlehem, if he is not born today in me?" And what does it
matter that Christ is coming tomorrow, if my heart is not open to receive
him today?

LOGION 39

Yeshua said:
The Pharisees and the scribes
have received the keys of knowledge
and hidden them.
They did not go within,
and those who wanted to go there
were prevented by them.
As for you, be as alert as the serpent
and as simple as the dove.

(CF. MATT 10:16, 23:13; LUKE 11:52.)

Although Yeshua appears in all the gospels as the very incarnation of gentleness and compassion when faced with those who are suffering, he manifests thunderous severity before those who pretend to guide and teach others yet do not practice what they preach. Though it now goes by other names, the hypocrisy of the scribes and Pharisees is still very much with us today. These are people who are supposed to have received the keys. They have learned the letters and the words of the holy books and have heard the good news of the love of God in which all are invited to participate. Why do they betray it?

Let us turn to Dostoyevsky's *The Brothers Karamazov,* to the chapter on the Grand Inquisitor, in order to shed some light on this. Is it not the Grand Inquisitor who rules the minds of such hypocrites? And does he not also exist in each of us? This is how he speaks to Christ: "You have revealed too great a freedom for men. It makes them unhappy, for they do not know what to do with it. But we have instructed them in what is right and what is wrong. We have told them what to do . . . They may be less free, but they are happier."

In the Grand Inquisitor we recognize the voice of all authoritarian systems that want to produce human happiness but without human participation in freedom. Thus the scribes and Pharisees have been given the keys of knowledge, but they do not want to use them to open the door for all. Instead, they seek to hoard the treasure of the Word for themselves—or, even worse, they seek to reduce the holy scriptures to a gross and vulgar level of interpretation. These people are very far indeed from "living the meaning" of the Word. At best, they offer the letter of it, devoid of the Spirit that brings it to life.

As early as Origen we find a complaint about priests who no longer transmit the spiritual meaning of the scriptures, who fail in their hermeneutical mission: "They distribute them like nuts to children, but without opening the hard shells, so that the children break their teeth. They never taste the almond, the core of the message."

Today, we have lost touch with the meaning of *initiation,* or *rite of passage.* The true hermeneutic art is one of offering a "passage" from one level of consciousness to another, so as to have access to the Spirit of the Word.

The early founders of Orthodox Christianity distinguished three general levels of scriptural interpretation:

1. The physical level, related to history
2. The psychic level, related to ethics
3. The spiritual level, related to ontology

Initiation means a passage through all these levels without denying or neglecting any part of the process. For example, we can read the Song of Songs as a tale of erotic romance between a shepherd and shepherdess, or as a symbolic story of the love between God and Israel or between Christ and the Church. Still another interpretation is that of St. Gregory of Nyssa and St. John of the Cross: It tells of the love affair between God and the soul, of the mystical union of the created and the uncreated.

This example illustrates a hermeneutic approach that respects all levels of meaning of scripture. Unfortunately, it is seldom practiced today, just as it was apparently seldom practiced in the time of Yeshua of Nazareth. By then the Torah had become a restrictive and guilt-producing body of rules and laws, instead of a law of freedom that could save human beings from what was most harmful and destructive in themselves and in the world.

Yeshua also reproached the scribes and Pharisees for turning the Word to their service instead of serving it. Indeed, it is possible to use scripture to gain personal power and dominate others—surely one of the most dangerous and perverted of powers. While pretending to speak in the name of God, offenders work on the minds of their recruits with manipulation disguised as guidance. This power has nothing to do with the true power of the Word, which is that of ever-greater love and service.

The knowledge communicated by sacred texts is one of attention and simplicity, as indicated by the following words of this logion: "[B]e as alert as the serpent and as simple as the dove." A gnostic is not a person with any special knowledge, but rather a simple human being with a clear and open heart and no self-concern or self-importance, someone who is attentive to what is in front of him or her. The gnosis taught by Yeshua is one that develops a meditative attitude toward what is, an attitude that is nondualist, nonrationalizing, and free of projection and judgment. Gnosis is simply seeing things as they are.

There is a remarkable beauty in Yeshua's image of serpent and dove. The serpent crawls upon the earth while the dove flies in the sky. Thus we are told to ground ourselves on earth without losing touch with our thrust upward into the skies. To hold both these animal qualities is to realize the union of opposites, of earth and heaven.

LOGION 40

Yeshua said:
A grapevine planted away from the Father
has no vitality.
It will be torn up by its roots
and will perish.

(CF. PROV 12:3–12, 15:6; ISAIAH 5:1–6; JER 2:21, 17:5; EZEK
19:10–14; DAN 4:14; MATT 3:10, 7:19, 15:31, 21:29; MARK
11:13–14; LUKE 13:6–9; JOHN 15:1,2,5,6; COL 2:7.)

This logion reminds us of the importance of roots and being grounded. To be grounded in the Father means to be rooted in the true origin of all existence. To be planted away from the Father results in being cut off from the Source. Even the purest water will soon stagnate when cut off from its source. It suffers the same fate as the branch, spoken of in the Gospel of John, that is cut from the vine.

The parable of the vine and its branches also offers a strong image of the unity that results when a community of faith is brought together. The real nature of this unity lies inside, like the sap that runs through the vine and branches. This unity can never occur from the outside when, like different branches, different religious traditions meet. Grafting the branches together would either damage them or link them in such an artificial way that their separateness would be even more apparent. But perhaps these different branches will be able to discover unity in their inner nature, in the silence of their common sap, which ultimately comes from the larger trunk that they had not seen before.

LOGION 41

Yeshua said:
Whoever has something in hand
will be given more.
Whoever has nothing,
even the little they have
will be taken away.

(CF. MATT 13:12, 25:29; MARK 4:25; LUKE 8:18, 19:26.)

The content of this logion is familiar from the canonical gospels, following the parable of the talents. At first glance, this conclusion may seem outrageously unjust. Those who have are to be given more while those who have not are to lose even what they have.

But this must be seen as an expression of the urgency of the demand, in all the gospels, that we bring our gifts to fruition, that we not neglect or waste them. It is based on the fundamental law that the more we give, the more we receive.

Thus the meaning of having "something in hand" has nothing to do with material wealth, but instead concerns the capacity to give of ourselves. It also means having love and self-knowledge, or gnosis. Without this gnosis, any possibility of understanding the world will be denied to us. Without this love, life loses its savor and its interest. Nothing astonishes us or reveals anything to us any longer. What we thought we knew, the power and possessions we thought we had, sooner or later turn to ashes. If we cannot give love, even the little we have will be taken from us.

LOGION 42

Yeshua said:

Be passersby.

(CF. JOHN 13:1; I COR 4–11, 7:31; HEB 11:9, 29:37.)

Christian tradition gives great significance to the theme of Passover, or Easter. The Hebrew word *pesakh* means "passage." The deeper meaning is that we are all temporary passengers and pilgrims here. The earth is a bridge and we do not build a house on a bridge. We must pass on. Time passes; everything, it seems, passes. What is it that does not pass?

It is a sign of psychic health to see ourselves as passersby, for we are in closer touch with reality. Just to know that our pain will pass makes it more bearable. And to know that our dearest pleasures will also pass gives us freedom from them, so we are not so sad when they are gone.

There is a story of a king who dreamed one night that he possessed a very special ring. Whenever he was unhappy and looked at the ring, a great calm and equanimity filled him. When he found himself agitated with enthusiasm and excitement, he looked at the ring and a great calm came to him so that he became peaceful in his fervor. When he woke up the next morning, he described the ring in detail to his ministers and commanded them to search the kingdom for such a ring or for someone who could make one.

After long searching, the ministers finally found such a ring on the finger of an old woman. There was nothing extraordinary about this woman, except perhaps for her serenity. She readily agreed to give her ring to the king, and it began to work as soon as he put it on his finger. In a few days he was cured of his manic-depressive tendencies, and his slavery to his changing moods came to an end. Beyond the extremes of laughter and tears, he discovered the great depth and beauty of a genuine smile.

One day he looked closely at the inner surface of the ring and noticed for the first time that there were tiny letters inscribed there. They read: "This, too, will pass."

Whether we find ourselves on a hospital bed or in the midst of the greatest experience of happiness, remembering this truth will serve us well.

The cause of suffering is our resistance to impermanence, the ever-changing flow of all things in life. Let pass what must pass. Dwell on that which is always alive.

To be a passerby is also to be moving toward the other shore, from the shadows to the light, from this world to the Father, as Yeshua taught—to move from what is always passing to what does not pass, to awaken to the life beyond birth and death, resurrected upon the other shore of ourselves. People said of St. Bernard that he had a very alert look, the appearance of someone who is constantly traveling, as if always on a pilgrimage to Jerusalem. Passersby see all things for the first and last time. They never look back and they savor each instant as the very place of passage of the Eternal Now.

The image of the bridge comes from an echo of this logion inscribed in Arabic letters upon the gateway of the ancient city of Fateh-pur-Sikri, now in the southern part of Delhi, built by the Moghul emperor Akbar. It says:

> The prophet Isa [Jesus], peace be unto him, said this:
> The world is a bridge.
> Pass over it,
> but do not make your home there.

These words are also attributed to Yeshua by a number of Muslim authors, notably Al-Ghazali (1059–1111).

LOGION 43

> The disciples asked him:
> "Who are you to say these things to us?"
> Yeshua replied:
> Do you not know me from what I say to you?
> Or have you become like those Judeans:
> If they love the tree,
> they despise the fruit.
> If they love the fruit,
> they despise the tree.
>
> (CF. MATT 11:2; JOHN 8:25, 14:8; LUKE 6:43–44.)

In the Gospel of John, the Pharisees ask Yeshua who he is, and he replies that his words have always said who he is.

Actually, Yeshua's teaching is not really that far from that of the Pharisees. The crucial difference is that they do not practice what they teach whereas he *is* what he teaches. He is transparent, for there is no dualism between words and action.

To listen, to hear, to meditate upon his words, is the way of access to the mystery of his Being. The creative meaning in his speech and the creative meaning that informs his acts are One.

The end of this logion reminds us that the fruit and the tree are also one and that apples do not grow on olive trees. Yeshua's words are the fruit of the Torah, the fulfillment of the Law and the prophets. He is the ripe fruit of the tree of Israel. But the Jewish Pharisees despise the fruit and the Gentile (or, later, Christian) Pharisees despise the tree.

The day when Judaism and Christianity are no longer at odds will be the day when the tree is proud of its fruit and the fruit embraces the tree with a love reaching down into the roots. In this clear light of Paradise the two are revealed to be One, and people will know the meaning of the Tree of Life.

LOGION 44

Yeshua said:
Whoever blasphemes against the Father
will be forgiven,
and whoever blasphemes against the Son
will be forgiven.
But whoever blasphemes against the Holy Spirit
will not be forgiven,
either on earth or in heaven.

(Cf. Matt 6:10, 12:31–32; Mark 3:28–29; Luke 12:10.)

We may be blocked from the insight that would enable us to see through the variety and multiplicity of creation toward the One who is its Source. This is a denial that does not recognize the Father. Or we might be blocked in our heart center, so that we are unable to see the beauty of human beingness or to feel awe at the divine compassion that can manifest in a human being. This is a denial that does not recognize the Son. But to be cut off from the Spirit, the very Breath that is the source of our life, is far more serious. It is a denial of our most intimate being.

This logion recalls the vision of God as Unity-in-Trinity. The Father symbolizes Transcendence, the Other, the Beyond. The Son[19] symbolizes Immanence, the Presence of Being that urges all things toward their destiny. The Holy Spirit is the link between Transcendence and Immanence.

In societies in which the free flow of Spirit is lacking, we often find people trapped in religions of one-sided transcendence, with God remaining outside and inaccessible. As the poet Jacques Prévert ironically wrote, the blasphemy becomes "Our Father who art in heaven, please stay right there where you are."

But the lack of Spirit can also lead to one-sided devotion to the Son, which is just as problematic. Here, humanity becomes its own god. This

---

19. [Here, the author uses the masculine term Son to refer to an Immanence that is traditionally considered the feminine aspect of God. There is no contradiction because (as is pointed out in other passages) the Christ is just as much feminine as masculine. "Son" is not meant here as it is in literalist Christian doctrine. —*Trans.*]

can lead to a humanism that lacks any opening to the transcendent dimension.

The Holy Spirit keeps us in touch with both the Transcendence beyond all experience and the Immanence within all experience. To blaspheme against the Spirit is to deny any possibility of a link between these two, to deny the Unity of Father and Son.

But why should this blasphemy against the Spirit be beyond all pardon? The Founders of the early Church put it this way: "God can do all things except one: force a human being to love Him." Hence, even God cannot overcome the obstinacy of those who destroy their most intimate links with their own Being, continually burning their only bridge to the other shore.

To refuse the Holy Spirit is to refuse all possibility of communion between the human and the divine. It is to refuse the grace forever offered by this communion and to imprison ourselves in the illusion of a separate self. If hell exists, it is only because God is Love and human beings are free. This freedom includes the power to say no to Love. Love cannot force open the door and still be Love.

LOGION 45

> Yeshua said:
> Grapes are not picked from thornbushes,
> nor figs from thistles,
> for they do not give fruit.
> The good offer goodness
> from the secret of their heart.
> The perverse offer perversity
> from the secret of their heart.
> That which is expressed
> is what overflows from the heart.
>
> (CF. MATT 7:16–18, 12:33–35; LUKE 6:43–45; GAL 5:19–23.)

"By their fruits shall you know them." This is the discrimination that Christ teaches throughout the gospels.

In his Epistle to the Galatians Paul expounds at length on the theme of this logion by contrasting the fruits of the Spirit with the fruits of the flesh. Here, *flesh* must be understood as *world* is understood in the Gospel of John—a restricted way of life in which humanity recognizes no need beyond its natural needs, no Law but its own laws, and refuses the notion of grace. In contrast to this, Paul goes so far as to say, "If the Holy Spirit leads you, then you are not under the law."

We are all too familiar with the fruits of this "flesh," this impoverished way of being: soulless sex, self-indulgence, materialism, idolatry, debauchery, power-seeking, pollution, discord, disputation, jealousy, hatred, violence, war . . . But the fruits of the Spirit are love, joy, peace, equanimity, kindness, confidence, service to others, and self-mastery. How can any law be above such fruits as these?

Thus the fruit reveals the nature of the tree, and the actions and words of individuals reveal the secret of their heart, the nature of the spirit that is inhabiting it.

LOGION 46

> Yeshua said:
> From Adam to John the Baptist,
> no one born of woman
> is higher than John the Baptist.
> Thus his eyes will not be destroyed.
> But I have said:
> Whoever among you becomes small
> will know the Kingdom, and be higher than John.
>
> (CF. MATT 11:11, 13:11; LUKE 7:28, 10:11; ROM 5:14.)

John the Baptist plays an important role in the Tradition. He is the archetype of the Precursor, the Friend of the Bridegroom. In Christian tradition he is the preparer of the way, called the "Roadbuilder for the coming of the Christ . . . lowering the high places, straightening the sharp turns, filling in the depressions, preparing a straight road for the Lord." On another level, the work of this archetype is to make us more balanced and peaceful individuals. John embodies and symbolizes the skillful work of asceticism, which can shrink our pride and straighten the tortuous and twisted places in our heart. It is a work that can liberate us from our depressive or despairing tendencies, helping us to rediscover our true nature, which allows grace to incarnate and radiate in us.

This Precursor archetype may show different faces to different people. Some may be led to an encounter with the uncreated Light, or the Christ, through the study of philosophy or science. For others, it might be art, poetry, sacred scripture, or falling in love. We have all experienced such presages of awakening. But we cannot remain in them indefinitely. When the gospels speak of those who wonder if John the Baptist might be the Christ himself, it is analogous to wondering whether some form of art, science, psychotherapy, or relationship might be our highest truth, our salvation . . . and it is the same mistake. Even if we arrive at the summit of the mountain, the sky is still far above us, for it is of another nature. At the summit of our experience, knowledge, or achievement, we are still far below with respect to this other nature, this Unknown—for it is consciousness of another order altogether, that of the Uncreated.

The smallest in the Kingdom is greater than John. And yet "his eyes will not be destroyed." This means that his vision is true as far as it goes, and should be followed. But it does not reach all the way into this new dimension. John the Baptist said as much himself: "He must increase, and I must decrease."

Once this new consciousness of Being is awakened in us, the Self must be allowed to increase and the ego must be allowed to diminish. According to Jung, this is the fundamental law of the process of individuation.

This is what Paul means by leaving more and more room for Christ within us, so that "it is no longer I who live, but Christ who lives in me." But this is accomplished through a day-to-day process whereby we continue to allow a little more light and peace to enter our lives.

LOGION 47

> Yeshua said:
> A man cannot ride two horses
> nor bend two bows.
> A servant cannot serve two masters,
> for he will honor one and disdain the other.
> No one drinks an old wine
> and then desires a new one.
> New wine is not put into old wineskins,
> for they will crack.
> Old wine is not put into new skins,
> for it will spoil.
> A patch of old cloth is not sewn
> onto a new garment,
> for it will tear.
>
> (CF. MATT 6:24, 9:17; MARK 2:21; LUKE 5:36–38, 16:13.)

The usual interpretation of this logion is simply that we cannot serve two masters: We must choose one or the other.

In the canonical gospels, this is further specified as a choice between God and money. This has been interpreted to mean that if you love money, you hate God; and if you love God, you must hate money. This interpretation has created enormous problems and has led to untold suffering. It encloses human beings in a dualistic attitude that is virtually guaranteed to lead to a "return of the repressed." Jean Cassien tells the story of a monk who gave up his considerable wealth in order to love God. Later, he became obsessively attached to a rubber eraser, so much so that he would never allow anyone else to touch it. As St. John of the Cross noted, it makes no difference whether a bird is tied with a chain or a thread—in either case, it cannot fly.

What is the way out of this either/or dualism?

What Yeshua seems to be saying here is that indeed, we cannot live in this kind of duality because we cannot love and hate at the same time. Loving God and hating anything are incompatible. What is needed is to put things in their proper places and order, to "render therefore unto

Caesar the things which be Caesar's, and unto God the things which would be God's."

But Caesar, too, has his ultimate source in God, as does money, a tool of communication and exchange that can be used for good or for evil. The important thing is not to worship money in any way, not to be dominated by it. This need not be a problem for those whose worship is only for God.

Thus we cannot live by setting one against the other and forcing ourselves to choose. It is an unbearable dualism and sooner or later will have serious consequences, which are well known in psychopathology. We must accept both, for we cannot love and loathe with one heart. We must learn to recognize the One through the duality, our only Master who can show us our way through the vast diversity and multiplicity of phenomena.

The logion goes on to say that we cannot drink both old and new wine together. They will spoil each other. Old wines and new wines each have their virtues—and we should neither oppose them nor mix them.

Tradition and innovation both have their good points. One must not be reduced to the other, for that only creates confusion. The gospels advise us to respect one principle without omitting a different principle. Two flowers of very different ages and colors can be placed harmoniously in the same vase without one eclipsing the other.

Indeed, new wine must not be put into old skins. (Experienced wine growers know that new wine will still undergo some fermentation, which can crack old barrels.) Some would go so far as to say that the new wine of the Spirit cannot remain in the old barrels of institutionalized religion. It will crack them, just as the wine of the Good News cracked the religious traditions of its day.

There is much truth to this. Surely we can find forms that are better adapted to the inspiration manifesting today without seeking at all costs to make it fit into old traditions. Our attempts have sometimes led to dreadful mixtures, but the truth is that both old and new have their own beauty and internal consistency. Again, difficulties can be avoided by not setting old and new against each other or blending them heedlessly. Drinkers of the old wine can respect new inspiration without fear of the strangeness of its words. And drinkers of the new wine can respect ancient tradition for the quality of inspiration that it has maintained through its authentic rites and practices.

This metaphor holds just as true in the realm of inner experience. When we are filled with the radically new wine of the consciousness of the Uncreated, with its infinite freedom, we should not attempt to make it fit into the categories of ordinary thought and logic. Yet this does not require any loss of respect for the value of thought and logic in their own domain.

The new-wine parable also applies to contemporary science. For example, quantum physics cannot be made to fit into the categories of Newtonian physics because its probabilistic logic is so different that it marks a discontinuity. But discontinuity does not necessitate opposition in either scientific discovery or levels of consciousness.

The Gospel of Thomas also implies that the wise know how to use both the old and the new. They are able to respect tradition without allowing it to block the radical newness of Spirit. Whatever wineskins may be used, it is important that the wine be of good quality and poured into the appropriate form so that nothing is spoiled and it retains its power to induce "sober drunkenness."

LOGION 48

> Yeshua said:
> If two make peace with each other
> in a single house,
> then they can say to the mountain: "Move!"
> And it will move.
>
> (Cf. MATT 2:25, 17:20, 18:19–20, 21:21; MARK 3:25, 11:22–23;
> LUKE 17:6; I COR 13:2.)

The power of peace is in Unity.

How could anyone thwart a human being who is in peace and in at-one-ment?

How could anyone thwart two or three who are in such complete accord?

Mountains—difficulties—recede. It is as if this atonement had support from Nature itself, from the One that is manifest in this accord.

Before we try to bring peace to others, we must begin at home and make peace with the various parts of ourselves—with our instinct, emotion, intellect, and so forth. As long as there is any division in ourselves, are not the obstacles we encounter a kind of expression of our own inner chaos?

St. Seraphim of Sarov said, "Find peace within you and a multitude will be saved alongside you." A peaceful, happy human being is a source of peace and happiness for humanity. How much more so with two or three together!

Clement of Alexandria interpreted moving mountains as a leveling of inequalities between human beings, so that true meeting is possible (cf. *Stromates*, II:11, et al.). From inner peace arises a manifestation of unity between beings, whereas the fear and envy of social divisions creates mountains between them.

In the canonical gospels it is faith that moves mountains. Yet what is faith if not the unity of mind and heart? When the "two" of intellect and emotion are united in one house, mountains can indeed be moved.

Faith is always associated with a movement of the thinking mind toward truth in an act of confidence. Faith is the total commitment of our being toward what has been recognized as true and righteous. This intimate and unqualified commitment has tremendous power as well as great lucidity. It is beyond reason, but not against it. In this clear and vivid force, what seem like mountains are revealed to be molehills.

LOGION 49

> Yeshua said:
> Blessed are you, the whole ones and the chosen ones.
> You will find the Kingdom,
> for you came from there,
> and you will return.
>
> (CF. JOHN 8:42, 16:27–28.)

Blessed and fortunate are the *monakhos*—we have translated this word as "simple" or "whole," rather than as "monks" or "those in solitude."

Solitude is only the condition of this process of unification of all our being so that we become truly undivided and *monos,* the image of the One. The monakhos are simultaneously "separate from all" and "one with all," as Evagrius Ponticus said. It is the solitude that opens into the heart of the world, that intercedes for the salvation of all beings. The monakhos seek and find the One who reigns in all and everything: the Root and the End.

To be chosen over and over again is to be open to this great wave of Life that is vibrating through us, from head to toe, from birth to death. It is to be One with Alpha and Omega.

LOGION 50

> Yeshua said:
> If they ask you from where you come,
> say:
> We were born of the Light,
> there where Light is born of Light.
> It holds true
> and is revealed within their image.
> If they ask you who you are,
> say:
> We are its children,
> the beloved of the Father, the Living One.
> If they ask you what is the sign of the Father in you,
> say:
> It is movement and it is repose.
>
> (CF. MATT 21:3; LUKE 1:7, 16:8, 17:10; JOHN 3:8, 8:14, 12:36;
> EPH 5:8; I THESS 5:5; ROM 9:26.)

In a famous conversation[20] with the philosopher Motovilov, who came to visit him in his hermitage, St. Seraphim said that gnosis is an experience of light. But his discourse was not about the nature of light; it was about participation in its uncreated radiance.

For St. Gregory Palamas and the monks of Mount Athos, the very goal of Christian life is the experience of the uncreated Light. They relate it to the stories of the burning bush, Mount Tabor, and the day of Resurrection. "It holds true," the logion tells us, like the inner meaning of Easter morning. This recalls a passage from the Chandogya Upanishad (III, 13, 7): "The light which shines from beyond the sky, beyond the highest of the highest worlds, beyond everything that is, is in truth the same light that shines inside human beingness."

The ancient triple question "Where do I come from? Where am I going? Who am I?" finds an unequivocal response in this logion. You

---

20. [An account of the full conversation and related information can be found at www.orthodoxinfo.com. —*Trans.*]

come from the Light, you are going toward the Light, you are the Light. This is the reality of the Living Son in us, who abides in the very heart of changing appearances.

The sign of our link with this luminous Reality is "movement and . . . repose." This is a union of opposites, the resolution of the seeming contradiction between action and contemplation: calmness within action and vitality within repose.

LOGION 51

> His disciples said to him:
> "When will the dead be at rest?"
> "When will the new world come?"
> He answered them:
> What you are waiting for has already come,
> but you do not see it.
>
> (CF. NUM 11:10; MATT 24:42; LUKE 17:20–21; JOHN 5:25; ACTS
> 14:13; ROM 8:19.)

We hear an echo of this logion in the Treatise on the Resurrection, another gnostic scripture found at Nag Hammadi: "Flee all divisions and all bonds, and you are already in the Resurrection . . . Why do you not consider yourself as resurrected now?"

What we have been waiting for, the peace and fullness we yearn for, is already here. It is not something that will come someday, someplace; it is always here and now.

In the Gospel of John, Yeshua reminds his disciples that whoever believes in eternal life does not relegate it to the future tense. Eternal life is in the very heart of this life. It is the uncreated dimension of our present life, which cannot die. To look for it elsewhere is to depart from it.

The Gospel of Philip says: "Those who say that the Lord died and then was resurrected are wrong; for he was first resurrected and then died." Yeshua had awakened to the Eternal Life within him. For us today, to be resurrected is to abide consciously in this dimension of boundless depth and love that neither death nor life can take away from us.

It is the end of all expectation—not in the sense of indifference or hopelessness, but in the direct knowledge that everything is infinitely given to us in every instant.

LOGION 52

> His disciples said to him:
> "Twenty-four prophets have spoken in Israel,
> and they all spoke of you."
> He said to them:
> You have disregarded the Living One
> who is in your presence,
> and you have spoken of the dead.
>
> (CF. NUM 3:12; DEUT 18:15; MATT 8:22; MARK 12:27; LUKE 1:70;
> JOHN 1:45, 8:53; ACTS 4:4; ROM 16:25.)

The fourth book of Esdras (14:44) says that the twenty-four books are considered the only ones of the ninety-four that are accessible to all and can be read in synagogues. The other seventy books are reserved for the sages. Revelation 4:4 speaks of twenty-four elders. We might be tempted to consider the possibility of a mythic transposition of the twenty-four divine zodiacal archetypes of Babylon, which ruled the cycles of the years.

In any case, in the Gospel of Thomas (and in quite different kinds of gnostic texts as well, such as the Pistis Sophia), neither prophets nor archons retain their usual primacy. What Yeshua has come to reveal is a dimension within us that is beyond time, beyond the twenty-four hours, beyond the recorded words of the twenty-four prophets of the past—a dimension that we are all too inclined to overlook. We ignore the Living One and persist in harboring trust in that which by its very nature is perishable and corruptible.

Another meaning of this logion is suggested by words from John 5:39: "You search the scriptures because you think that in them you have eternal life; yet it is they that bear witness to me." The "me" that is spoken of here is not the existential *me* of the historical person known as Jesus of Nazareth. It is the essential I of Logos, the Creative Intelligence that holds together all things and that can be witnessed just as much in the book of nature as in the books of scripture. The intent of sacred scripture is not to distract and burden our minds with all sorts of debates and interpretations, but rather to help us open to the One who is alive in us here and now.

There is a point beyond which referral to the authority of sacred tradition, of others' words, becomes merely a way of avoiding direct experience ourselves. My friend's insight cannot help me if I do not open my own eyes. The words of the greatest prophets and seers are useful only if they help us to learn to see. If we repeat their words without living them, the words die. As it says in II Corinthians, "[T]he letter kills, but the Spirit gives life."

LOGION 53

> His disciples asked him:
> "Is circumcision useful or not?"
> He replied:
> If it were useful, fathers would engender sons born circumcised
> from their mothers.
> Rather, it is the circumcision in spirit that is truly useful.
>
> (CF. JOHN 4:24; ROM 2:25–29; I COR 7:19; GAL 5:6; COL 2:11.)

For pious Jews, circumcision was the inscription in living flesh of man's covenant with God. It symbolized the truth that everything that lives and gives life belongs to God. But what good is such an outer sign of alliance without the participation of the heart? It can become degraded into a mere badge of belonging to an ethnic group and thereby no longer a sign of belonging to the One God.

The spiritual circumcision of which Yeshua speaks is related not to the foreskin, but to the ego. It is this ego, with its old skin of concepts and habits, that is to be circumcised. The Sacred Embrace with the Living One will then become deep and uncontaminated. This purity of heart and spirit in the ego's silence is the true circumcision, the true sign of covenant and Union. It is not merely a return to what is "natural," but a return to our true nature as well.

The fourteenth-century Indian poet Kabir, born in a Muslim milieu, echoes this logion when he remonstrates those who observe merely the outer form of the law:

> *So sure of your righteousness, you practice circumcision;*
> *But I do not agree with you, my brothers!*
> *If God wanted me circumcised,*
> *Could he not do it himself?*

LOGION 54

Blessed are you, the poor,
for yours is the Kingdom of Heaven.

(CF. MATT 5:3; LUKE 6:20; JOHN 2:5.)

We find this same saying in Matthew and in Luke.

It would seem that for Yeshua of Nazareth, poverty is the necessary condition in order for the Spirit of God to reign in us and in order for heaven to have a place on earth. To have the mind-set of the rich is to believe that we deserve the best and that it can be bought, but this completely misses the Essential. True happiness and true love can never be bought. In contrast to this, to be poor in spirit is to know that we deserve nothing and that everything we receive is a gift. The slightest smile that cheers, the least sunbeam that shines is received with gratitude, as a flash of the Kingdom.

Meister Eckhart often commented on poverty, pointing out that this beatitude renders us pure, empty, and capable of receiving God. A human being who is totally poor, totally empty, cannot but be fulfilled. In one of his sermons he says: "When God finds you ready and empty, he must act and fill you to overflowing with himself, just as sunlight must flood and fill the clear, pure air. He cannot fail to do this when he finds you so empty and bare." In another sermon he says, "The poor one perceives nothing, knows nothing, has nothing." Of course, this does not refer to some unconscious or unfeeling state, but rather to one in which we are totally free of our knowledge, possessions, and desires.

This detachment or freedom from the objects of creation allows us both to experience divine love and to discover our uncreated essence. Poverty-stricken in willfulness, in knowing, and in possessing, I hold to the Root and know myself as "cause of myself according to my eternal being and not according to what I become, which is temporal. This is why I was never born and, in accord with my unborn nature, can never die."[21]

---

21. Quotes from Meister Eckhart, respectively, from the Sermons: *Et cum factus esset Jesus* and *Beati pauperes spiritu.*

LOGION 55

Yeshua said:

Whoever cannot free themselves from their father and their
   mother
cannot become my disciple.
Whoever cannot free themselves from their brother and sister
and does not bear their cross as I do
is not worthy of me.

(CF. MATT 10:37–38; LUKE 14:26–27; MARK 8:34–35.)

Yeshua's invitation is one of freedom with respect to our father and mother and their desires, thoughts, and social conditioning. It also means being free from our brothers and sisters, our peers, and all the related judgments and customs of the surrounding society. This is obviously no small matter, yet it is the only way we can become who we truly are. Just as physical autonomy cannot begin without cutting the umbilical cord, psychic and even spiritual autonomy cannot begin without a kind of cut.

We must acknowledge what has nourished us. Yet we must go further and "bear our cross"—that is, accept and face ourselves in our full dimensions, the horizontal and the vertical, "[t]hat you may have the power to comprehend with all the saints what is the breadth, length, height, and depth, and to know the love of Christ which surpasses all knowledge," as Paul said in his letter to the Ephesians.

Some of the early patristic writings also speak of the cross as the "great book of the art of love," the open book of a realized human being who loves without boundaries, with "a love stronger than death." This open book of Love and Freedom transforms all events of everyday life. Everything is fuel for its fire, which transforms even rubbish and filth into living light.

The first step on this road is freedom with respect to our family, peers, and society.

LOGION 56

Yeshua said:
Whoever knows the world
discovers a corpse.
And whoever discovers a corpse
cannot be contained by the world.

(CF. JOHN 1:10, 3:1; HEB 11:38.)

What is an inanimate body—a body without *anima,* or soul—if not a corpse? When the informing principle withdraws from a body, it no longer lives as a whole and quickly decomposes.

To seek to know a body, a system, or a world without contact with the soul that informs it and gives it its unity and wholeness is, sooner or later, to find ourselves with a corpse. It is to discover the nonexistence of the world in and of itself. As the prologue to the Gospel of John says, without the Logos, the Creative Intelligence, *nihil,* nothing.

Meister Eckhart was condemned for saying openly what the gospels say implicitly: "All creatures are pure nothingness; I am not saying that they are minuscule, for that would make them something: They are pure nothingness." This may seem radical, but it is actually another way of expressing the completely Orthodox doctrine that no relative existence is real in itself; it has reality only through its participation in Absolute Being.

In short: No soul, no body—or rather, a body without a soul is only a decomposing corpse.

This is not a melancholy teaching. When we recognize our nothingness we thereby discover the Source of who we really are. Consciously dissolved in it, we can say: "No other being but Him" or "I am That" or, with Yeshua the Christ, "Before Abraham was, I am." Time and space cannot contain who we really are. Only I AM can contain it.

LOGION 57

Yeshua said:
The Kingdom of the Father is like the man
who had some good seed.
His enemy came at night and sowed weeds
among the good seed.
The man would not allow them to pull up the weeds,
saying, "I fear you might pull up the wheat as well."
Indeed, at harvesttime, the weeds will be conspicuous.
They will be pulled up and burned.

(CF. MATT 13:24–43.)

The very attempt to deal with evil typically stirs up strife in us and among us. What Yeshua teaches here is a nondualistic attitude with regard to evil. Do not try to exterminate it, because you may harm the good seed at the same time. Who can judge? Often good and evil are thoroughly intermixed.

It is not good for any of us to be aggressive and violent—yet we must avoid aggression toward these attributes in ourselves, for that can vitiate our own energy. The power they contain can indeed be used to attack someone, yet it can also help someone to carry a burden. That powerful energy can be used either to attack someone or to help someone carry a burden.

It is not good for any of us to be hypocritical—yet we must not cripple our intelligence and subtlety of mind in an effort to attack our own hypocrisy, for such finesse can be used to deceive someone, but it can also be used to enlighten.

We must accept this primordial ambiguity in ourselves. What matters is our heartfelt attitude. This will determine which of our acts are encouraged to grow and mature: those of the good seed or those of the bad. The most important thing is to shower everything, good and bad, with intelligence and kindness. All that is problematic can then be dealt with easily at harvesttime, or maturity. Our frowns and sneers will then melt away in the beauty of our countenance.

INNER TRADITIONS

BEAR & CO.

BEAR CUB BOOKS

HEALING · ARTS · PRESS

DESTINY BOOKS

Park Street Press

BINDU BOOKS

Inner Traditions • Bear & Company

P.O. Box 388
Rochester, VT 05767-0388
U.S.A.

Affix
Postage
Stamp
Here

PLEASE SEND US THIS CARD TO RECEIVE OUR LATEST CATALOG.

Book in which this card was found _____

☐ Check here if you would like to receive our catalog via e-mail.

Name _____ Company _____

Address _____ Phone _____

City _____ State _____ Zip _____ Country _____

E-mail address _____

Please check the following area(s) of interest to you:

☐ Health   ☐ Self-help   ☐ Science/Nature   ☐ Shamanism

☐ Ancient Mysteries   ☐ New Age/Spirituality   ☐ Ethnobotany   ☐ Martial Arts

☐ Spanish Language   ☐ Sexuality/Tantra   ☐ Children   ☐ Teen

Please send a catalog to my friend:

Name _____ Company _____

Address _____ Phone _____

City _____ State _____ Zip _____ Country _____

Order at 1-800-246-8648 • Fax (802) 767-3726

E-mail: customerservice@InnerTraditions.com • Web site: www.InnerTraditions.com

LOGION 58

> Yeshua said:
> Blessed are those who have undergone ordeals.
> They have entered into life.

(CF. PSALMS 33:19; JAMES 1:12; I PETER 3:14.)

Popular wisdom agrees that people who have never suffered are lacking in maturity; there is a dimension of life that "they wouldn't understand." For those who are committed to the path of self-knowledge, trials and difficulties are teachings. Suffering is accepted, but with neither resignation nor complicity. In this way, ordeals can serve as aids to enlightenment and gnosis. Absurdity, pain, illness, solitude, death—sooner or later we will meet them all. Yet it is possible to completely accept and transcend them. Life is to be sought and discovered in every circumstance. Our suffering can be authentically shared and understood only by those who have also passed through the experience of suffering. Without this shared experience, their reassurances are hollow and it is better that they remain silent when faced with someone in agony. If we really want to offer someone who is suffering a transfusion of peace and serenity, the best we can do is to be in touch with that in ourselves which is already beyond death.

LOGION 59

> Yeshua said:
> Look to the Living One
> while you are alive.
> If you wait until you are dead,
> you will search for the vision in vain.

> (CF. JOHN 6:50, 8:21, 12:21, 16:16.)

Dostoyevsky said, "Love life more than the meaning of life!" Only through intense, unconditional love of life will its meaning be revealed. We must take full advantage of this space-time in which we find ourselves. Relative and unsatisfying though it is, it is still our only chance to experience the Living One. We must not wait for death to show us how we have been ignoring and missing life. We are born to die, but more important, we are born to live. This clearly demands courage—yet what greater encouragement is there to live fully than knowing the Living One?

LOGION 60

> They saw a Samaritan carrying a lamb,
> entering into Judea.
> He said to his disciples:
> What will the man do with the lamb?
> They answered:
> "He will kill it and eat it."
> He told them:
> As long as it is alive, he will not eat it,
> but only if he kills it and it becomes a cadaver.
> They said: "He cannot do otherwise."
> He told them:
> Seek a place in Repose.
> Do not become cadavers,
> lest you be eaten.
>
> (CF. REV 5:6; HEB 12:2.)

The lamb symbolizes innocence, vulnerability, the gift of ourselves, and the power of love. How can we protect the life of this lamb and keep from killing it in ourselves? The cadaver of the lamb is the hardened heart, the stagnant persona that lacks innocent repose, purity of heart, and the invincible force of humility.

To avoid becoming a cadaver to be eaten means to keep ourselves free and open to the Essential, rather than caught up in the rewards of doing and possessing. It means protecting our freedom to be.

The lamb here is the Passover lamb, the lamb who is the passerby . . . living our migratory being to its fullest.

LOGION 61

Yeshua said:
Two will lie on a single bed.
One will die, the other will live.
Salome asked him:
"Who are you, Sir?
Where do you come from, you who
lie on my bed and eat at my table?"
Yeshua replied:
I come from the One who is Openness.
What comes from my Father has been given to me.
Salome answered:
"I am your disciple."
Yeshua told her:
That is why I say that when disciples are open,
they are filled with light.
When they are divided,
they are filled with darkness.

(CF. MATT 24:40–41; LUKE 17:34.)

As long as there are two in bed, the two have not become One. If this persists over time, one of them will begin to dominate the other. "One will die, the other will live." It is a dualism that implies a relationship based on power of one sort or another, both in and out of bed. Two who are One in bed recognize the Presence of Being that is the source of each of them, in all their otherness.

Salome is the intimate friend of Yeshua and the initiate also spoken of in the Pistis Sophia. During a time when Yeshua lies on her bed and eats at her table, she asks him who he is, where he comes from, and what is the origin of his communion.

He answers:

I come from the One who is Openness.

Rilke once said that Openness is the least blasphemous name for God. It is the name that is the least defining and qualifying. Openness is the infinite Space within the very heart of space, containing all and contained by nothing.

The whole process of human transformation is one of opening on all levels: the physical (release of stress), the psychic (unraveling the knots of memory), and the spiritual (allowing love, light, and forgiveness to live and radiate in us). The goal of this transformation is to dwell in Openness, where the body is open to the energies of the cosmos, the heart is open to a deep compassion, and the mind is as clear as a mirror, serenely reflecting the multitude of appearances.

A totally open human being is not formless, but is instead capable of allowing the One to manifest. The Unity of all things then becomes manifest in and through that human form. As long as there is any fear, constriction, closure, division of the heart, or dualism, the light cannot enter. We can close the shutters on all the windows of the house, which is so much the worse for the air inside, yet the sun goes on shining.

> Salome answered:
> "I am your disciple."

She has made herself the abode of Openness, a house that welcomes the breeze, a body that has become transparent, like a crystal flooded with light.

LOGION 62

> Yeshua said:
> I reveal my mysteries
> to those who become worthy.
> Do not let your left hand know
> what your right hand is doing.
>
> (CF. MATT 6:3–4, 13:10-11; MARK 4:10–12; LUKE 8:9–10.)

God gives to each according to his or her capacity to receive. The process of opening to higher consciousness really means becoming more and more *capax Dei,* capable of God, receptive to the clear light—in other words, worthy of the mysteries.

Thus the left hand must not know what the right hand is doing. It must not harbor memories or attachments to the fruits of this divine Action. Only in this way can it remain open and able to feel, in its naked palm, the freshness of the present moment.

LOGION 63

> Yeshua said:
> There was once a rich man with a great amount of money
> who said: "I will use my money for sowing,
> reaping, planting, and filling my silos with grain
> so that I will never lack for anything."
> Such was the thought of his heart.
> Yet that night, he died.
> Those who have ears,
> Let them hear!
>
> (CF. LUKE 12:16–21; JOHN 4:12; I COR 14:25.)

Seeking security, accumulating and holding on to wealth, whether in material form or in the form of power and achievement—none of this ever gives us true security. It can all disappear in an instant. Impermanence and death have dominion over the best-laid plans.

Our deepest longing is infinite, and only the Infinite can satisfy it. Finite substitutes, even when we are successful in attaining them, only intensify our pain of lack. The deeper lesson of this logion is that we must fully accept this deficit, this longing, this void in ourselves. What is more, we must keep it open, like a great window through which the unknown can enter and penetrate the very heart of our darkness.

Those who live with this window wide open can no longer be robbed by death, for they have already given everything.

LOGION 64

Yeshua said:

There was a man who invited some visitors. After preparing
the meal, he sent his servant

to summon the guests.

The servant went to the first one and said "My master invites
you."

The man answered: "I have business with some merchants who
are arriving this evening. Please excuse me from the dinner."

The servant went to the next one and said "My master invites
you."

The man answered: "I have just bought a house and need one
day more, so I cannot come."

The servant went to another guest and said "My master invites
you."

The man answered: "My friend is getting married and I must
prepare the food. Excuse me."

The servant returned to his master and said:

"Those you have invited to dinner cannot come."

His master replied:

"Then go out on the roads and invite whoever you find
to dine with me.

Buyers and merchants will not enter my Father's dwelling."

(Cf. Matt 22:1–10; Luke 14:15–24; Mark 11:15–17; John 2:14.)

As with all scriptural writings, this parable can be read on at least two levels: a literal/factual level and a psychic or "psychological" level.[22] On the
literal level it is simply a story of invited guests who were all unable to
come to dinner because of seemingly valid reasons. The disappointed host
then generously opens his doors to feed anyone who happens to be passing by.

But on a deeper level, it is the story of lack of interest and lack of love

---

22. [Throughout his writings, the author uses the word *psychic* in its original sense, referring to the *psyche*, or soul. Not to be confused with *pneuma*, or spirit, it is the intermedi-
ary realm between physical and spiritual reality and includes everything that we now call
psychology. —Trans.]

in response to a supremely important invitation. The ingenious human mind always finds the best excuses to justify not answering the inner call. Invited to our own wedding, the union of the created and the Uncreated in us, we find that we have more important things to do. We are so busy, so preoccupied with our tasks. Who will deliver us from this cold war that we have declared upon ourselves?

In order to rediscover the authentic Self, the busy doer-ego must halt. It must take a *vacation* in the original sense of the word: "create vacancy."

The first step is to rediscover our desire for the Essential. What do we truly want most? What do we want our life to be about? This questioning can begin to re-set our priorities.

Then, with maturity, we simply stop fabricating excuses and justifications. We become responsible for our acts—able to respond to both our refusals and our enthusiasms. And we no longer give in to the temptation to blame others—spouses, friends, enemies—for our lack of desire and availability.

Beyond these levels of interpretation, a more metaphysical reading is possible. These buyers and merchants who cannot enter into the house of the Father are the hyperactive, acquisitive mind. As with love and happiness, truth and freedom can never be bought—nor can they be possessed. Truth and freedom are from a higher order of reality than possession can comprehend.

Meister Eckhart pointed out that this "merchant" mentality even leads people to try to bargain with God. To them, God is like a divine milk cow who will take care of their needs and desires.

God (symbolized as the Father in the language of this logion) cannot be approached in this way. He is free, the very essence of gratuity. He resists any attempt at possession or attainment on our part and is immune to our manipulations. Yet he gives himself totally to those whose minds are unassuming, accessible, uncalculating, and neither grasping nor expecting. Those who are not seeking peace and fulfillment (symbolized by the passersby on the road) will receive it in abundance and enter into the abode of the Father. Variously translated as "dwelling," "house," or "abode," this is a term also used in the Gospel of John. It is the place of the Source of Life.

This logion reminds us again that those who are empty, open, without preoccupation, and attentive to the Presence are in touch with earth and with heaven. They abide in the origin of both, and the Father manifests through them as through the Son.

LOGION 65

Yeshua said:
A good man had a vineyard,
which he gave to tenants to work
and harvest the fruit for him.
He sent his servant to collect the fruit of the vine.
The tenants seized the servant
and beat him nearly to death.
The servant reported this to his master, who thought:
"Perhaps they didn't recognize him."
And he sent another servant, who was also beaten.
Then the master sent his own son,
thinking: "Perhaps they will treat him with respect."
When the tenants realized that he was the inheritor of the
    vineyard,
they seized him and killed him.
Those who have ears,
Let them hear!

(CF. MATT 21:33–41; MARK 12:1–9; LUKE 20:9–16; ISAIAH 5:1–2.)

The standard interpretation of this well-known parable is that God has planted his "vine" in this world in the form of his servants, the sages and prophets, but people refuse to respect them or listen to their message.

But in addition to his servants, he sends his son, a holy one who incarnates the Presence, Image, and Likeness of the Father in the heart of this space-time. The drama of the killing of the son is the killing of the Christ in ourselves. It is the same madness, the same murder: stifling the likeness of God, or Love, in ourselves and preventing the vine of the Living One from offering its fruit.

LOGION 66

Yeshua said:
Show me the stone rejected by the builders.
That is the cornerstone.

(CF. MATT 21:42-43; MARK 12:10–11; LUKE 20:17–18.)

Can a society be built without Love or, in another term, without God? Can it hold together without this cornerstone?

Such a society holds together through common interests but collapses through special interests.

Love has been excluded from our theories of economics, as well as from our educational curricula. Sometimes people even exclude it from their lives. We can exist without love, without God. But what is such an existence worth?

In our own life we must look deeply enough to examine honestly what we have habitually rejected from the edifice of our personality. Might it be a certain desire, a certain longing, or even an experience of hell?

The rejected cornerstone can be hidden in the most surprising places. Sometimes our wholeness wells up from the very heart of what we have repressed.

LOGION 67

> Yeshua said:
> Those who know the All
> yet do not know themselves
> are deprived of everything.

(CF. MATT 16:26; MARK 8:36; LUKE 9:25.)

What good is it to own the entire universe and lose our own soul?

What is the value of the greatest knowledge if it knows not the agency of knowing? Vast knowledge without inner transformation is an illusion. It is mere show.

Job himself exclaimed to God: "I knew you only by hearsay. Now I know you in my flesh; my eyes have seen you!" To move from hearsay to realization is to pass from words and beliefs to wholeness in action, to make the outer and the inner as one.

This self-knowledge, so fundamental to the Gospel of Thomas, has nothing to do with self-analysis or narcissistic introspection. It is a process of keenly observing our reactions and emotions without judging or explaining them. In this attentive regard, neutral and compassionate, we discover what is and who we are.

LOGION 68

Yeshua said:
Blessed are you when they hate you
and persecute you.
There is a place where you are not persecuted
that they will never find.

(CF. MATT 5:11; LUKE 6:22; JOHN 13:33.)

In every human being there is a place that hatred and persecution can never reach: the Self, the uncreated Being beyond the identification of "I" as suffering victim. This is the space of inalienable freedom that empowers us to say, with Christ, "My life cannot be taken, for I have already given it"—or the famous words: "Forgive them, for they know not what they do."

Blame and persecution may even be considered beatitudes, inasmuch as they awaken in us an authentic Love for our enemies, putting us in touch with that freedom which no circumstance can ever affect.

This is the place of Repose, the abode of God.

LOGION 69

> Yeshua said:
> Blessed are those
> who have been persecuted in their hearts,
> for they have known the Father in Truth.
> Blessed are those who are hungry,
> for they will be fulfilled.
>
> (Cf. MATT 5:6; LUKE 6:22; JOHN 4:23–24, 10:15, 14:7.)

Those who have experienced a persecution so cruel that it breaks the heart know that loving our enemies is neither simple nor natural. It belongs to a higher order of nature. Those who have truly known the transcendent Source know that only It can engender such an attitude.

Blessed also are those who are not satisfied with themselves. They are hungry because they refuse to live superficially and they make use of difficulties to go deeper. They will receive a food worthy of their hunger and drink from a spring worthy of their thirst.

LOGION 70

Yeshua said:
When you bring forth *that* within you,
then *that* will save you.
If you do not,
then *that* will kill you.

(CF. MATT 13:12; MARK 4:25; LUKE 8:18, 19:26.)

In the canonical gospels, after the parable of the talents, it is written: "To him who has, more will be given; to him who has not, even what he has will be taken away." (Cf. the commentary on logion 41, page 128.)

In this logion, Love or Being is the mysterious *that*, the thing that can save us or kill us, according to whether we bring it forth or neglect it. Without it, all is desolation.

Another reading interprets *that* as gnosis—without it, the universe remains radically alien and incomprehensible.

It is true that things seem to be given in unreasonable abundance to those who live in love and gnosis, for they are able to marvel at the vast richness in the tiniest manifestation of being. To those who lack love and self-knowledge, however, life sooner or later becomes stale and depleted. Even what they have will be taken away.

LOGION 71

> Yeshua said:
> I will overturn this house
> and none will be able to rebuild it.
>
> (CF. MATT 26:61, 27:40; MARK 14:58; JOHN 2:19; ACTS 6:14;
> JOB 12:14.)

What is the house, or edifice, that is to be overturned?

"Destroy this temple, and in three days I will raise it up" is attributed to Yeshua in the Gospel of John. Some would be tempted to mix this passage with this logion and interpret the "house" as referring to his body and its overturning as symbolizing the Resurrection's power over form and matter. But the "house" in this logion actually refers to the psychic and mental constructions whose vanity the Christ reveals.

All that is constructed will be deconstructed. Once we have experienced this truth directly, we no longer worry about what part of us will remain or not remain after death.

All the constructions of our minds, our concepts and our dreams, are bound to be overturned. What always abides is this Awakening, this pure I Am, which nothing can deconstruct because it was never constructed.

LOGION 72

> A man said to him:
> "Speak to my brothers,
> that they may share with me
> my father's property."
> Yeshua answered him:
> Who made me into a divider?
> Turning to his disciples,
> he said:
> Who am I, to divide?
>
> (CF. GEN 19:9; EX 2:14; MATT 12:25–26; LUKE 2:49, 10:23,
> 12:13–15.)

This man would like to reduce Yeshua to his own level of dualistic consciousness and induce him to take sides. But Yeshua is consistent with his teaching about the trap of judgment and he refuses to become an arbiter in this family dispute.

This radical nonjudgmental quality is one of his most striking characteristics and often angers and perplexes those who follow him. He dines with Nicodemus, the Pharisee, and visits with Matthew, the tax collector. His followers include both virgins and prostitutes.

It is the essence of individuals that always seems to interest Yeshua, not the labels and reputations that others give them. Where others see a whore, he sees a woman who is a human being. Refusing to take one side against the other, his engagement is of another order entirely, one that is beyond duality. "When you make the two into One" (see logion 22), then what belongs to you belongs to the All and to the Other. Here, the notion of "private property" becomes privation of the Other.

In this logion a *divider* means one who breaks wholeness into a multiplicity of fragments and factions. There is a radically different meaning of *division:* "a multiplication, where each receives his or her due." There is a different meaning of *sharing* that renders unto each his or her due. It is symbolized in the story of the multiplication of loaves, an abundance that engenders unity among people.

Yeshua has come into the world not to take sides in its conflicts, but to expose the nature of conflict so that in facing their differences, people may begin to respect Otherness and to discover the good of complement and communion.

LOGION 73

> Yeshua said:
> The harvest is abundant
> but the workers are few.
> Pray the Master to send
> more workers to the harvest.
>
> (CF. MATT 9:37–38; LUKE 10:2.)

Harvest is the time of ripening, when the wheat yields its grain and the vine its grapes. To assist the harvest in a spiritual sense is to work to help the divine seed, already planted in everyone, to have a good chance to grow, ripen, and bear its fruit of light.

The field to be cultivated is immense. All human beings bear within them a grain of mustard whose calling is to become a great tree, a spark that longs to be fanned into a blazing fire. What is lacking is workers, men and women who are able to cultivate this field of consciousness so that the fruit of Awakening can come to harvest.

To pray the Master to send more workers to the harvest is to ask God for holy ones who remind people what is really happening in their field of consciousness, what is sprouting and growing in the depths.

It is also to ask the Master for the strength and insight to be a worker in our own field, so that the embryo of the divine in us can develop toward the day when we emerge from the womb of space-time and awaken to the Light of the Uncreated.

LOGION 74

> The Master said:
> There are many who stand round the well,
> but no one to go down into it.

Origen quotes this saying of Yeshua in his *Contra Celse* (VIII, 15–16). Indeed, many people hang about, staring into the well, speaking of its springs, imagining how its waters taste. But words do nothing for their thirst!

There are very few who are prepared to descend or to dig. Yet, as Meister Eckhart often reminds us, "the Spring is always there." In order to drink from it, we must forget all our talk about it from the time when we were bystanders and be prepared to descend into the depths of our earth and clear away the excess dirt so that it can gush forth and fill the well.

We descend each day and dig according to the measure of our thirst, drinking from our own well, refreshing our face with its waters.

LOGION 75

Yeshua said:
Many are standing by the door,
but only those who are alone and simple [*monakhos*]
can enter the bridal chamber.

(CF. MATT 9:15, 12:46–47; MARK 2:19; LUKE 5:34; JOHN 3:29, 18:16.)

Just as in the previous logion, there are many bystanders who speak, preach, and dream of love. But few of them really go through the door and begin to love truly and completely.

It is those who are alone and simple who enter the bridal chamber, because the unity they have realized and the solitude they have embraced have made them capable of meeting the Other as Other, without circumscribing them by their own lacks and desires. Only they truly know the meaning of the wedding.

Communion among two or more of such *monakhoi* is like the flow of water through a network of underground channels connecting each spring intimately with the others while the brims of the individual wells remain distant from one another. Thus the wells are united in their depths and in their fullness. This is a symbol of Union without separation or confusion.

This logion also suggests that among those who stand before the door to the Kingdom, the few who go through are those who have experienced their solitude fully so that they manifest simplicity, transparence, and the peace of essential Being. Only they will know the bridal chamber of the wedding of Created and Uncreated, of God and Human, the Union without separation or confusion.

LOGION 76

The Kingdom of the Father
is like the merchant
who had a load of goods to sell.
Then he saw a pearl.
The merchant was wise
and sold his goods to buy the pearl.
You too should pursue
that treasure which is everlasting,
there where moths never go
nor worms devour.

(CF. MATT 13:45–46; LUKE 12:33–34; MARK 9:48; JOHN 6:27;
ACTS 12:23.)

In many gnostic texts (see the Gospel of Philip), the pearl is used as a symbol of the Self or uncreated Being. This may derive from Iranian gnostic teachings, for the Persian word *gowhar* means both "precious stone" and "quintessence."

One of the pearl's characteristics is that it is filled with light but also reflects it. In the beginning, in Paradise, a human being was a pearl, filled with light inside and outside. Thus the pearl also signifies the state of grace to which we can return through love and gnosis. Even legends of the miracles of the saints attest to the transformation of bodily matter into a pearl.

To rediscover our own pearl, we must know how to let go of all that is superficial and nonessential. Again, it is a question of abandoning our calculating, bargaining tendencies, for the tiny and insignificant thing that we have been ignoring may turn out to be the real treasure.

Where our treasure is placed, there is our heart placed. If it is in the realm of the perishable, the worm and the moth will find it. If it is in the uncreated Essence, it will remain as it is.

Here is a possible extension of this parable, illustrating the wisdom of the merchant's choice:

As a merchant was sailing home, a violent storm arose and sank the ship. Those aboard escaped with their lives, but all their merchandise was destroyed. Yet the wise merchant still had his precious pearl, which was hanging on its necklace beneath his shirt.

When your pearl, the treasure of the Self, is kept safely in the locket of your heart, what can you lose, even in the ultimate shipwreck?

LOGION 77

> Yeshua said:
> I am the Light
> that shines on everyone.
> I am the All.
> The All came forth from me
> and the All came into me.
> Split the wood, and I am there.
> Turn over the stone,
> and there you will find me.
>
> (Cf. John 3:31, 8:12; Eph 4:6; II Thess 2:4; Isaiah 55:11;
> Rom 11:36; I Cor 8:6.)

When Yeshua says "I am the All," he refers to the fact that he manifests in himself the integration of all polarities and opposites. He incarnates the union of the human and the divine, the finite and the infinite, time and eternity.

We might say that the Christ takes on all human faces, none of which is alien to him. He has manifested the face of human transfiguration and that of human disfiguration. He has been the sage who speaks from the mountaintop, the slave, and the sheep being led to slaughter. He shows the face of the most dazzling light and the face of the deepest darkness, the face of suffering and the face of beatitude. He has passed through all states of human beingness, including death.

Thus when he says "I am the All," he does not mean some outer (and rather vague) totality, but rather the power of integration of all polarities contained in humanity and in the cosmos, or *pleroma* (a Greek word, sometimes translated as "fullness" and often used by gnostics, as well as by Paul and John in the canonical gospels). Nothing is to be excluded, but everything is to be *transfigured*, integrated—even the absurd, evil, and death. This is shown in the story of the Christ.

In psychological terms we may say that the Christ is alive in us when we are totally ourselves, excluding nothing of what we are. It is when we are no longer fragmented, no longer made up of more or less well-chosen parts sewn imperfectly together.

The moments of direct experience of Being are moments of totality when we are free of the fragmentary aspect of time. This is the eternal Now.

There are two very different ways of reading the last lines of this logion. A moralistic interpretation might be summed up thus: "Split the wood and lift heavy stones, but know that I am beside you in this work." This was the interpretation of the famous German biblical scholar Joachim Jeremias (*Les Paroles inconnues de Jésus* [Paris: Éditions du Cerf, 1970], 105):

> For a disciple of Jesus, work is not a danger, a burden, nor a hardship, but the very presence of the Lord! "You will find me when you break up stones, and I am there while you split the wood." In Matthew 18:20 Jesus promises to come to those who pray in his name; here, he promises to come to those who do hard work in his name.

In contrast to this, a metaphysical interpretation of the logion is that all things participate in the very essence of Being, according to their mode and degree. We could say of the creative Intelligence: It flowers as a tree in springtime, it is heavy as a stone, it sings as a bird, and it becomes conscious of itself as a human being. The Christ, or *theanthropos,*[23] here remembers and evokes the different stages of existence of the Cosmos. It is in this sense that he can say, "I am the All." This cosmic Presence of the logos, or the "All in All," as Paul would say, has too often been ignored in Western Christianity for fear of pantheism.

This interpretation of the logion certainly implies no worshipping of stone or wood, but it does recognize the immanence of the Living One in everything that exists. As St. Francis said, "Brother Sun, sister Moon . . ."

---

23. [The Greek *theos* + *anthropos* means the union of the human and divine within us and is seen here and in logion 81 as a higher stage of evolution. In logion 81, it is analogous to the butterfly that is transformed from a caterpillar. —*Trans.*]

LOGION 78

Yeshua said:

Why do you roam the countryside?

To see some reeds shaken by the wind?

To see people like your kings and courtiers

in elegant clothes?

They wear fine clothes,

but they cannot know the truth.

(CF. ISAIAH 24:21; MATT 11:7–8, 20:25; LUKE 24–25; JOHN 8:32;
ACTS 12:21; REV 6:15.)

The first question in this logion is "Why do you roam the countryside?"
The Kingdom is not to be found in any place.

Second in the logion is the assertion that we may be deceived by the
dazzling appearance of those who wear fine clothes. We should seek
beings who are naked, not those dressed in impressive personas. Yeshua is
the naked man, the one who is not playing some role. But even so, our
tendency is to make him into a great personality, an idol.

The truth—*aletheia* in Greek, meaning "non-forgetting"—is a
process of unveiling. It requires us to put aside our illusions, our dress-up
games with the Self. If we are naked in the presence of Love, how can we
fear the cold?

LOGION 79

> A woman in the crowd said to him:
> "Blessed are the womb that bore you
> and the breasts that nursed you!"
> He answered:
> Blessed are those who listen
> to the Word of the Father
> and truly follow it,
> for the day will come
> when you will say:
> Blessed are the womb that has never borne
> and the breasts that have never nursed.
>
> (CF. LUKE 11:27–38, 21:23–29; MATT 24:19; MARK 13:17.)

There is kinship of the blood, but there is also kinship of the spirit. To be of Yeshua's family is to hear and live the Word. It brings news of the ever-present Source, which can transform us into its likeness, our true nature.

The end of this logion recalls the relative nature of reproduction. What good is it to perpetuate biological existence in space-time if we have lost touch with the meaning of it all? "Birth is a fatal disease," as the saying goes. The lesson of this dark humor is echoed in a passage quoted by H.-Ch. Puech, from the Nag Hammadi scripture known as the Dialogue of the Savior: "Whoever is born of the truth does not die. Whoever is born of woman, can only die."

Again, the teaching is that physical birth and reproduction are inadequate. As John 3:5 says, we must also be "born of the Spirit."

LOGION 80

> Yeshua said:
> Whoever knows the world
> discovers the body.
> But the world is unworthy
> of whoever discovers the body.

To observe and truly know the world is to discover endlessly an animated, living body whose parts are profoundly interconnected.

Discovering the great cosmic body brings us nearer to our own soul, that which animates, informs, and gives life to the body. The gnostic teaching is that we must marry the soul of the world. As Nietzsche said, "It is in true love that the soul embraces the world."

The body is beautiful as the world, the flesh of God, is beautiful. But only love can free us from the trap of it. The world is just a sacrament— a sacrament of a Presence that is real but cannot be grasped.

We can touch the earth as we touch the body—as if it were a fragile skin, an envelope for the Breath and the Abyss.

LOGION 81

> Yeshua said:
> Whoever has become rich,
> may he become king;
> Whoever has power,
> may he renounce it.

(CF. I COR 4:8; I TIM 3–5.)

Yeshua comes not to abolish, but to fulfill!

The butterfly's purpose is to complete or fulfill the caterpillar's destiny. Likewise, the stage of theanthropos (see footnote 23, page 178) is a fulfillment of ordinary human beingness—after we have first become fully and simply human. We cannot renounce something that we do not truly possess. Before surrendering our ego, we must have an ego to surrender!

This is one of the dangers encountered by those who commit themselves to a spiritual path. They may imagine they are transcending the ordinary, human stage of existence, whereas they have yet to live it fully.

In this logion, Yeshua advises us to fully realize our worldly potential—symbolized by becoming wealthy and powerful—so as to truly see the vanity of this achievement, for if we hold back, we will harbor the bitter illusion of having missed something. The butterfly does not come into being by crushing the caterpillar; instead the latter must be allowed to grow in order to reach the threshold of mutation, of Passage into another form—the butterfly.

Jung defines the process of *individuation* thus: First, we realize the "self" as a social being; then we see its relative and illusory nature and begin to make space for the Self. Our previous values of attainment and success give way to Being and Transcendence. The balloon must be blown up to its fullest before it can be ready—at the slightest jolt—to pop and reveal its true nature, which is pure Space.

LOGION 82

> Yeshua said:
> Whoever is near to me
> is near to the fire.
> Whoever is far from me
> is far from the Kingdom.
>
> (CF. MATT 3:11; MARK 9:48–49, 12:34; LUKE 12:49.)

J. E. Ménard considered this logion to be one of the best examples of evidence that the Gospel of Thomas represents a tradition that is both independent of the canonical texts of the New Testament and parallel to them. We find it quoted in early Christian writings, such as Origen's *Homily on Jeremiah* (20:3) and the *Commentary on the Psalms,* by Didymus of Alexandria (88:8). Jeremias also notes that this logion is mentioned by Ephrem and by Ignatius.

Thus the early Christians saw the fire in the Christ as a return of the fire of the burning bush. To approach the Christ is to approach the fire and to hear the same voice of the unnamable: I AM.

If that fire burns us, it is because we have not yet become fire ourselves. The only cure for "that affliction called Jesus" (as Muslim mysticism has expressed it) is to become the Christ—in other words, to make room for the Christ to manifest inside us, to allow our dry, dead wood to catch fire, burst into flames, and shine like the light of the Pentecost.

LOGION 83

Yeshua said:
When images become visible to people,
the light that is in them is hidden.
In the icon of the light of the Father
it will be manifest
and the icon veiled by the light.

(CF. COL 1:15–17.)

The vast multiplicity of images hides the Light. Sometimes, like polished stones, physical objects reflect a dazzling light. This distracts and captures our vision.

But the Son is the Icon that manifests the true Light, rather than hiding that light in reflections. It is like a spiritual diamond in which the light of the Father can shine fully. "The Son is the visible aspect of the invisible Father," as Ireneus said. When the Presence is realized in human embodiment, it is the Icon of the Father.

The Letter to the Colossians is even more explicit: "He is the image of the invisible God, first-born of all creatures, for it is in him that all things are created in heaven and on earth, visible and invisible . . . He is before all things, and all things subsist in him."

This is an Icon that, rather than hiding the light as ordinary images do, is itself hidden by the light, which envelops it totally. The revelation of the Christ, far from putting an end to the Mystery, only deepens it.

LOGION 84

> Yeshua said:
> When you see
> your true likeness,
> you rejoice.
> But when you see your icons,
> those that were before you existed,
> that never die and never manifest,
> what grandeur!
>
> (CF. LUKE 13:28; I COR 13:12; II COR 3:18.)

Gnosis has nothing to do with external imitation or with a desire to resemble someone—least of all the Christ. The imitation of Christ can result only in mimicry or caricature. The Christ is not an external person, a model to be imitated, but instead an inner source that is to be allowed to flow and is to be followed.

There is a patristic tradition that says that on the Day of Judgment we will be asked not whether we were like St. Francis or like Jesus Christ, but whether we were ourselves.

Each of us must become who we are. In the terms of this logion, this means to realize the icon that the hand of the Father (*pneuma*, Spirit) has drawn and implanted in us as the Son (our true identity).

To discover our essential icon is to discover who we are before we were born. This is the Image of God, which is never born and never dies. Its discovery is cause for rejoicing and grandeur beyond words, for it is the direct discovery of the Uncreated in the heart of the creature.

LOGION 85

> Yeshua said:
> Adam was produced by a great power
> and a great wealth,
> yet he was not worthy of you.
> If he had been worthy,
> he would not have known death.
>
> (CF. ROM 5:12–17.)

In Jewish apocalyptic writing and in Syrian theological writings there are a number of stories about Adam that are related to this logion. There is also an Armenian legend holding that Eve saw Adam after his death, resplendent in his luminous body, which was like the bodies they both had in Paradise. An analogous vision is found in the Jewish apocryphal text *Vita Adae et Evae*. According to a number of rabbinical sources, Adam, the First Man, partook of the glory of God before his fall (cf. *Genesis Rabba* XI:2). Adam was even said to have been the light of the world, a being whose heel outshone the sun (cf. Philo, *De Opificio Mundi*, etc.)

Adam was a man of light until he tasted the fruit of the Tree of Knowledge of Good and Evil, the tree of dualistic and subjective knowledge ("What makes me happy I call good, what makes me unhappy I call evil"). It could also be described as the tree of egocentric knowledge. To eat of its mortal fruit is to elevate the small self, the ego, to the status of critic and judge of what is good and bad.

Gnosis is the surrender of this form of egocentric, "mortal" knowledge to the theocentric, or nondual, knowledge of the Tree of Life. As St. John of the Cross said, "May I know all things from God, not from myself; for I can know only an effect from its cause, never a cause from its effect." Then the critical or judging aspect, with its memories, desires, and fears, ceases to reside in our personality. Only God, the divine Self, can accomplish this. It is then that we cease to eat the mortal fruit and take nourishment instead from the Living One in all things.

LOGION 86

> Yeshua said:
> Foxes have their holes
> and birds have their nests.
> The Son of Man has no place
> to lay his head and rest.

(CF. MATT 8:20, 11:28; LUKE 9:58; I KINGS 19:20.)

In the canonical gospels, this saying is prefaced by a disciple's declaration, "Master, I will follow you wherever you go," which gives Yeshua the opportunity to remind him that whoever takes this path will have no abode in this world of time.

Our "animal" aspect has a legitimate need for a home, territory, or nest. How could that be wrong? But the divine dimension of our being cannot find its repose in these things. Thus the Son of Man has no place to lay his head and rest. We can go further and say that he has not even the slightest notion of a place to lay his head, for his abode is in Openness. His home is the open sea, not in waters where anchors can be cast.

"If you want to know God, then it is not sufficient to become like the Son; you must become the Son himself," said Meister Eckhart. This means abandoning all anchors in order to find our repose in that Openness which John called the "bosom of the Father."

In the Gospel of Truth, it is the head of the Father that is the poetic metaphor for the repose of gnostics: "They have his head, which for them is repose." How could we find meaning in such a thing as the head of God? Perhaps we can by imagining ourselves as a bird floating in the infinity of Space, both soaring and at rest, hearing only the song of the wind in our wings, leaving behind no trace.

LOGION 87

> Yeshua said:
> Wretched is the body
> that depends on another body.
> Wretched is the soul
> that depends on both.

As long as we have not consummated the wedding of Unity in ourselves, we still dwell in the cycles ruled by dependence and attachment. This is dualistic sexual desire: One body needs another body in order to experience wholeness.

A child born of such a relation of mutual dependency has no choice but to enter into the cycle of alienation and gratification. Thus the same pattern of lack and craving is transmitted through generation after generation.

It is rare that parents desire a child truly for itself. From birth on, the child becomes subtly "responsible" for its parents' love and will be induced to feel guilty if it does not participate in the maintenance of their state of dependency.

Wretched, then, is the soul that depends on both; yet blessed indeed is the soul that is reborn from a love that is free and unconditional!

LOGION 88

> Yeshua said:
> Angels and prophets
> will come to you
> and give you what is yours.
> And you, too, should give what you have
> and ask yourselves:
> When will the time come
> for them to take what is theirs?
>
> (CF. MATT 10:8, 16:27; MARK 8:38; LUKE 9:26; REV 22:6.)

Each of us has an "angel"—a higher level of awakened consciousness that is far wiser than our ordinary consciousness. To pay attention to the voice of our angel or the voice of the prophets is to gradually expand and deepen our way of seeing so that we share more and more of the angel's vision. It is also to discover our true capacity for radiance.

In order not to lose the light given us (see the commentary on logion 33, page 115), it must be shared. The same is true of love. We must give it in order to keep it—yet we must not fall prey to the illusion that we are giving a "thing."

Gnosis, like faith, is transmitted not like information nor like a microbe. It is witnessed. When we witness it, the fire that already smolders within us can burst into flame.

LOGION 89

Yeshua said:
Why do you wash the outside of the cup?
Do you not understand
that the one who made the outside
also made the inside?

(CF. MATT 7:14, 23:215–26; LUKE 2:49, 11:39–40.)

This is yet another way in which Yeshua invites us to realize the nonduality of Being and appearance, inner and outer. To abandon duplicity and hypocrisy is to rediscover transparency.

It is also to discover that the same One is both inside and outside. The space inside the cup is the same space that contains the Universe. One moment of true silence, and we are in the heart of that Silence from which all creative words arise.

LOGION 90

> Yeshua said:
> Come to me;
> my yoke is good,
> my command is gentle,
> and you will find repose within you.
>
> (CF. MATT 11:28–30; ECCUS 51:23–26.)

Ancient writings have spoken of the "yoke of Wisdom." What is a yoke if not a uniting? When two horses are yoked, their powers and their movements are harmonized, and the carriage goes forward as if pulled by one.

On a deeper level, the yoke of wisdom makes "the two into One." It may rightly be called a yoga, for the etymology[24] of *yoke* and *yoga* is the same: to unite, to bring together what was separate or divided—body, heart, and mind.

Yeshua tells us that his yoke is good and its authority is gentle, a metaphor also seen in the Old Testament book Ecclesiasticus (Sirach). In 51:23–26 it is Wisdom who speaks: "Come close to me, you who are ignorant, and enter my school. Why do you claim to be in lack and why do you endure such thirst? I have opened my mouth to speak; pay for it without money and place your neck under the yoke so your soul can receive instruction. It is very near, within your reach."

The Gospel of Matthew adds: "Take my yoke, and learn of me that I am gentle and humble of heart, for you will find repose."

The Christ does not offer knowledge that works miracles, unveils the mysteries, or heals the sick, but instead offers gentleness and humility. This is the path of peace and Repose. We would look in vain to find a modern university curriculum that values gentleness and humility. Our education is based rather on competition, dominance, and power. Nevertheless, we can verify in our own life experience that the doors of true self-knowledge remain locked to those keys. It is to the dual keys of gentleness and humility that they open. To carry out a task with gentleness is to act more deeply in communion with the depths of what Is. To

---

24. [The common ancestor of the words *yoke* (*joug* in French) and *yoga* (Sanskrit) is the Indo-European root *yeug-*, "to unite." —*Trans.*]

walk lightly upon the earth is to realize how sacred the earth truly is.

Humility, like humus, is close to the earth. Sooner or later it becomes a source of fertility and growth. It allows others to be and it accepts its own limits as well as its grandeur. It is the open allowing of the Kingdom in oneself and in others.

LOGION 91

> They said to him:
> "Tell us who you are
> so that we may believe in you."
> He answered them:
> You search the face
> of heaven and earth,
> but you do not recognize
> the one who is in your presence
> and you do not know how to experience
> the present moment.
>
> (CF. MATT 16:2; LUKE 12:54–56; MARK 8:11; JOHN 6:30, 7:3–5,
> 7:27–28, 14:8–9.)

We are always asking for signs and omens so that we may believe. It is as if we want to be compelled from outside ourselves. But Yeshua offers no proofs, omens, or explanations. He is what he Is. All who question must encounter him in the present if they want to see.

He reminds us once again that what we are looking for is already here and now. Here and now are the place and time to recognize, to experience, to taste the vastness of the present moment in all its dimensions of time, of space, and of beyond space-time.

The gnostic is the child of the Now.

LOGION 92

> Yeshua said:
> Seek and you shall find.
> Yet those things
> you asked me about before
> and which I did not tell you
> I am willing to reveal now,
> but you no longer ask.

(CF. MATT 17:7–8; LUKE 11:9–10; JOHN 12:23, 13:7, 16:4.)

From instant to instant we must be ready and open to discover what is being shown to us. This will stabilize in us the right quality of attention and availability.

Seeking and finding become one movement. The Grail may appear at the very moment we stop searching for it. The answer is given to us at the very moment when we let go of the question.

LOGION 93

Do not give sacred things to dogs,
for they may treat them as dung.
Do not throw pearls to swine,
for they may treat them as rubbish.

(CF. MATT 7:6; LUKE 14:35.)

The poet Paul Éluard said, "I see the world as I am." Likewise, we listen to the words of sacred writings at our own level. We transform them according to our degree of understanding, rather than letting ourselves be transformed by them and thereby participating in the Christ intelligence.

In a famous story by Flaubert, two characters named Bouvard and Pécuchet are so obsessed with the practicalities of working their farm that they decide not to waste time looking at the sky because it is not edible. If you "throw pearls to swine," indifferent to the beauty of their light, the creatures will look only for what is edible in them. Likewise, there exists a way of reading scripture so that it is reduced to an object for dissection and analysis, which is downright piglike. If we experience no desire to resonate with the radiance of a text, we cannot hope to find its deeper meaning.

"Holy things are for holy ones," says the liturgy of St. John Chrysostom. We cannot enter into the depths of the sacred without a transformation of consciousness, a "tuning" of what is most sacred within us to what is most sacred without.

Some eyes transform everything they see into depravity. The eyes of the saints never see others as diabolical because they no longer harbor the diabolical[25] within themselves. Where some see only evil, the saints see only God.

---

25. From *diabolos*, originally from the Greek *diaballein*, "to hurl division," "to slander," "to divide."

LOGION 94

> Yeshua said:
>
> Whoever seeks will find;
>
> whoever knocks from inside, it will open to them.
>
> (CF. MATT 7:8; LUKE 11:10.)

"Ask and you shall receive," the canonical gospels say. But for what should we ask? Do we really know what is good for us, much less what is good for others?

As logion 14 suggests, we truly do not know how to pray. Better to allow the Spirit to pray in us, and say, with the Lord's Prayer, "Thy Kingdom come, thy will be done . . ." Otherwise, we risk either praying for some event that does not transpire or praying for an event that does transpire but which is not the best thing for us.

As the famous proverb goes: "More tears are shed over answered prayers than unanswered prayers." What is good in the short run may reveal itself as very bad in the long run—and vice versa. It may be best to keep silent yet remain alive to the thirst and longing in one's heart.

According to the Gospel of Luke, there is only one prayer that can never go unanswered. "If you who are corrupt are able to give good things to your children, how much more will your Father give of the Holy Spirit to those who ask?"

"Knock and it shall be opened," say the canonical gospels. But it is well to remember that the door does not always open in the way we expect. It is like the story of a man who knocked on a door, then pounded it and pushed it and kicked it, all to no avail. Finally, when he sank down exhausted, the door opened . . . but inward, in the opposite way.

LOGION 95

Yeshua said:
If you have money,
do not lend it with interest,
but give it to the one
who will never pay you back.

(CF. EX 22:24; DEUT 23:20; MATT 5:42; LUKE 6:30.)

There is a certain altruism that is a sign of real transformation of the heart.

To love is to expect nothing in return. We give much as the rose offers its fragrance, with no thought of repayment. To love, to give, or to loan in such a disinterested way (not to be confused with indifference) is undoubtedly the purest witnessing of the Good News.

What we have received freely, we give freely!

As this sense of freedom penetrates deeply into our existence, we experience a certain lightness that will lead us sooner or later to this insight: "All is absurd" is transformed into "All is grace."

LOGION 96

> Yeshua said:
> The Kingdom of the Father
> is like the dough in which a woman
> has hidden some yeast.
> It becomes transformed into good bread.
> Those who have ears,
> let them hear!
>
> (CF. MATT 13:33; LUKE 13:20–21; I COR 5:6; GAL 5:9.)

This parable occurs also in Luke, where it is specified that the woman uses "three measures" of flour to make the dough.

What is this yeast that leavens the dough of humanity in its threefold nature of body, soul, and spirit? Some say love, others say gnosis. But how can they be separated? The light of love expands the body, heart, soul, and mind, opening us to knowledge of the spirit. It strengthens us so that we stand upright, as on an Easter morning.

The creative Intelligence, that tiny seed of infinity, is at work within us. It is that which urges and leads us on, from the state of flour or shapeless dough to that of a good, well-baked bread.

But the dough also needs time to rise and must be kneaded by the woman—Sophia, or Wisdom—before it will be ready to be transformed by the divine Fire.

This is the fulfillment of the mission of the seed of light within us.

LOGION 97

> Yeshua said:
> The Kingdom of the Father
> is like the woman who carried a jar of flour.
> After she walked a long way,
> the handle of the jar broke
> and the flour began to spill behind her along the road.
> Heedless, she noticed nothing.
> When she arrived, she set down the jar
> and found it empty.
>
> (CF. PROV 7:19; MATT 26:7; II COR 4:7; ROM 9:22.)

The closest parallel to this logion is found in the Gospel of Truth:

> Those whom he has anointed
> are gnostics,
> for they are like full vessels,
> which it is normally the custom to seal.
> But when the oil of one type is poured,
> the vessel is emptied, and the cause of its defect
> is the place where its oil flows out.
> But in the flawless vase,
> no seal is broken, and nothing is emptied.

We are like the woman with the jar containing flour, the purpose of which is to be transformed into good bread. But the road of Transfiguration is long. Handles can break; our connection with the Word can be lost; flour can leak away. The longer we are oblivious to the loss, the worse it is. We lose touch with the creative Intelligence and its teachings go in one ear and out the other.

When we arrive, we discover—not without shock and bitterness—that we have been wasting our time, wasting our life. But it is too late: The jar is empty.

In this logion, Yeshua warns us against heedlessness. Such lack of attention and care recalls the story of the wise and foolish virgins in Matthew 25, where the lesson is also about vigilance.

The Valentinian gnostics taught that there is a danger that Sophia (Wisdom) will stray and become lost in the "forgetfulness of Being"—unconsciousness. Gnosis is not some kind of acquired knowledge; it is a more and more vivid consciousness of every step of the way: mind and body attentive to the nearness of Being.

LOGION 98

Yeshua said:
The Kingdom of the Father
is like the man who wanted to kill
a man of power.
First, he unsheathed his sword at home
and thrust it into the wall to test his strength.
Then he was able to kill the man of power.

(CF. I ROM 18:11; MATT 26:51; LUKE 14:28–32; EPH 2:14; EZEK 12:1–2.)

The man of power (or the one who claims to have power) is our own ego, with all its illusion, pretense, and puffed-up self-image. It can be killed only by first attacking the wall of division that separates us from God and from each other. Piercing a hole in the wall, we can begin to open up a passage to the other side.

When this passage is examined, we can see that the man of power can be killed because all his power—indeed his very identity—resides in opposition. The ego is an immense tautness, a defense mechanism. When it takes over as "the man of power," it opposes the flow of life that carries and guides us.

A purely moral reading of this logion is also possible: In contrast to the heedless woman who lets all her flour leak out of the jar, we have here a symbol of vigilance (as in logia 21, 76, and 103) that prevents evil from having its way.

We must have a firm hand and a steadfast mind in order to deal with the morbid impulses that exist within us. The "enemy of Life" is a real force inside ourselves that we must learn to unmask.

LOGION 99

His disciples said to him:
"Your brothers and your mother are waiting outside."
He replied:
Those who do my Father's will
are my brothers and my mother.
It is they who will enter the Kingdom of God.

(CF. MATT 12:46–50; MARK 3:31–35; LUKE 8:19–21; JOHN 15:6.)

Once more Yeshua places kinship and family ties in a spiritual perspective. The bonds of blood are not enough. They have nothing to do with the Kingdom, where a higher value is placed on a common intelligence of the heart, an orientation to the unique priority of the Essential.

It is in a shared recognition of this value that we become brothers and sisters in true spiritual kinship. The Father is a symbol of the transcendent root of all true fellowship. If we kill the Father, we also kill spiritual kinship.

Moses understood that the true unity of a people derives from their relationship to the Transcendent. When this is reduced to mere social order or State, then the door opens to all the varieties of conformity and totalitarianism, which are caricatures of authentic unity and harmony among individuals. Mere social unity can create perhaps allies, but not brothers and sisters.

LOGION 100

> They showed Yeshua a gold coin
> and said to him:
> "Caesar's agents demand that we pay taxes."
> He answered them:
> Give to Caesar what is Caesar's,
> give to God what is God's,
> and give to me what is mine.
>
> (CF. MATT 22:17–21; MARK 12:14–17; LUKE 20:22–25; JOHN 17:10.)

"Give to Caesar what is Caesar's"—this must be done first. We must establish an appropriate relationship with others and with the social order.

"[G]ive to God what is God's"—all praise and adoration are for God alone, the Source and Goal of all things. This is also an act of insight: Seeing through effects, we recognize their Cause, even though it remains unnamable and unknown.

To render unto Yeshua what is his is to discover him as a bridge between humanity and divinity, between Caesar and God. To do this is to become as he is. As he says in the Pistis Sophia: "Every human being is I, and I am every human being."

In some gnostic texts we encounter the theme of the Savior who must be saved. According to this theme, Yeshua the Christ can be totally free only when all his sparks of divinity, now dispersed in matter, are reunited. This spark of Spirit in us, which is his, must be awakened in order to re-ascend to the Father.

LOGION 101

Yeshua said:
Whoever does not hate their father and mother
as I do,
cannot become my disciple.
And whoever does not love their father and mother
as I do,
cannot become my disciple.
For my mother made me to die,
but my true mother gave me Life.

(CF. MATT 10:37, 19:29; MARK 10:29; LUKE 14:26, 18:29; GEN
3:20; JOHN 10:28.)

The emphasis here is on loving—and refusing to love—as Yeshua does.
We love our mother and father for what they are, but we do not love their
tendencies to perpetuate a web of neurotic codependency. Such a relationship makes us oblivious to our second birth and to the true mother
who engendered us not to die, but to know true life.

In Hebrew the word *ruah*, translated as "spirit" or "breath," is feminine. In the context of a patriarchal society, Yeshua dared to offer privi-
leged revelations to women (to Mary Magdalene and to the Samaritan
woman, for example), and his gnostic successors emphasized the feminine
gender of *ruah* in an effort to restore the rightful place of the feminine
and maternal aspect of Divinity.

Of course, God, the Uncreated beyond all images, is neither masculine
nor feminine. But it is important to have a balance in the symbols we use
in trying to speak of the Unnamable. This is why Sophia, who is Wisdom
and also the Divine Mother, has such an important place in gnostic texts.
In the Acts of Thomas (27, 50), the name Mother is used to invoke the
Spirit. In Manichean writings she is often called Mother of Life, and in
the Gospel of Philip it is said that Adam received the Breath from his
mother.

In the Armenian tradition of Adam and Eve, the Messiah is the Son
of the ruah, the Holy Spirit. There is also a parallel in the fragments that
remain of the Gospel of the Hebrews, where the Holy Spirit speaks of

Yeshua as her firstborn son at his baptism and Yeshua speaks of her as his mother when being transported to Tabor. The Master also advises his disciples to be children of the Holy Spirit, like himself (see the Apocryphon of James, 6, 19, 20). Again, in the Gospel of Philip, the Holy Spirit seems to be the celestial companion of the Father.[26]

Surely our goal in all this must not be to crystallize or manipulate these symbols, but to comprehend their deeper meanings. It is obvious that Being includes as many "feminine" qualities as "masculine." Does not the Hebrew Bible include God the compassionate Mother as well as God the harshly judging Father?

Discipline and forbearance, truth and kindness, are among the metaphysical aspects of the celestial Father and Mother. The Son is the Image and Likeness of both, incarnating the two in One.

---

26. [For these two references to Philip, see logion 80 and logion 17, respectively, in Leloup, *The Gospel of Philip* (Rochester, Vt.: Inner Traditions, 2004). —*Trans.*]

LOGION 102

> Yeshua said:
> Wretched are the Pharisees.
> They are like the dog
> lying in the cow's manger.
> He cannot eat,
> and will not let the cows eat.
>
> (CF. PROV 14:4; ISAIAH 56:10; MATT 23:13–27; LUKE 2:7.)

The Pharisee in this logion is an unfortunate man. He thinks he has knowledge, yet he does not even know himself. His teachings can amount only to a distraction from the essential, usurping the very place of the Living One in the minds of his listeners.

He has no idea that he prevents others from knowing themselves, for he does not commune with the Living One. His readiness to shower his listeners with precepts, rules, and advice that he does not practice himself is an obstacle to their living fully.

Wretched is he who speaks of joy and love through lips of bitterness and teeth of censure.

LOGION 103

Yeshua said:
Blessed are they who know
at what time of night the thieves will come.
They will be awake,
gathering their strength
and strapping on their belts,
before the thieves arrive.

(CF. MATT 24:36, 43–44; LUKE 11:8, 21–22; I PETER 1–13.)

To stay awake is to be centered, to gather strength and not waste it. This is a condition for maintaining calm and confidence during times of trial, when the thieves, the enemies of Life, come to rob our energies.

We may also know the time of the thieves' arrival. Once more, this refers to self-knowledge: knowing our own tendencies toward weakness or depression without judging ourselves. It is a calm knowledge of our darkest doubts and desires.

LOGION 104

> They said to him:
> "Come, let us pray and fast today."
> Yeshua answered:
> What wrong have I done?
> How have I been defeated?
> When the bridegroom leaves the bridal chamber,
> that will be the time to fast and pray.
>
> (CF. MATT 9:14–15; MARK 2:18–20; LUKE 5:33–35; JOHN 3:39,
> 8:34; ROM 12:21.)

When you are with others, do you think longingly of them? No, for you are *with* them.

When God is truly present, there is no need to pray or fast. His Presence fills everything. The bridal chamber is permeated with that fragrance.

Yet it happens that the Bridegroom leaves the chamber. In other words, we leave the state of Union between created and Uncreated. Then is the time for praying and fasting, so that we may return.

Rabbinical tradition speaks of the "exile of the Shekhina." To return is to end our own exile of her, to find repose in her high, holy chamber.

LOGION 105

> Yeshua said:
> He who knows his father and his mother,
> will they call him the son of a whore?
>
> (CF. JOHN 8:18–19, 41–44.)

Ménard translates this logion as "Whoever knows his father and mother will be called the son of a whore." He interpreted "knowing one's father and mother" as a symbol of bondage to the flesh and prostitution to matter.

But of what father and mother does this logion really speak? Is it not the divine Father and Mother spoken of earlier?

Furthermore, there is a real possibility that this logion contains a copyist's error: The Coptic *p'sère m'porné* (son of whore) is very close to *p'sère m'prôme* (son of man). Indeed, the latter term occurs in the very next logion. According to Rudolf Kasser, this is deliberate, serving as a link between the two logia. If this is true, then the meaning is clear: A gnostic who knows his divine Father and Mother will be called a Son of Man.

Logion 106

> Yeshua said:
> When you make the two into One,
> you will be a Son of Man.
> And when you say:
> Mountain, move!
> It will move.
>
> (Cf. Matt 17:20; Luke 17:6; Mark 11:22–23.)

As in logion 22 and elsewhere, the teaching here is about the Union of all dualities: matter and spirit, male and female, created and uncreated, and so forth. In realizing this Union in ourselves, we become a Son of Man. Again, this symbolic term has nothing to do with a masculine bias of any kind, but rather with becoming fully and divinely human.

When faith, peace, and unity reign, all laws are transcended. Even mountains cooperate and obstacles recede before the passage of the Living One.

In the *Libri Graduum* (col 737:24), discussing Jeremiah 31:17, it is said that we each must become a living Son of Man, reborn in Christ, living as Adam lived before his fall into dualism.

The *Libri Graduum* says, "Pray that they all become Sons of Man," through the integration and realization of all their potential.

LOGION 107

> Yeshua said:
> The Kingdom is like the shepherd
> with a hundred sheep.
> One of them disappeared—
> it was the most beautiful.
> The shepherd left the other ninety-nine sheep
> and looked only for that one
> until he found it.
> After his great effort he said to the lamb:
> I love you more than the other ninety-nine.
>
> (CF. MATT 18:12–13; LUKE 15:4–8.)

There are a number of possible interpretations of this famous parable of the lost sheep. Let us begin with that of Valentinus, who is often called a gnostic but who would be better described as influenced by gnostics. It is important to bear in mind the distinction between gnosis and gnosticism, sometimes written as Gnosticism. The latter is limited to certain historical phenomena that were influential around the time of early Christianity and are often associated with it. The former is an attitude of the heart and mind oriented toward the apprehension of Divine Presence, regardless of what era or culture it manifests in or what religious language it uses.

For Valentinus, Yeshua is the shepherd who leaves the ninety-nine sheep that have not strayed and rejoices in finding the one who has. Valentinus gave great significance to the numbers ninety-nine and one, for in those days there was a method of counting up to ninety-nine with the left hand and moving to the right hand for one hundred. Thus, the strayed sheep represents completion and the One. It is the most beautiful sheep because it transcends multiplicity and opens the shift to a higher state of consciousness.

This same interpretation is found in the Gospel of Truth: "It is he, the shepherd, who has left the ninety-nine lambs who did not stray. He went to search for the one who strayed, and rejoiced when he found it, for ninety-nine is a number counted on the left hand. But when he found the One, the total number shifted to the right hand."

A different interpretation has taken its inspiration from the canonical gospels. It emphasizes the infinite mercy of God, which desires for all to be saved and for all to attain to the fullness of Truth. There is more rejoicing, then, for one sinner who repents than for the ninety-nine righteous who have no need to repent.

The Gospel of Luke follows the story of the lost sheep with the parable of the lost piece of silver and that of the prodigal son. All these demonstrate the depth of God's caring and compassion.

A more psychological interpretation is also possible. The sheep strays from the others as an act of liberation and maturity. We must leave the "herd" in order to find our true self. Then we can return to the flock, but with a heart that is free and cleansed by the love and compassion of the shepherd. Henceforth, rather than submitting to the shepherd's presence, we enjoy it in mutual affection.

Finally, a more metaphysical reading reminds us that when we stray, we lose awareness of the One, the Self, and of our highest potential. We lose our center, which alone can bring about a harmony of our different levels of being, our multiplicity, as represented by the other sheep. This strayed lamb is not unlike a goat that catalyzes the unity of the flock and also serves as a symbol of our senses, thoughts, and emotions, which are always ready to explore but also go astray. This is why it is so important for this particular goatlike sheep to find its center, for then the other aspects will come to order around it. As Heidegger might say, the Shepherd of Being will rejoice.

LOGION 108

> Yeshua said:
> Whoever drinks from my mouth
> will become like me
> and I will become them
> and what was hidden from them will be revealed.

> (CF. MATT 26:48; MARK 14:44; JOHN 6:53, 7:37.)

There is a passage from John that expresses the same truth as this logion, though in a very different tone: "Unless you eat the flesh of the Son of man and drink his blood, you have not life in yourselves."

Our goal is not just to follow the Christ, but to allow ourselves to be filled with his substance, in-formed by his Word, and to become him.

We must trace back John's words to the very Breath of the mouth of Christ. Jewish tradition says that Moses died from a kiss of God. The butterfly flew into the burning bush and became fire.

In logion 82 (page 183), Yeshua speaks of the same fire. When we allow ourselves to be consumed by it, what remains of us? Him!

LOGION 109

> Yeshua said:
> The Kingdom is like the man
> who had a hidden treasure in his field.
> He did not know it was there.
> When he died, he left the field to his son,
> who knew nothing and sold the field.
> The buyer came to plow the field
> and found the treasure while working.
> He began to lend money at interest
> to all who wanted it.
>
> (CF. MATT 13:44; LUKE 14:18.)

According to some interpretations, the owner is a Jew, the son a Christian, and the buyer a gnostic. The treasure is the spiritual one hidden in every human being (cf. Clement of Alexandria, III 36:2). The Naasenes considered the treasure to be the Kingdom of Heaven, which resides in the gnostic. The mention of "interest" might be a symbol for the multiplication of spiritual riches when they are shared (cf. Hippolytus, *Elenchos* V, and the Gospel of Philip, logion 22).

In a more general sense, this parable illustrates that most people have no inkling of the treasure that is hidden within them. "The Self, which is embedded in the heart of every creature, is smaller than the infinitely small and more luminous than the infinitely great," according to the Katha Upanishad. We overlook the Presence of this treasure. Even those who claim to be disciples of the Christ are ignorant of their heritage. The one who discovers it is the passerby, the stranger who patiently works his field.

LOGION 110

> Yeshua said:
> Whoever has found the world
> and become wealthy,
> may they renounce the world.
>
> (CF. MATT 16:24.)

As in logion 81 (page 182), Yeshua reminds us that we cannot renounce something unless we possess it. It is too easy to renounce what we lack. This does not mean that we literally have to experience having great wealth or power in order to see the impermanence and vanity of these, which cannot buy what we most deeply long for. We must not forget, however, that overcoming ego-centered consciousness is an achievement of our humanity, not some kind of amputation or castration of our desire-driven destiny. The Transpersonal is an immersion of the whole human being in the divine dimension. It is not a regression to some pre-personal state of union with Nature. The impersonal beauty of a mountain or a jewel is not the same as the transpersonal beauty of a man or woman suffused by grace.

There is a story of a gnostic who lived in austere simplicity in spite of his family wealth and connections and diplomas. One day a visitor asked him:

"When did you decide to renounce riches and the world and why did you do it?"

"I never renounced the world," the gnostic replied. "I have never relinquished anything; it is the world that has renounced me. It is riches that have abandoned me—no doubt because I no longer needed them."

In his Ascent to Mount Carmel, St. John of the Cross also shows that it is not we who renounce the world but actually the world that renounces us. That which had the power to thrill us suddenly leaves us indifferent. Encounters and entertainments that used to fascinate us we now find boring. The same may apply to certain religious practices—they may have consoled us at one time, but now they leave us cold. This has nothing to do with apathy; it is the vital sign of our entry into a more profound contemplation, subtler than the outer senses and often less "worldly." This is the meaning of the embrace of nakedness, as in logion 37, page 120.

LOGION 111

> Yeshua said:
> The heavens and the earth will roll up before you.
> The living who come from the Living
> will know neither fear nor death,
> for it is said:
> Whoever has self-knowledge,
> the world cannot contain them.
>
> (CF. ISAIAH 34:4; MATT 24:34; MARK 13:31; LUKE 21:33; JOHN
> 8:51; HEB 1:12; REV 6:14.)

For some commentators, logion 111 should be the last. It speaks of the end of the world (apocalypse and *parousia*), and of that self-knowledge that enables us to remain serene before whatever is to happen. In this context it is useful to consider the deeper meanings of these three Greek words: *apokalupsis, parousia,* and *gnosis.*

Apokalupsis literally means "unveiling." ("Revelation" is the exact equivalent, based on Latin.) The day of the Apocalypse is the day of Unveiling of what Is. In this sense we all have our times of apocalypse, which may be pleasurable or painful. The term is not reserved for the end of the world as is normally imagined. But it is the end of *a* world— that of the representations and constructions of our mind. We see things no longer as we think and imagine them to be, but as they are. Our little world that we have created begins to crumble and we enter into the real one. A proverb says: "Those who are asleep live separately in their own worlds. Those who are awake live together in the same world."

The day of the Apocalypse is also the day when the reality of God is revealed to us. The First Letter of John says: "Then we will be like him, for we will see him as he is." Is it a joyful day, or a terrible one? We will see Love and we will also see how little we have loved. We will see that we are living beings who come from the Living One and see also how little we have rejoiced in this. We will see that we are light born of the Light and we will see how much time we have wasted playing with shadows.

The day of the Apocalypse is also the day of Parousia. The Greek word *parousia* means "presence." Neither of these terms is reserved to refer to some future return of Christ—that is, the Second Coming at the end of time. We can already experience moments of parousia when the Presence makes itself totally felt in us. "It fills all; it is not I who live, but Christ in me," as Paul said.

A holy being is someone filled with the Spirit, completely inhabited by the Presence of Love. Such a being is already the incarnation of the end of the world and the end of humanity—that is to say, the goal and final cause, the Plenitude and Presence that are always calling us.

Gnosis is the recognition of the Self. It alone makes possible the realization of the Apocalypse and Parousia in the true sense of these words. Self-knowledge is indeed a process of apokalupsis, of progressive unveiling, one mask dropping after another, from apocalypse to apocalypse. This is how we discover ourselves as we truly are.

In this nakedness the Presence, or Parousia of Being, can become manifest. When our cup is emptied of all its stagnant contents, there is room for new wine.

Apokalupsis, parousia, gnosis: This threefold path of individual transformation is also the foundation of the transformation of the world. Can the manifestation of the Kingdom, the transformation of all humanity, be furthered in any way? The only realistic response is this: We can hope to transform the world only if we transform ourselves. There is only one place where our action can be truly effective, and that is in ourselves. This recalls the story of the man to whom God appeared in a dream, asking him to save the world, and he promised the Lord that he would. When he woke up, he resolved to get to work immediately. But being a practical man, he began to reflect, asking himself some pragmatic questions: "Where should I start? Clearly, it must be in my own country. But where in my own country can I most effectively begin? Surely in my hometown, which I know so well. But what part of town should I begin working in? Obviously, in my own home. But who in my family can I most effectively begin to save? Myself."

The relationship among apokalupsis, parousia, and gnosis can serve to clarify this passage from the First Letter of John (3:2–3): "Beloved, now are we children of God [gnosis] and it is not yet made manifest what we shall be. We know that if he shall be manifested [parousia-apokalupsis], we shall be like him [gnosis, parousia]; for we shall see him even as he is [apokalupsis]. And every one that hath this hope set on him purifieth himself, even as he is pure [gnosis].[27]

---

27. [The Greek terms inserted by the author are only to illustrate the deeper meaning of this passage from the New Testament. They do not refer to the original Greek words of the passage, which are different. —*Trans.*]

LOGION 112

> Yeshua said:
> Wretched is the flesh
> that depends on the soul;
> wretched is the soul
> that depends on the flesh.

Yeshua is not saying that the flesh is bad and the soul is good, and still less is he saying that the body is real and the soul is some kind of illusion. Again, he refuses to enter into the dualism of matter vs. spirit. What he laments in this logion is dependence: the failure of respect and autonomy in the relation between soul and body. Dependence in this sense is a form of confusion that prevents each aspect from functioning on its own level in a natural manner appropriate to its own wholeness. The pleasures of the flesh are not the same as those of the soul; each should have its proper place and order of experience.

Another interpretation of this logion sees Yeshua reminding us that we become wretched when we are reduced to the "psychosomatic" level of existence. Only the presence of pneuma (breath, spirit) can make us free in all our dimensions of being. *Psyche* (soul) and *soma* (body) are necessary, but are not sufficient. In the presence of pneuma, we no longer confuse the two, nor do we oppose them.

LOGION 113

The disciples asked him:
"When will the Kingdom come?"
Yeshua answered:
It will not come by watching for it.
No one will be saying, Look, here it is!
or, Look, there it is!
The Kingdom of the Father
is spread out over the whole earth,
and people do not see it.

(CF. LUKE 17:20–21; MATT 24:3; I COR 2:9; HEB 11:1.)

Rather than asking questions about where God is, it would be better to ask: "Where is God not?" Everything is a manifestation of his Presence; all that exists participates in his Existence.

We might object, "But is God also present in evil, in suffering, and in the massacre of innocents?" It is said that as a child was being led to the ovens in the Dachau concentration camp, a man shouted out with all the rage and indignation of a broken heart: "But where is God now?" His friend, a fellow prisoner, raised a finger and pointed directly to the child. "God is there." Indeed, God is there—innocent, persecuted, led to the ovens, crucified by the monstrosity of human ignorance.

Yeshua's teaching is always reminding us that God is everywhere, in everything that is. It is in suffering as well as in beauty. It blossoms in the redness of a poppy and it is crushed in the child run over by a truck. Who dares to see this fully?

Whether a Presence that radiates or a Presence that is being crucified, it is everywhere and fills everything. This is why Yeshua says, in Matthew 25:40, "What you do to the least of my brothers, you do to me." It is a matter not of searching here or there for some special manifestation, but of opening our eyes to what is already before us, here and now (see logion 5, page 73) and caring for all that is.

Yet one place where God is prevented from manifesting is in the heart that is closed to love, the heart that refuses forgiveness and revels in bitterness. Hell is truly the incapacity to love.

Another place from which God is banished is the intellect that closes itself off from the light of its source, the mind that no longer seeks true understanding and indulges in a doubt that is only a defense of its ignorance.

The Tradition tells us that Christ descended into the hell realms, those dark states of consciousness whose denizens have extinguished all desire to love and all desire to understand. There he encountered the inevitable: suffering, absurdity, treachery, death. He encountered the Beast of human folly and did not flinch. Even in these hells he looked at those whom he encountered with the same regard of love and compassion with which he looked upon his friends, upon Thomas, John, and his beloved Miriam, upon Zacchaeus, the adulterous woman, and the rabble of the sick and wretched who so often pulled at his coat. He had seen to the bottom of the worst hells of the human soul and never ceased to love. And if any of those denizens glimpsed, even for an instant, the infinite compassion of that regard, how could they not have the capacity to leave even the worst of hells and live anew?

LOGION 114

Simon Peter said to him:
Mary should leave us,
for women are not worthy of the Life.
Yeshua answered:
This is how I will guide her
so that she becomes Man.
She, too, will become a living breath like you Men.
Any woman who makes herself a Man
will enter into the Kingdom of God.

(CF. MATT 19:12.)

It is instructive to contrast this logion with the following long passage from the Gospel of Mary Magdalene.[28] In that gospel we again find Peter the representative of a repressive, patriarchal attitude toward women. We also find there the theme of the "perfected" Human Being, but in a different expression: as those who have integrated the masculine and feminine in themselves, whatever their biological sex happens to be.

After saying this, the Blessed One
greeted them all, saying:
"Peace be with you—may my Peace
arise and be fulfilled within you!
Be vigilant, and allow no one to mislead you
by saying:
'Here it is!' or
'There it is!'
For it is within you
that the Son of Man dwells.
Go to him,
for those who seek him, find him.
Walk forth,
and announce the gospel of the Kingdom.
Impose no law
other than that which I have witnessed.
Do not add more laws to those given in the Torah,
lest you become bound by them."

28. Quoted from Leloup, *The Gospel of Mary Magdalene* (Rochester, Vt.: Inner Traditions, 2002).

Having said all this, he departed.
The disciples were in sorrow,
shedding many tears, and saying:
"How are we to go among the unbelievers
and announce the gospel of the Kingdom of the Son of Man?
They did not spare his life,
so why should they spare ours?"
Then Mary arose,
embraced them all, and began to speak to her brothers:
"Do not remain in sorrow and doubt,
for his Grace will guide you and comfort you.
Instead, let us praise his greatness,
for he has prepared us for this.
He is calling upon us to become fully human [Anthropos]."
Thus Mary turned their hearts toward the Good,
and they began to discuss the meaning of the Teacher's words.
Peter said to Mary:
"Sister, we know that the Teacher loved you
differently from other women.
Tell us whatever you remember
of any words he told you
which we have not yet heard."
Mary said to them:
"I will now speak to you
of that which has not been given to you to hear."

Mary goes on to describe how Christ appeared to her in a vision, telling her, "You are blessed, for the sight of me does not disturb you"; and, "There where is the *noûs,* lies the treasure." Then the Savior instructs her in the art of visionary gnosis, which is neither sensory perception nor perception of the psyche or intellect, but rather a state of opening that mystics call the noûs, or the fine point where the highest region of the soul merges with spirit.

In this Openness that reaches to the depths of being, the uncreated in humanity is One with the uncreated in God (see Meister Eckhart).

Mary finishes her long: "Henceforth I travel toward Repose, where time rests in the Eternity of Time; I go now into Silence."

Having said all this, Mary became silent,
for it was in silence that the Teacher spoke to her.

Then Andrew began to speak, and said to his brothers:

"Tell me, what do you think of these things she has been telling
us?

As for me, I do not believe

that the Teacher would speak like this.

These ideas are too different from those we have known."

And Peter added:

"How is it possible that the Teacher talked

in this manner with a woman

about secrets of which we ourselves are ignorant?

Must we change our customs,

and listen to this woman?

Did he really choose her, and prefer her to us?"

Then Mary wept

and answered him:

"My brother Peter, what can you be thinking?

Do you believe that this is just my own imagination,

that I invented this vision?

Or do you believe that I would lie about our Teacher?"

At this, Levi spoke up:

"Peter, you have always been hot-tempered,

and now we see you repudiating a woman

just as our adversaries do.

Yet if the Teacher held her worthy,

who are you to reject her?

Surely the Teacher knew her very well,

for he loved her more than us.

Therefore let us atone,

and become fully human [Anthropos]

so that the Teacher can take root in us.

Let us grow as he demanded of us,

and walk forth to spread the gospel

without trying to lay down any rules and laws

other than those he witnessed."

Thus both these gospels show evidence of Peter's difficulty in
acknowledging the rightful place of woman—which is not unrelated to
the more general difficulty of acknowledging the rightful place of gnosis.

Levi invites the disciples to take the path of the Anthropos, or fully
realized human being (not *andros*, meaning "male"). No matter what their

gender happens to be, if they let themselves be guided and inspired by the Breath of the Living One, it will lead them to a fullness and an integration of masculine and feminine.

This approach may also help us to understand a difficult passage in Matthew 19:11–12: "Not all will understand this language, but only those for whom it is given: There are eunuchs who are born thus from their mother's womb; there are eunuchs who have been made thus by the actions of men; and there are eunuchs who have made themselves thus for the Kingdom of Heaven." Gnostic tradition, dismissing the literalistic notion that communion with the creative Intelligence would ever require castration of its creatures, interprets the word *eunuch* as a gloss. Yeshua would actually have used *androgyne*. The redactors of Matthew, however, may have judged that the latter word (like many words, for that matter!) could easily give rise to misunderstanding: People might interpret it as an advocacy of sexual androgyny, thus giving rise to a confused fascination with people who manifest a curious mixture of male and female.

But the word *androgyne* was meant by gnostics in the spiritual sense of the integration of our masculine and feminine polarities so as to know the Totality of who we are. As was said in the commentary on logion 22 (page 99), this opens the door to a higher love that derives from fullness rather than lack so that we are able at last to love others "as Christ loved us."

But as the Gospel of Thomas and the Gospel of Mary often repeat: "Those who have ears, let them hear!" In order to be able to hear, though, we must engage with the teaching of the first logion of the Gospel of Thomas and ask ourselves if we are truly living the interpretation of these words in our body, heart, and mind. Only then can the creative words of the Living Yeshua give rise to the new Anthropos in us, in the image and likeness of the Eternal Son.

If, however, the words of this logion[27] fail to offer us ever-deeper insight or to make us more loving and alive, then let us forget them and be inspired by the Spirit to find other words of joy and strength.

---

27. [A number of scholars now consider logion 114 to be an inauthentic, later addition. There are two arguments: First is its quasi-misogynist style of language, which is not characteristic of Yeshua's discourse in the rest of this gospel (nor with his discourse in the Gospel of Mary, as the author demonstrates); and second is its anticlimactic placement, tacked on, as it were, right after the sublime logion 113, which would seem an appropriate ending for the gospel. —*Trans.*]

Resources

www.gospelthomas.com

Peter Kirby's site offers an excellent online display of the Coptic-English interlinear text of Thomas, as well as the Oxyrhynchus Greek fragments and useful notes and links.

www.gospels.net/thomas

The original Greek of the Oxyrhynchus fragments can be downloaded here, along with an interlinear literal translation.

www.geocities.com/Athens/9068

Michael W. Grondin's "Codex II Student Resource Center" has valuable material on the Gospel of Thomas, Codex II, and Coptic resources.

http://home.epix.net/~miser17/Thomas.html

Stevan Davies's "Gospel of Thomas Homepage" has many valuable resources and links.

www.earlychristianwritings.com
www.gospels.net

These are two useful sites where canonical and gnostic scriptures can be consulted together.

BIBLIOGRAPHY

Alter, Robert. *The World of Biblical Literature.* New York: Basic Books, 1992.

Barnstone, Willis. *The Other Bible.* New York: Harper, 1984.

Barnstone, Willis, and Marvin Meyer. *The Gnostic Bible: Gnostic Texts of Mystical Wisdom from the Ancient and Medieval Worlds.* Boston: Shambhala, 2003.

Campbell, Joseph. *Occidental Mythology.* New York: Penguin, 1991.

Corbin, Henry. *The Man of Light in Iranian Sufism.* Boulder, Colo.: Shambhala, 1978.

———. *The Voyage and the Messenger.* Berkeley, Calif.: North Atlantic, 1998.

Davies, Stevan, and Andrew Harvey. *The Gospel of Thomas.* Boston: Shambhala, 2004.

Eckhart, Meister. *Selected Writings.* London: Penguin, 1994.

———. *Sermons and Treatises.* New York: Lilian Barber Press, 1987.

Funk, et al. *The Jesus Seminar: The Five Gospels.* Sonoma, Calif.: Polebridge, 1993.

John of the Cross. *The Collected Works of St. John of the Cross.* Washington, D.C.: ICS Publications, 1991.

Josephus (Flavius Josephus). *Complete Works.* Grand Rapids, Mich.: Kregel Publishing, 1981.

Jung, C. G., and Robert A. Segal. *The Gnostic Jung.* London: Routledge, 1992.

Kasser, Rudolf. *L'Évangile selon Thomas: Rétroversion et théologie.* Switzerland: Neuchâtel, 1961.

Koester, Helmut. *The Other Gospels: Non-Canonical Gospel Texts.* Cambridge: Lutterworth, 2001.

Layton, Bentley. *The Gnostic Scriptures: A New Translation with Annotations.* Garden City, N.Y.: Anchor, 1995.

Leloup, Jean-Yves. *The Gospel of Mary Magdalene.* Rochester, Vt.: Inner Traditions, 2002.

———. *The Gospel of Philip*. Rochester, Vt.: Inner Traditions, 2004.

Mack, Burton. *Who Wrote the New Testament?* New York: HarperCollins, 1995.

Meyer, Marvin. *The Unknown Sayings of Jesus*. San Francisco: HarperSanFrancisco, 1998.

Meyer, Marvin, and Harold Bloom. *The Gospel of Thomas*. New York: Harper, 1992.

Mitchell, Stephen. *The Gospel According to Jesus*. San Francisco: Harper Perennial, 1993.

Needleman, Jacob. *Lost Christianity*. New York: Jeremy Tarcher, 2003.

Neusner, Jacob. *Judaism in the Beginning of Christianity*. Minneapolis: Fortress Press, 1984.

Pagels, Elaine. *Beyond Belief*. New York: Vintage, 2004.

———. *The Gnostic Gospels*. New York: Vintage, 1989.

Patterson, Meyer, et al. *The Q-Thomas Reader*. Sonoma, Calif.: Polebridge, 1990.

Patterson, Stephen. *The Gospel of Thomas and Jesus*. Sonoma, Calif.: Polebridge, 1993.

Philo of Alexandria. *The Works of Philo, Complete and Unabridged*. Mahwah, N.J.: Paulist Press, 1993.

Quispel, Giles. *Jewish and Gnostic Man*. Putnam, Conn.: Spring Publications, 1986.

Riley, Gregory J. *Resurrection Reconsidered: Thomas and John in Controversy*. Minneapolis: Augsburg Fortress Publishers, 1995.

Robinson, James. *The Nag Hammadi Library*, rev. ed. New York: Harper, 1990.